HARLEY-DAVIDSON
XR-750

Allan Girdler

Motorbooks International
Publishers & Wholesalers ®

101182

First published in 1991 by Motorbooks International Publishers & Wholesalers, PO Box 2, 729 Prospect Avenue, Osceola, WI 54020 USA

The information in this book is true and complete to the best of our knowledge. All recommendations are made without any guarantee on the part of the author or publisher, who also disclaim any liability incurred in connection with the use of this data or specific details

We recognize that some words, model names and designations, for example, mentioned herein are the property of the trademark holder. We use them for identification purposes only. This is not an official publication

Motorbooks International books are also available at discounts in bulk quantity for industrial or sales-promotional use. For details write to Special Sales Manager at the Publisher's address

Library of Congress Cataloging-in-Publication Data
Girdler, Allan.
    Harley-Davidson XR-750 / Allan Girdler.
        p.   cm.
    Includes index.
    ISBN 0-87938-510-3
    1. Harley-Davidson motorcycle—History.   I. Title.
TL448.H3G55   1991
629.227′5—dc20   90-24879

On the front cover: Jay Springsteen at speed on his Harley-Davidson XR-750. *James F. Quinn*

Printed and bound in the United States of America

Contents

Introduction and Acknowledgments 4

Part I Development

Chapter 1   **Prelude**   6

Chapter 2   **The Iron Maiden**   14

Chapter 3   **Aluminum Rules**   33

Part II The Racing Record

Chapter 4   **The First Batch, 1972–76**   46

Chapter 5   **Willy and Jay, 1977–79**   77

Chapter 6   **The Rivals Return, 1980–83**   95

Chapter 7   **The Big Red Ones, 1984–87**   114

Chapter 8   **Return of the Native, 1988–90**   127

Part III Tuning

Chapter 9   **Race Preparation**   141

Index   174

Introduction
and
Acknowledgments

One of journalism's subtler risks is that the man who becomes a police reporter eventually becomes more police than reporter.

As you can see from the photo, this happened to me. When I was 17 I got my first motorcycle, a big Harley-Davidson older than I was. I read the magazines and knew the names of the stars, but I was never brave enough to race motorcycles and I wasn't much of a fan.

Then I fell in with the guys at *Cycle World*. I became a contributor, joined the staff, went to the races and discovered Grand National/AMA/Camel Pro flat-track/dirt-track racing. I believed then and believe now that it's the most exciting, most sporting, fairest and all-around best racing in the world and yes, I've reported Grand Prix bikes and cars, and Indy and stocks. Been there and done that, and dirt track is best.

Which of course meant I just had to have one. Late in 1981 I bought the lower half of an iron XR-750 engine, and a frame made in 1972, modified in 1975 and ridden that year by Jay Springsteen to his first national win. No kidding. I even got Jay to sit in the saddle, never mind that he didn't recognize anything on the bike.

I scrounged up piles of secondhand parts, haunted swap meets, worked with the clerks at the Department of Motor Vehicles and got a license plate, then spent three years getting the collection of secondhand parts to run like a motorcycle.

You see half the results here, after the vintage TT races at Sturgis, South Dakota, in August 1990. That's my XR in racing trim, with the full number being 86D, the bartender's code for Throw That Man Out. I was hopelessly slow, as always, but as you can tell from the grin, if a thing is worth doing, it's worth doing badly. (The suit, by the way, belonged to Corky Keener, the former team rider, even though it was used by him after he left the team.)

The second half of my fascination with Harley-Davidson's XR-750 led to creating this book.

Nothing in my reporting career had prepared me for the XR's longevity, flexibility, durability or the sheer number of good and bad breaks and quirks of fate that illuminate the model's—and the sport's—past twenty years. The more I learned in the course of magazine reporting, then writing guides to Harleys and a history of Harley racing, kept me digging deeper and with more understanding until I had the full history of this model.

Except that right this minute, two days before I ship the package to the publisher, I am still learning.

But that's OK, because my teachers say they're in the same boat.

Which brings us to that. For one more superlative, I've never met a more open group of competitors than the Camel Pro family. I can only compliment them by saying the professional riders and tuners are like a pack of wolves, unrelentingly fierce in their pursuit of the quarry, yet unfailingly supportive of and fair with each other in the pits and on the road.

Every person I spoke with answered honestly. I never got turned down, nor was I steered wrong. Sorry to have to single out people, but my special thanks go to Pieter Zylstra, Bob Conway, Brent Thompson, Carroll Resweber, Al Stangler, Ken Tolbert, Ricky Graham, Tex Peel, Mert Lawwill, Bill Werner, Terry Poovey, Jay Springsteen, Steve Storz, Scott Parker, Jon Cornwell, Corky Keener and Vera Cherry.

One more bow. He retired several years before I began this book, and he moved away, out of racing.

But I still had my piles of notes and transcripts, and everybody who's had anything to do with AMA racing since the present rules were implemented knows that behind the XR-750 was one man, the man to whom this book is dedicated: Dick O'Brien. Thanks Dick, in behalf of all of us who've thrilled to that deceptively calm howl and streak of orange and black that is the Harley-Davidson XR-750.

Allan Girdler
Rainbow, California
November 1990

5

Part I Development

Chapter 1

Prelude

Motorcycleracing should be one word, so quickly did the first race follow in the wake of the first motorcycles.

Racing and sport were naturals. It might not have been obvious that the car would evolve into a wagon with the comforts of home, but any young man (and not a few young women) at the turn of the century could tell instantly that the motorcycle was the horse given magical powers. For as long as we've recorded

Board tracks flourished in the excessive 1920s, with speeds up to 120 mph and far more accidents and deaths than we'd tolerate now. The rider here is Harley factory teamster Curley Fredericks, and the machine has a 45 deg. V-twin with overhead intake valves and exhaust valves in the cylinders. There are no brakes, and the front suspension had perhaps 1 in. of travel. Harley-Davidson

history, speed has been a measure of success, so about the time we hit the year 1900, we put men astride machines and turned them loose on the track and the guys who did best, were best.

Here we are getting close to the year 2000 and it's still the same.

Except now we have history. We can look at the results of nine decades of competition and some of the names are footnotes, and some, well, they made history.

Few machines have made more history, in the sense of winning races against worthy competition and under the control of fair rules, for a longer period of time than the Harley-Davidson XR-750.

This is the story of how it was done, and of the people who did it. Not to give away the game, but Harley's XR has always been a triumph (sorry, chaps) of determination and skill and, yes, cunning in the face of the odds and sometimes the establishment.

There's more to this than names and numbers.

And there's more to the XR story than just the XR. If we can argue that the XR is the most successful racer of all time, and the plan is to argue just that, we must also pay tribute to other times and situations, simply because if it hadn't been for the convergence of factors unique in racing, none of what follows could have taken place.

The Motor Company

Harley-Davidson, the company, came into being in 1903, not long after the invention of the motorcycle. Young Mr. Harley and his partners the three Davidson brothers were craftsmen, pragmatic engineers and enthusiasts, not always in that order. They rode what they built; indeed, they initially built so they could ride and then went into business because other people asked to buy their machines. In the very early days the partners rode in competition, and won.

But the company didn't have a professional racing team, nor did they build racing bikes, or even

6

Technology arrived early. This is a peak, the eight-valve Harley, so called because it had four valves per cylinder in 1927, about when Harley-Davidson taught the Japanese how to make motorcycles. Again it's a V-twin with no *brakes, minimum suspension and that at the front only. The plunger at the front of the fuel tank is the oil pump: every lap or so, the rider would deliver another shot of lube to the crankcases.* Harley-Davidson

sponsor any professionals. The partners felt such efforts were sort of frivolous and distracted from the real job, which was to build good, solid road machines.

Not that they opposed sport in itself. Quoting an H-D ad from 1911, "No, we don't believe in racing and we don't make a practice of it, but when Harley-Davidson owners win races on their stock machines, hundreds of miles from the factory, we can't help crowing about it."

Motorcycles were a booming business and scores of companies competed. By 1914, just crowing from afar wasn't enough. Harley-Davidson formed a factory team, to run against the teams from Indian, Cyclone, Emblem and a score of others.

This ushered in the first of several motorcycle racing Golden Ages. Racing teams meant racing engines, with multiple cylinders, overhead camshafts, multiple-valve heads—nearly every high-tech feature the car people stumbled across years later had appeared on racing motorcycles before World War I.

The Harley team gave at least as good as it got. The team was called The Wrecking Crew because the squad was capable of sweeping the board. The racing itself evolved from runs on public roads to oval dirt tracks first built for horse racing and on special board tracks, high bankings that allowed incredible speeds inches from the packed grandstands.

Board track racing was a spectacle, as dangerous as it sounds and looks. Through the 1910s and 1920s, as speeds increased and engines became more and more powerful, engine size was reduced (and the board tracks abandoned) to keep things within reason.

Then came the 1930s and economic hardship. At the broad base, the motorcycle was in serious, nearly fatal, trouble. By that time, mass production from Ford and GM had reduced the cost of a car to that of a motorcycle, never mind taking along the family and keeping warm and dry. Motorcycles were sport; discretionary expenditure as they say in financial circles. Sales all but stopped and the scores of motorcycle companies became less than a handful.

Harley-Davidson was at the top of the tiny pile. There was one factory team, the Harley team. It consisted of one person, Joe Petrali. Not to take anything away from Petrali, who was an exceptional talent as a rider and tuner, but when one man wins all the national championship races in a season, as Petrali did in 1935, it says as much about the lack of competition as it does about the winner.

Clearly, something had to be done, and it was.

Birth of Class C

Motorcycle enthusiasm was at an all-time low. The American Motorcycle (now Motorcyclist) Association (AMA) was supposed to be a user club, but

Specialized racing machines were too expensive for the economically depressed 1930s, and the AMA invented production racing, clumsily known as Class C. The idea was, you rode to the race on your daily bike, stripped the extras and raced. The racer here, Griff Kathcart, seems to have done just that for the Wisconsin State Fair of 1937. The model is a WLDR, the sports 750, and the front brake innards have been removed while the license plate is still on the rear fender. They raced with foot clutch and hand shift, the lever on the side of the fuel tank. Harley-Davidson

membership had slumped and the bills weren't paid and Harley and Indian had to take up the slack.

To be fair, yes, the two factories wanted to stay in business. They wanted racing to stay in business, too, and they knew that if riders didn't have fun, they wouldn't ride.

So, pushed if not shoved by the factories behind the scenes, the AMA invented a new kind of racing, arguably the most fair in principle ever devised.

In theory, it was Olympian; in fact, it was production racing. The AMA decreed that professional racing would from then on be done with production machines, motorcycles that anybody could buy. The bikes could be stripped of things like lights and brakes—we'll get to the brake part later—but the machine had to begin as a stock model, as catalogued by the maker, and the modifications were limited and subject to inspection.

The theory was that every rider would begin at the same place. Every part could be bought over the counter, so the races would be won by those who tuned and rode and worked the best. By dint of careful planning, detailed examination and the occasional blind eye, the system worked then, and it still does.

The second factor involved the races themselves. In all other places and venues, motorcycle or car, there are series and championships and exclusionary rules for one class. There's stock car racing and sprint car racing. There's speedway and road racing, pavement and grass and cinders and so forth. Midget races have their own league and the jalopy stocks don't take part. This is the way it's always been.

But not in the AMA's new rules. The club decided it would also be easier and cheaper for the average racer to use the same bike for all the races in his area. Thus, there were national championship races for short tracks (quarter-mile or less), half-mile ovals, mile ovals and road courses, even though in the 1930s and 1940s the road race course was apt to be at least part dirt or even, as at Daytona Beach, half sand.

There were a few exceptions. Presumably because hill climb machines were so specialized anyway, that type remained with its own rules. And because the unique form of race that had turns in both directions and at least one jump—known as TT or TT Steeplechase for reasons lost in time—had been open to big bikes when the little ones ran the other professional classes, TT races were open, contested by big men on big, as in 74 ci, motorcycles.

Much later, when the big bikes proved tricky and there was a choice of smaller engine, short track was limited to production engines of 250 cc, or 15 ci, but the principle remained.

The principle was unique, and it meant that the top men had to be adaptable, flexible and willing to learn and develop new skills. Which they did, although only a handful of riders have won national races in all of the five types.

The actual rules from 1938 had one other factor. Harley and Indian both made sporting machines of 45 ci, or 750 cc capacity. There was a handful of dealers in the United States selling imports, and the sporting machine from those shops generally had 500 cc. But the Harley and Indian were sidevalve (flathead) engines and the imports, read here English, had overhead valves.

Because the factories and dealers and AMA all wanted guys to run what they could bring, the national championship rules limited engines to 750 cc sidevalves and 500 cc overhead valves, as sold to the public. The machines were supposed to be stripped of road equipment like stands and tool boxes and lights and even, on the ovals, of brakes. This was as much habit as anything else, but the board track and purely racing machines didn't use brakes, supposedly because if they slowed too quickly, they'd be hit. Motorcycle racers are oddly traditional, and the riders and rule makers at the time had all been raised without brakes, so they ruled them out.

Still, being fair, that wasn't nearly as dangerous as it sounds to us, who are perhaps as traditional and habit-formed as our grandfathers were. High-compression engines slow quickly on closed throttle, and the riders could throw the bikes into sideways skids that stopped them short.

If the AMA made one mistake with the new rules, it was the name. The former professional classes had been called A and B, the license levels. The new one was labeled Class C.

Darn. The club knew what was meant. The public, though, knew that Class C ball was minor league, and a Class C sticker on the cafe door meant the health department was concerned.

Even so, the rules worked. Professional racing did revive well in advance of the economy. Riders with ambition could begin at a reasonable level and work up and the races were just as closely contested, perhaps even more so, than they'd been with the pure racing machines.

The Production Racers

The new bikes followed a pattern. Both Harley and Indian produced 750 V-twins, sidevalve as mentioned, with hand shift and foot clutch; as they did when the motorcycle was invented, Harley had the shift lever on the left side of the fuel tank and the throttle on the right side of the handlebar, while Indian was the reverse. (Next time you wish to test your powers of concentration, climb off an old Indian onto an old Harley.)

But both were sidevalve with the rear wheel held rigid in the frame and the front moving an inch or two on links and springs. Drum brakes, of course, and only three forward speeds. That was just as well because shifting was difficult in TT and illegal on the ovals. The rules said you could shift to get up to speed but not in the turns. Safety again, or so the rule makers said. But just as with the other clauses, it didn't seem to hurt the racing.

Moving to mechanical history, in 1938 the sporting production Harley-Davidson, the model listed with the AMA and stripped for racing by owners, was the W series. Harley-Davidson has used letters to designate engines since the very first: The W series 750 followed the D-type 750, while the E was a 1000 cc V-twin that supplemented the V, a 1200.

Next in line, H-D adds letters, so the W's hotter brother was the WL, the L meaning higher output in Harley's book. Then came the WLD and the WLDR, the R meaning racing version.

Here's the first of the arrangements. All the parties were slightly guilty of helping the racers. If there were no frames suitable for American racing from the English factory, the dealers were allowed to arrange for frames that did work. And it was cheaper and easier to sell a stripped bike direct than to charge for equipment the racing owner would throw away. This happened in turn because while the rules expected the bike to be raced by the owner, who'd ridden it to the track, it didn't take more than a few seasons for

Harley's sport bikes were modernized in 1952, with unit construction, hand clutch and foot shift, but still with side-valve engine. This is the racing version of the K model, the KR. Note the telescopic forks and the rigid rear wheel, mounted in a subframe that bolts to castings behind the seat and the primary cover. There were no brakes, and the pad on the rear fender is a perch for a rider crouched down on the tank. Harley-Davidson

The KR evolved. This is Mert Lawwill's KRTT, the road racer, circa 1965. Still sidevalve, but with drum brakes and suspension, front and rear. Harley-Davidson

sporting owners to lend their prepared machines to guys who were better on the straight than in the shop.

And what that meant was that in 1941 Harley-Davidson introduced the WR, W for sidevalve 750 with attached three-speed gearbox, R for racing only and no lights or brakes but with heavier gears and a full choice of large and small oil and fuel tanks.

There was a pause for the war. In 1952, racing having resumed, Harley-Davidson introduced the K model road bike. It was nearly all-new and modern. The K had suspension front and rear, foot shift and hand clutch: the shift lever was on the right, same as the English bikes had and done for competitive purposes, as the big Harleys went from left-hand shift to left-foot shift.

The K engine was unit, with the gearbox housed at the rear of the engine cases. Even with all the new parts, the K retained sidevalves, for reasons of economy and (the factory said) low maintenance.

With the road-going K model came the KR, the racing version. The KR and K differed more than did the WD and WR. The KR engine didn't just have hot cams, the valves were inclined toward the bore, for better flow. The cylinder heads were intricately shaped, as was the surface of the cylinder between the bore and the valves. The main bearings were ball,

rather than roller, and the KR had a magneto at the front of the cases, where a K carried its generator.

By this time, suspension and brakes were accepted for road racing and the KR came with its own frame that could be adapted. There was a subframe that held the rear hub rigidly, and there was a swing arm and shock and springs, for rear suspension. The racer could unbolt one system and bolt on the other. The parts book had an astonishingly long list of gears and hubs and camshafts and oil tanks, even wheels of different diameter. At the same time, the K and KR engines looked nearly alike on the outside and could be swapped; that is, a KR engine would fit right into a K frame, and vice versa. The KR was a production racing motorcycle, sold to the public, and so were all the parts. It was also a direct sibling of the K and later KH, just as the rules required and the spirit of the rules had hoped for.

This was a period of change, in that Indian went out of business and the imports, the British, came in to ensure the competition nature seems to need. And the racing was close, as the 500 cc ohv singles and twins were just about equal, on the terms of power to weight, with the larger sidevalve 750s. There was some grumbling and there were debates over the no-shifting rule and the limits the AMA imposed on compression ratio: on one hand, the compression ratio limit meant you didn't need to worry about fuel, and the engine would last longer. On the other, a sidevalve engine can't use as high a compression ratio as an ohv engine can, so one type was limited and the other wasn't.

Overhead Valves

The major breach with the spirit of the production class came in 1957. Harley-Davidson admitted that the sidevalve's day was done, and introduced the Sportster, an ohv 900 cc replacement for the KH. Frame, suspension, brakes, styling and basic engine all looked the same or very close. In detail, the new engine had a shorter stroke and larger bore and a host of other differences. But the engines would swap, bolt into each other's mounts and they did share parts.

Thing was, while Harley-Davidson introduced a stripped sports version of the Sportster, the XLC, and later a racing machine for the TT class, the XLR, the KR remained in limited production and remained as the bike used by the factory and private customers in the AMA's national championship.

This probably made sense at the time. The KR *was* a production racer, for sale to customers. The parts were available and because a host of smart and hungry tuners had spent a generation delving into the black art of sidevalve tuning, the obsolete old engine

was coaxed into more and better power. It could still win races, and it was more practical to keep racing with the old version of the road bike than it would have been to design and produce a direct rival to the English 500s. It may not have hurt that H-D management remembered that Indian went out of business in part because that company tried to compete directly with the English.

But, in the long run, the KR was an evolutionary leftover, the equivalent of a shark in that it was an outmoded, even archaic design still alive because it filled its limited niche so well.

On the personal side, the Harley-Davidson racing department had been one man; then it grew into a department, with an engineer and team manager—except the real power was one of the founding fathers' sons. He liked racing and was a sportsman and a fair man. But it was a family company and there were some silly incidents. For example, if a tuner got $5 for gas and a rider got $5 for gas, they were in trouble if the boss found out they'd driven to the race together.

The team became professional about the time the Sportster was born, with the arrival of Dick O'Brien. He'd been a tuner at a Harley dealership, specializing in two-strokes of all things. O'Brien was big and bluff, rough and tough and at the same time a soft touch. He was a self-taught engineer and willing to listen and

Dirt track evolved. By 1970, with the trusty KR defending the team until the XR-750 arrived in force, Cal Rayborn's KR had Ceriani forks and rear suspension but still no brakes. *Note the horizontal backbone of the frame, the cross-over of backbone and downtubes at the steering head, and the profile of the KR engine.*

learn. He backed his people even when they were wrong, which is the true test of leadership, and he argued the factory into giving the team what was needed to do the job. Not incidentally, he took the orange and black used on Harley-Davidson packaging and made those colors the team colors, a move so effective in the marketing sense and so obvious when it was done that of course it hadn't occurred to anybody else.

A Hint of Things to Come

We are now up to the mid 1960s. The KR still lived, and guys with factory help were winning the national title year after year. The team had OB, as everybody called him, at the helm and there was what we'd now call a network of outside builders and tuners and suppliers, and an inside system of partnerships—rider and tuner, or sometimes, Mert Lawwill for one, riders who also did their own modification and maintenance.

The opposition had been growing. First, the British had an increasing share of the market. BSA, Triumph and Norton had AMA teams, and belonged to the various committees. They were also growing in that the buyers wanted 650s, so the 500s became less typical. And the road bikes had suspension and brakes, while the stripped and rigid frames were a joke, a legal fiction pretending to be a production motorcycle.

Especially to those with a vested interest, the old sidevalve-overhead formula became unfair. There were proposals to open the national class, to make the rule one size and devil take valve location. The proponents of this change became the majority, and in 1968, the AMA's competition committee adopted the new system: the national championship would be contested on production motorcycles, at least 200 examples of which had to have been constructed. The specifications had to be on file and approved by the AMA. In 1969, the oval track nationals would be run for bikes with 750 cc, no limit on valve configuration, compression ratio or number of cylinders. (That was because back in the 1930s, Indian had made inline four-cylinder engines. They weren't racers, nobody thought such an engine could possibly be a racer, thus everybody was so committed to twins that the rules didn't bother to specify them.)

The KR era ended in a blaze of dramas, plural. Just to show that the equivalency formula was fair, that who rode and tuned mattered as much as what the bike began as, the 1968 Daytona race was one of the KR's finest hours. The team, seven riders, lined up

Brakeless racing wasn't merely safer than you'd think. It also had style, witness Lawwill about to touch his cases to the ground with braced foot and power on. He's pursued by Chuck Palmgren, Triumph; Dick Mann, BSA; and Cal Rayborn, H-D. Harley-Davidson

It's Daytona, 1968 and Dick O'Brien's dream is about to come true. The team, from left, is Bart Markel, Mert Lawwill, Dan Haaby, Cal Rayborn, Roger Reiman, Fred Nix and Walt Fulton, Jr. It's the first year for orange-and-black livery. The team will blitz the field on the first lap and Rayborn will win the 200. Harley-Davidson

on KRTTs (the TT meant suspension and brakes) wearing full fairings and painted orange, white and black. H-D teamster Roger Reiman was fast qualifier, and the incredible Cal Rayborn (much more about him later) won the race. Not only did he win, he lapped the rest of the field.

Against that, Gary Nixon won the championship in 1968, riding for Triumph.

Then came 1969. The new rules said 1969 would be 750s on the dirt tracks, the old 500–750 split on the road courses. So Cal Rayborn won Daytona again, although it was a fluke. The team bikes were slower than they'd been the previous year, it rained and the race was postponed. During the week's delay they found what had been wrong and fixed it. Don't let anybody tell you there's no such thing as racing luck.

Next, Nazareth, Pennsylvania, and the national race on the longest mile track, 1⅛ to be exact. This was going to be the confrontation, the day the ohv 750s showed their stuff. Nixon had two bikes wearing his number-one plate. One was a 650 cc Triumph twin, the other a 750 cc triple. Yes, three cylinders. The Triumph factory had rented the track earlier, so Nixon had the gearing and the lines down pat. There were BSA triples and twins, and Nortons.

There weren't any new Harleys. Rumor had the team preparing ohv versions of the KR. Rumor added, when the team arrived with trucks filled with KRs, that Harley-Davidson had assumed they could promise to build 200 and race on that promise, but that the AMA had said no, build first, then race.

The team wouldn't talk. Instead, team member Fred Nix went out on the old flathead. It was brakeless and had the rigid rear: O'Brien had decided in 1968 that the riders could use brakes or swing arm suspension if they chose. Nix wasn't one for experimental tactics.

Nix was fast qualifier, at 42.06 sec. Nixon was next, at 42.08 sec.

When the checkered flag waved, after fifty laps, Nix was half a straight ahead.

Nixon could dish it out, and he could take it. A reporter rushed up and asked, "What happened?"

"I got beat, is what," Nixon said.

And at the end of the season Mert Lawwill, star of *On Any Sunday* and a man who never hesitated to trust his own judgment, was the new national champion, on his own KRs with factory help.

But everybody knew it couldn't go on, that the overhead-valve engines were better and that Harley-Davidson would have to do something, and right now.

What they did, of course, was the XR-750.

Chapter 2

The Iron Maiden

Minutes from the AMA's Competition Congress late in 1968 show that the original proposal for revising the national championship rules called for an engine limit of 650 cc. Walter Davidson, of the family whose name is on the door, moved that the limit be raised to 750 cc and Dudley Perkins, the dean of Harley-Davidson dealers, seconded the motion. The motion was approved, 27 to 15.

Then Davidson moved that the new rules be delayed until 1970. The second came from Bart Markel but this time the Harley forces lost, 24 to 19.

As demonstrated by the sticker on the air cleaner when the XR-750 was introduced at the 1970 Houston show, Harley-Davidson wasn't beyond a bit of bravado. As we learn later, they surely knew by then that they were in trouble. Cycle World

What does this mean? First, that clearly there were lots of Harley ties to the AMA and the rule makers.

Second, that although they had influence, they didn't have control.

In turn, that doesn't mean that Davidson, Perkins and Markel were unfair or even lacking in sportsmanship. Instead, they wanted to be fair and survive, at the same time.

And they were in trouble. Due to nothing except coincidence, along about the time the British gained an influence in the AMA and the old equivalency formula began to look outmoded, Harley-Davidson the company got into hot water.

Honda's dazzling little machines and creative marketing efforts, along with a sort of national willingness to do new things, had reinvented the motorcycle in America. There was a boom and Harley-Davidson was caught unprepared. The firm was still family owned, then it went public and then had to be saved by what Wall Street calls a White Knight, a bigger corporation that steps in and protects the small one from the invaders and exploiters.

In Harley's case, salvation came in the form of American Machine and Foundry, better known as AMF. The families retained some minority stock and management influence while production was expanded. This hurt quality and that snatched away time and resources, just when the racing department, which wasn't all that important in the AMF view, needed help.

O'Brien and crew had seen the crisis forming on the horizon a long time before it became a dark cloud. But along with the financial limits, the AMA's political turmoil made various people in and out of H-D and the AMA worried about or resentful of each other.

So first, while OB and staff had begun experimenting with a 750 cc racing engine as early as 1965, designer Pieter Zylstra actually did the drawings and designs for the new engine in just four months.

The XR Engine

Now we go way back, to the basic Harley-Davidson technique and terminology.

The new racing engine was closely based on, and descended from, that unit V-twin of 1952. Engine and gearbox were one structure, and the structure consisted of four cavities.

The structure was made up of the engine cases, two halves, left and right, split vertically down the middle. The front and center cavity formed by the two case halves was the actual crankcase.

Except that Harley-Davidson engines don't have crankshafts. They have a pair of flywheels, left and right. The flywheels are big discs; iron sometimes, in this example steel. The disc has a shaft through its center, projecting outboard, and a hole, offset by half the distance of the stroke from the center. The flywheels are joined by a crankpin. On the crankpin ride a pair of connecting rods. They are fork and blade, that is, one rod has a thick lower section and the other rod has two paired thin sections and the thick center slides between the two thin ones. They also call this male and female for reasons we can deduce without more detail.

The flywheels thus joined are supported by main bearings pressed into the case halves and into which go the two outboard shafts, called the sprocket shaft on the left, the gearshaft on the right.

The sprocket shaft runs through the left-side main bearing and a seal, into the cavity on the left. There's a sprocket, the engine sprocket, that goes on the shaft, then a three-row primary drive chain running back to the clutch hub.

The center rear cavity is for the gearbox, the transmission. There's the mainshaft and countershaft, which collectively carry four pairs of gears for four forward speeds. The output sprocket is on the right side (the rider's right, when seated) of the gearbox and the clutch is on the left, with activation via a four-piece pushrod running through the rear shaft. Why four pieces? Because the clutch pressure plate is spinning 3000 to 4000 rpm at full speed and the clutch arm is stationary, so each part of the shaft is spinning slower from one to the other and they don't wear.

The right-side cavity is the gearcase, or timing case. The gearshaft comes through the right-side main bearing and then drives sets of gears. One set is the cams, four lobes laid out in an arc, riding in ball bearings set in the case and in the timing cover. The cams are arranged exhaust, intake, intake, exhaust. They activate roller tappets which move pushrods that go

The first (iron-topped) version of the XR-750 was clearly based on the mass-production XL Sportster. Heads and barrels were modified stock and the cases looked identical. Frame, running gear and suspension were virtually copied from the last of the KRTTs. Notice the lack of brakes, the Ceriani *forks and Girling shocks and the perfect lines of the fiberglass tank and seat and fender. The oil tank is slung below the seat via springs and rubber straps. The snapdown seat cover harkens back to dirt-track sprint cars.* Harley-Davidson

The XR's straight pipes and the large—and quickly discarded—air cleaner mimic the Sportster and there's still a passage through the output sprocket cover for a kick-start shaft. It's a long reach from the rearset footpeg to the right-side shift lever (one down, three up), but these bikes raced mostly in high gear. Harley-Davidson

Harley-Davidson was careful to prove that they'd built the required 200 examples of the XR-750, so they took this photo of endless rows of XRs. Alas, half the machines were scrapped for tax accounting purposes after they'd been parked right here for several years, unsold. Harley-Davidson

to rocker arms in the rocker boxes atop the cylinder heads. At the front of the train of gears driving the cams is a gear that drives the generator in the XL engine or the magneto (more about this later) for the KR or XR or XLR engine.

The center top of the geartrain in the timing case drives a tachometer for an XR, the early ones anyway, or the magneto on the road machine.

Now we come to an operation so important you probably should take notes. The oiling system is made up of several oiling *systems* and it is much more important than would first appear.

At the rear of the timing case is the drive for first, the oil pump, which is actually two pumps. The XR engine, like the earlier XL and KR and K engines, uses a dry sump: there's a tank for the oil supply, located separately from the engine, and the oil is delivered to the engine and then collected and pumped back to the tank. At any given time the engine will contain only a few fluid ounces of oil—or that's all it should have. If the oil isn't moved back to the tank as rapidly and efficiently as it was moved to the engine, the crankcase and gearcase will fill with oil. This is known as wet sumping and it means disaster. At best, the engine slows with the friction of churning the oil. At worst, the engine literally drowns in its own oil.

The XR's oil pump has two levels, two sets of gears that are spun and have just enough clearance to scoop oil and send it through the lines and passages. The gears are a precision fit, and so are the covers and the pump body and shafts and so on. I used to make dry runs at the kitchen table, putting the upper gears into the case, then inserting the driveshaft with the woodruff key and slipping the shaft through the body just right, twisting so the rod that held the drive gear would clear and so forth. All this so when I was ready to actually put the pump together, with the gaskets coated in quick-drying adhesive, I could do it without getting the gaskets out of place, or letting the adhesive dry. It takes the exact amount, see, because if you don't use enough, the pump leaks, and if you use too much, there's internal clearance and you start the engine and look down and see all the oil that seeped into the crankcase now being pumped out the timing case breather and onto your boots or the shop floor, depending on whether you're wearing your good boots or the ones that don't matter.

So, why is this a problem, getting it just right?

Because of the nature of the engine. We have a narrow-angle, 45 deg. included, V-twin. The configuration is classic and permanent Harley-Davidson and it's a good one because it fits so nicely. It's also awkward, as we'll see.

The two cylinders are aligned fore and aft. That's done with the one crankpin, with both connecting rods riding on it, and with the fork and blade design of the rods' lower ends. The alignment eliminates any side to side motion or vibration.

But if you visualize the operation of the engine, say at 100 rpm, you'll see the pistons and rods going up and down together, in sequence, forming a sort of an arc, galumph, galumph, galumph. The flywheels are counterweighted to offset this, but those weights are merely revolving around the shafts, so they can't perfectly balance the ups and downs of the pistons and rods.

More important to the oil system, when the pistons go up, they leave behind them a partial vacuum in the crankcase. And when they come down, they create pressure. You've got an engine going aahh–chuff, aah–chuff at the same time it's going galumph, galumph.

That sounds silly, spelled out like that. But the picture is painted and the point is made and we can see that the vibration and more so the internal pressure can make it difficult to deliver the correct amount of oil to parts and systems subjected to such variations.

To deal with that, the XR (again like the KR and the K and the XL) had atop the oil pump a timed breather, a rotating drum with holes. This drum was driven with the oil pump and the slot lined up with passages to the outside. When all was correct, air could go out and come in, at the right time and in the right volume, to counter the ups and downs of the pistons and rods.

Getting back to the other basics, O'Brien and staff had almost no time to design and build the engine,

make that the complete motorcycle. They had limited funds and limited attention from management.

So they played the cards they had. They had the XLR engine, a version of the XL Sportster, but with hot cams and ball bearings and stronger internals shared with the KR.

The KR's bore was 2.75 in., stroke was 3.8 in. and nominal displacement was, of course, 750 cc. The XL and XLR engines had the same stroke but a bore of 3 in., and displaced 883 cc, or 900 in the ads.

The XR began with the XLR's engine cases, designed and sized for ball main and camshaft bearings, and with an oil pump that ran at one quarter engine speed, rather than half speed, the way the road engines did. As mentioned, you want the right amount of oil at the right time.

The XR also began with the XLR's wider crankpin, much thicker and therefore stiffer, than the XL's pin.

But the pin was closer to the center of the flywheels because the XR neatly met the 750 cc limit with a shorter stroke, 3.2 in. Just for the record, then, the XR and KR had different bores and strokes for the same displacement. Nor did they share cases. The old and new racing engines looked a lot alike, but they were more different than they looked. And the XR wasn't merely a KR with overhead valves.

The XR got XL cylinders, shortened by 0.3 in., which worked out to one fin worth of iron.

Right, iron. The XL's barrels and heads were cast iron, so when they made the TT racing engine they made larger ports and installed bigger valves in the basic casting and when they got the XR out of the XLR, they retained the old material.

Why? Economy, one must guess. Harley-Davidson went to aluminum heads with the big twins, the Shovelheads, in 1966. The Shovelheads and XL heads looked similar and used the same basic pattern, so H-D's foundry could have done alloy XL heads. But they didn't.

The XR cylinder heads were iron, virtually identical to the XLR heads, with two large valves in the classic hemispherical combustion chamber dome, and with domed pistons jutting into the chamber. The pistons came from Offenhauser, the car racing engine people, whose midget engine, a 1500 cc four, by chance had the same bore and stroke as the XR engine.

The camshaft lift and timing were evolved out of the KR cam spec, and allowed for the higher revs that the ohv heads and shorter stroke would permit. There were straight exhaust pipes sized to provide extraction, that is, the pulses would resonate in such a way as to pull the exhaust gas out of the cylinder at a selected engine speed. And because the engine's vee was narrow with the intakes at the center, there was one carburetor, a Tillotson with one venturi.

The XR Chassis

This evolved engine went into a frame and chassis done in the same way. By the time serious work

Close to the steering head of the original XR frame, one can see the details of the cast-alloy Ceriani clamps, and the overlapping of the front tubes and backbone. Note that the main backbone tube is horizontal and the brace is at an angle. Note also that the steering head itself extends well below the backbone. That was done to raise the engine cradle, and thus the engine, in relation to the forks.

began on the XR, the AMA rules and restrictions had come a long way from the production, ride-it-to-the-track ideal of 1938. Harley-Davidson produced the only complete for-sale dirt track bike, so the others were allowed special models with their own frames and various components supplied from elsewhere.

That let the Harley guys do their own development work. The best, for instance Lawwill, had done modifications to the KR parts until they were only KR in name. Lawwill was helped by his backing from dealer Dudley Perkins and by the work of Jim Belland, who was trained as a biologist, paid to be a salesman at Perkins' showroom but whose true vocation was racing.

The team had reworked the thinking behind the KR frame, which was steel tubing with cast-iron junctions, and some of the better road racing frames, notably the Norton Featherbed designed by two Irish brothers.

Customers still got the rigid KR with optional parts to add suspension and become the KRTT, but the team and selected privateers had gone to a frame

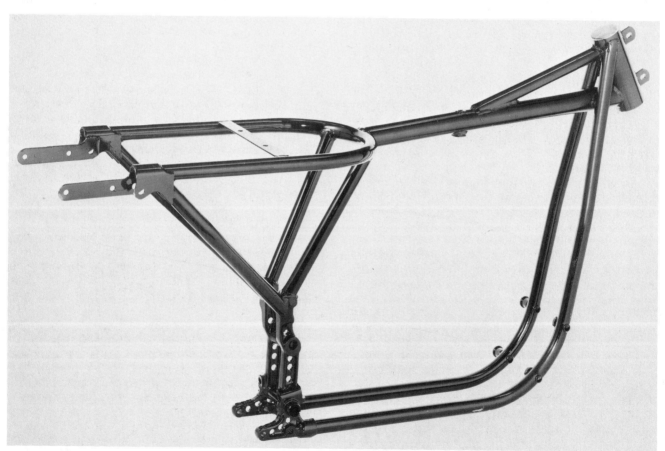

Looking back here, this is the last KR frame, which was adapted to the first XR. I used this photo because the factory doesn't have one of the XR. Visible here is the double-tube engine cradle, the triangulated extension to carry the seat and the rear shock mounts and best of all, the casting known as the twin tomahawks, at lower left. The rear engine mount bolts to the lower right of the casting and the swing-arm-pivot bolt runs through the top, just below the highest lightening hole. The holes through the front right of the cradle are for the front engine mount, and the boss at the middle of the backbone is for a stay between backbone and cylinder heads. Harley-Davidson

Soon as the XR-750 appeared—this is Lawwill in 1970—it was revised. The object beneath his left elbow is the air cleaner for the rear carb, which faces forward. The frame has shorter shocks and the fork tubes are higher in the clamps, to lower the high and heavy engine. Harley-Davidson

with straight backbone, called the Highboy, or one with backbone bent to wrap close to the cylinder heads and to lower the steering head, called the Lowboy. The Lowboy was mostly for road racing, except that it and Belland's TT frames were the inspiration for the XR frame.

The XR frame was made of 4130 steel tubing, with a large single backbone tube, paired front downtubes that wrapped beneath the engine and paired triangles joining the rear shock mounts, the backbone and the rear engine mount.

The triangles, the rear of the front tubes, the swing arm pivot and the rear engine mount all came together at a casting, called the twin tomahawks because the thing was shaped like a pair of those instruments. Such a casting was unique in racing by then and looks like a mistake, except that Lawwill says you have to spend lots of time and money fabricating the frame section that performs the same function while the casting costs a dollar or two.

All the parts and ideas in the frame were conventional and established, or so the designers believed. The swing arm rode in Timkin bearings, the forks were Ceriani and the shock absorbers came from Girling. Brakes were an option on the track and in the catalog, so the first XR was displayed with spool hubs front and rear.

A lovely 2 gal. fuel tank and slick seat and rear fender were done in fiberglass by the Wixom brothers, who'd designed the fairings for the KR road racers. The 3 qt. oil tank mounted below the seat behind the engine. Wheels were laced spokes, 19 in. diameter, and the tires were semi-knob, certified for road use as the rules required. The alloy cases and oil tank were polished, the barrels were silver, the heads black and the fiberglass was team orange.

The XR-750 was lovely. Period. It was in balance and alignment, the very avatar of a production dirt track racer.

An Omen of the Future

It was shown, with appropriate fanfare, at the show held in conjunction with the opening of the 1970 racing season at the Houston Astrodome. The magazines and newspapers had been timed, with early press sessions, so they hit the stands at showtime.

All the timing was perfect, or so it seemed. The racing shop did the prototype and first handful of frames, then an outside outfit produced the rest of the batch of 200. All the frames were fitted with engines and wheels and tires and were lined up in a warehouse, where the AMA officials solemnly counted the full number, as required.

Officially the XR-750 weighed 317 lb. dry, and had a wheelbase of 54 in.—that's nominal, because suspension tuning often means a given bike will be an inch or so longer or shorter on any given day.

There was one odd note, to which little attention was paid at the time.

Dick O'Brien did an extensive introduction of the bike, in *Cycle.* He was just back home from testing at

Daytona. He didn't reveal lap times, but professed satisfaction. Then he said the engine produced "about 62 bhp at 6200 rpm."

Editor Cook Neilson protested, saying that first, the new engine had to wind higher than that, and that because the KR was nearly as powerful at lower speeds and the XLR was more powerful at the same speed and so forth, the XR had to have more power. OB repeated his statement. Neilson knew how fast Cal Rayborn, winner of the Daytona race in 1968 and 1969, expected to go in 1970. Neilson reckoned the new engine had to have at least 70 bhp and that O'Brien was being modest, or wanted to mislead the other teams.

Would that it had been so.

The season began well, as Lawwill won the Houston short-track race on his Harley-Davidson-Aermacchi 250 cc single-cylinder Sprint. Mark Brelsford at least got his TT bike, the fabled Belland-built *Goliath,* into the final, where he finished ninth: the indoor track wasn't kind to the big machines, but Brelsford always had the touch and outrode men who were outwardly stronger and should have done better on the heavyweights.

Then came Daytona, and disaster.

The factory team was loosely organized back then, at least in part because of the other struggles in The Motor Company. Four riders flew the flag at the beach in 1970: defending champion Mert Lawwill, protégé Mark Brelsford, pavement genius Cal Rayborn and old pro Bart Markel.

Lawwill did most of his own tuning, and Brelsford was with him. Markel also kept his own counsel, while Rayborn was under the wing of Len Andres, a former H-D dealer who'd tuned his son Brad to a national title and three Daytona wins. Rayborn was an extra step from the factory because he preferred pavement to dirt and had persuaded Harley to let him ride a Yamaha in lightweight races. H-D had nothing that could compete with the little two-stroke—in fact the other Japanese factories were in the same boat—so Rayborn couldn't do the home club any harm.

In the event, O'Brien must have known things were worse than he was letting on, because when the truck got to the track, the engines were wearing twin carburetors. Short, curbed stubs had been fitted to the intake ports so the carbs sat together on the right. So extreme a bend couldn't have helped, but it was better than having the staggered intake pulses pulling through the same venturi.

One of the low points, Lawwill at Daytona Beach, 1970. The road-race version was a kit, with four-shoe drum front brake, fairing, seat screen and 6 gal. fuel tank built for the late KRTTs, and with 18 in. rear wheel so the newer road-race tires would fit. The iron engine produced more heat than it could take and road racing, with literally miles of wide open throttle, was the worst place the engine could have gone. All the new engines blew up before the rest of the racers got warmed up. Harley-Davidson

The machines were all-new. The frames were high sorts of Lowboy, wrapped around the taller engine but with lowered steering heads: one of the factory tips handed out later was to cut a full inch off the bottom of the steering head and tack it back on the top. The wheels were 18 in. diameter, the better to use the new road racing tires. Four-shoe Fontana drum brakes, that would grace the factory road racers until 1973, were mounted; disc brakes weren't reliable in those first applications, or so the traditionalists thought. All four of the XRs wore longer exhaust pipes, tuned for torque, and an airbox to feed cool air to the carbs. Markel's engine had a scoop to deliver air to the rear cylinder, while Cal's entire fairing was offset 1 in. to the left, the better to ensure adequate airflow.

The opposition showed up in force, with force. The Triumph triple, tested later by a magazine, had a full 80 bhp, and the Kawasaki two-stroke triple had 75.

In 1970 qualifying was done with a dash down the front straight. Gene Romero and Triumph had top time, 157 mph. The Harleys couldn't break 150; they were no faster than the old flatheads had been and they didn't make the top ten.

The four new bikes retired, with melted engines, and the best Harley-Davidson was Walt Fulton's old and private KR, in sixth.

The Harley team "never seemed to have it their way," said *Cycle News,* while *Cycle World* commented they "were never in the hunt."

The XR won its dirt debut, Lawwill up, at a non-national half-mile at Ascot. But Brelsford rode an old KR at the first Sacramento mile of the year and Mert wasn't in the final. At Phoenix, Mert was second and Brelsford fifth and Rayborn out of the running. Strange comment, quoted from *Cycle News:* "There isn't much to say [about the new XRs] except they need work. Cal said some frame work would also help."

At the Kent road race, Rayborn's engine blew up, Markel and Brelsford didn't qualify and Lawwill was a dismal thirteenth. There was an entirely different style of disaster at Atlanta, when labor troubles at the airport meant nobody would unload the bikes from the airplane. As if to make up for that, Lawwill won the Cumberland national and Mark was fifth, despite being "plagued with mechanical problems," as *Cycle News* said.

Evidently. All the XRs retired from the Talladega road race, Lawwill coasted to a stop with a grounded kill button at Reading while Cal's engine blew again.

Canadian privateer Dave Sehl won on Louisville's tricky limestone half-mile, despite a blown oil line that had him riding the last six laps with crossed fingers. Rayborn was second, a crippled engine put Lawwill next to last, "riding 20 mph with a disgusted expression on his face," and Brelsford was behind him. At Loudon, Cal was thrown off and broke his wrist, Brelsford's ignition failed as Lawwill trailed in

twelfth. Mert rode his KR at Hinsdale while "more ill luck plagued the XR," and Brelsford's magneto failed again. At Columbus, Sehl won, Brelsford was fourth and it was Lawwill's turn to have mechanical failure.

They couldn't make the show for the San Jose mile. Mert's engine lunched itself again while Brelsford put on a spectacular display of wide-open-throttle, feet-up, power slides. To no avail. The machine didn't have the power to make the program.

Just about then Triumph certified its 750 twin for AMA dirt-track racing, while a magazine test showed the BSA triple, as tuned for the mile, weighed 380 lb. but had 83 bhp. Direct comparison is tough here because nobody actually weighed the XR at the time. The magazines simply took the factory's word. Years later, guys in the shop said the dirt version, minus brakes, weighed about 340 lb. topped off, and had 62 to 65 bhp with the first twin-carb heads. So the iron version was well behind the competition.

One more result: Brelsford flung his XR into top time at the Santa Rosa mile. In the national Mert was seventh, Brelsford ninth and Cal sixteenth.

Then came an exposé.

The Flaws

For background, as they say in diplomatic circles, twenty years ago the reporters worked in gee-gosh-golly mode. They tended to think they were part of the circus, and they forgot that the fans and readers hadn't been with them in the pits. Thus, while the dismal finishes and cryptic remarks let the fans work out that the new Harley-Davidson wasn't the sensational winner it was supposed to be, nobody had actually written any such thing.

Until Ed Youngblood, who later became head of the AMA but who was editor of *Cycle News East* in 1970, got together with a disappointed tuner and told all. (Twenty years later Youngblood still won't say who the informant was; Dick O'Brien may be retired, but he still has respect.)

Even then, the article was almost apologetic. Youngblood wrote that "too many people jumped into the 1970 season thinking they had found an easy way to the checkered flag."

Well yes, they did think that. They thought that in part because that's what Harley-Davidson ads said, and in part because that's what the magazines told them. As *Cycle Guide* put it, when you bought an XR-750 you got "a race ready dirt track racer."

Never mind. Based on what *Cycle News* said in 1970, and on what even OB and crew admitted when the new engine came out in 1972, and on recollections and firsthand experience in the years since, here's what was wrong with the iron XR:

First, the basic material of the barrels and heads, namely cast iron. Useful stuff in many applications, the iron simply retained too much heat for a racing application.

Next, the pistons. Harley-Davidson made the same mistake some car racers made at the same time, and assumed that if an Offy engine will work on oval tracks, so will the engines (or their pieces, in this case) work in other applications. They forgot that American dirt and oval racing cars then ran on alcohol, which is as good at taking away heat as iron is at retaining it. Gasoline burns hotter and the Offy pistons in those early XR engines burned and melted. That's what took the team out of Daytona and out of every other road race that season.

Next, the flywheels. Recall that because there wasn't room for the retaining nuts as used on the XL and XLR mainshafts and flywheels, the plan was to press the shafts into the XR flywheels with extra firmness.

The XR engine, like the KR before it, used ball bearings for the mainshafts. The street engines had roller bearings and bushings. Ball bearings have less friction, which is why they're used for racing. But they will not tolerate any misalignment. Anytime you press two flywheels onto a crankpin and press the shafts into the flywheels, you are going to have some misalignment.

Not much, though. One of the Harley racing secrets, the skill behind the famous engines, is the time and talent to make this alignment as perfect as the human hand and machine measurement can make it.

That still isn't perfect. And when it's not perfect, the weak link between those intolerant ball bearings and the ever-so-slightly untrue shafts, wheels and pins was the pressed-in mainshafts. They came loose, with the horrible damage you can only imagine.

Here's a historical note nobody can explain even now. I said you can't imagine because I, the author and owner of an iron XR engine, know firsthand what the damage looks like.

I was surprised. The introductory story *Cycle* did on the XR mentioned the weak link of the shafts and said the shafts would be welded to the flywheels.

But mine, engine No. 36, were merely pressed into place. And when I got a replacement right-side flywheel, it came from the warehouse of Len Andres, the tuner for Cal Rayborn during this time. And that flywheel, which must have come direct from the factory, sent by people who had to know how important it would be, was merely pressed into place.

I had mine welded. And there's a much better cure, a permanent fix for the whole problem, coming in the next chapter.

Back to the flaws. Even without the structural shortcoming listed, the XR wasn't a good engine because it didn't have as much power as it was supposed to have, nor as much as the competition had. Studies done during that first season showed that the ports were the wrong shape, the single carb didn't flow enough air in the right sequence and the valves were too big.

A flaw of even more importance was the shape of the combustion chamber. Back in the early 1950s, when H-D was working on the design for the Sportster XL engine, the classic hemispherical combustion chamber, with its deep dome and two valves at right angles to each other, was the way to do things in performance mode.

But the oil companies kept improving their products, the car companies increased compression ratios to match octane ratings and the hemispherical chamber became more like a hemi-orange peel. The combustion chamber was all wrong in shape for controlling the flame front and the expansion of heated air, which is how engines get their power.

Another pause here. This was a boom time for professional AMA racing. A national race would have as many as 175 licensed experts show up for time trials to determine who'd be the forty-eight qualified riders to go for the sixteen starting places in the main event.

There should have been a good market for machines, and there was, with Harleys, Nortons, BSAs, Triumphs and Yamahas, even an occasional Honda, certified for AMA racing.

Even so, practically speaking, the XR-750 was the only big dirt racer on the market, but the customers were more wary, or more aware, than one might have expected. Jumping ahead here, by the end of the iron engine's time, just a few more than half the production run, something more than 100 machines, had been sold, or assigned to the team, favored tuners and so forth. (Exact accounting isn't possible. Some complete machines were parted out, and other piles of parts became complete machines and which of these does one count as a motorcycle?)

But Harley-Davidson did have customers who bought XR-750s. For those buyers, H-D had bulletins and instructions.

First, they said, retard the ignition setting, from 50 deg. BTDC to 35–40 deg. There was a double meaning here, in that first, such a large amount of advance indicates that it took a long time for the flame front to fill the chamber, which is a sign of a poor design, and second, retarding was needed because of pre-ignition, another sign of the same problem.

Next, there was a long list of internal modifications for the oil pump and passageways. More flow was needed, to clear oil from the crankcase and to use oil to carry heat away from trouble spots, especially the cylinder heads. The instructions said to be extra careful with the timing of the breather. They didn't give the reason, but what had happened was, nobody had remembered that the engine now wound much tighter and that meant the timing for the opening and closing of the valve that ventilated the crankcase was different. Or should have been.

The factory recommended a new breather, installed for the primary case. There was a one-way valve between crankcase and primary, and the pressure in the crankcase was putting pressure into the primary and the gearbox, which wasn't good.

And the private owner was supposed to reduce the compression ratio by cutting ¼ in. off the top of the piston. The compression ratio had been a nominal—that means measured from bottom to top of stroke, without regard for when the valves close and compression actually begins—figure of 9.5:1. With cuts, it should have been measured at 6.7:1, not much more than the old sidevalve engine used to run.

Were these backward steps? Yes, in that the reduction in spark advance and compression ratio meant the engine produced less power as it generated less heat. And the owners were told to fit an oil cooler, installed in the feed from oil pump to cylinder heads.

Cal Rayborn's earlier cryptic comment about the frame referred to another plain fact: the new bike didn't handle well. The bulletins didn't say this, but they did show the owner how to cut 1 in. off the bottom of the steering head and put it back on the top, and suggested shock and springs that were 1 in. shorter. Both changes would of course lower the bike.

Developing the Engine

There's never enough time to do it right but there's always enough time to do it over.

While the racing shop was doing what it could for the customers, the shop and the team and the factory-backed tuners were also doing what they could.

Some of this, the dual carbs, has been mentioned. That took place right away. We can infer now that O'Brien knew he had a power problem well before the XRs ever arrived at Daytona Beach.

Next came cylinder heads with the front intake and exhaust in the stock locations, but with the rear barrel's intake moved to the left front. The front carb pointed to the rear, on the right, and the rear carb pointed to the front, on the left.

The fourth version of the iron heads used two front heads, with intakes at right rear and the two carbs pointing to the rear, on the right. The front exhaust was on the right and the rear exhaust on the left.

This was, as they say, labor intensive. Bill Werner, who'd been hired as a race shop mechanic four years earlier and who'd been given the crash-speed job of assembling all those 1970 XRs, had the task of building twelve sets of parallel-carb heads. It took Werner and another man six months of filling, brazing, trimming, boring and such. It also did what *Cycle* called figurative violence to the AMA rule that the stock castings be used for cylinder heads. Well, they began as stock, was the best excuse the factory had.

Naturally, the flywheels used by the team were welded up. As cited earlier, there's evidence that the customer parts went out without welding, and the customers took their chances: nothing in the factory bulletins in my file mentions that weakness.

The major internal changes done to team engines began with the connecting rods. Lawwill did this one and agrees it's one of those theories that everybody can debate.

The third try for a working cylinder head involved plugging the rear intake, as seen on the stock head, left, and carving out a new intake port next to it but facing the other side, for a second carb. This did great violence to the notion of a stock casting but the factory got away with it, perhaps because it didn't do that much good. The fitting between the old and new ports is a drain from the rockerbox. Ted Pratt

23

Here's the iron XR head sequence. At the bottom, the XR and XLR heads, with angled intakes to one, central carburetor. Then the bent intakes, to two carbs in the center of the vee. Then the cross-over intakes, mildly modified front head on the right, the relocated rear head on the left. At the top, the last version and the one that was practice for the alloy engine, with two carbs at right rear, the rear exhaust on the right and the front one exiting to the left. Ted Pratt

But anyway, imagine a connecting rod as long as a football field. If the crankpin rotates, say 30 deg. off top dead center, the angle of this infinitely long connecting rod will hardly have changed at all and the piston will still be pushing almost straight down, rather than making the flywheels revolve.

Now make that connecting rod as short as it can be, an inch or two, and yes, this time the same 30 deg. of rotation cocks the rod at an angle and the down motion of the piston has become rotation of the flywheels. True, such a short rod won't have enough clearance within the other moving parts and even more true, cocking the rod will jam the piston against the cylinder wall. And more thought will reveal that changing the length of the connecting rod will also change the length of time the piston is moving down, or holding still or accelerating or decelerating, and this means more work is needed getting the valve and camshaft timings and sequences right.

In the long and theoretical run, there seems to be an optimum rod length based on a percentage of the engine's stroke, and varied by builders and tuners with hunches of their own.

In this case, team engines had 1 in. taken out of their connecting rods. This gave more power and quicker power. It also meant that the cylinder had to be trimmed by an inch, which removed the mounting flange by which the barrel was held to the cases, so the heads and barrels were changed so through bolts ran from the heads to the cases, holding the barrels in between.

The ports were redone when they were moved, naturally, and the valves were made smaller. The team got new pistons and cut down the domes while machining out the combustion chambers so there was more chamber and less slice of orange peel. And the spark plugs were moved from the side of the chamber to the top, the better to speed up and control flame travel.

Toward the very end of the program, when the alloy engine was well under way, the team iron engines got forged flywheels with the mainshafts an integral part of the discs. The one-piece flywheels took care of the flex problem, and, obviously they didn't come loose.

We are compressing time here. Improvements for the iron engine began before the thing made its official debut, as noted. And work carried on well past the official replacement, as we'll see shortly. But for the record, with all the changes and a good set of team parallel-carb heads, the later iron XR engines cranked out 68 or so bhp, on the engine dynamometer.

Developing the Chassis

The other problem, the one Rayborn hinted at, was handling.

Plainly put, the XR-750 didn't handle at all well. The flaw was basic: the frame size and engine location and so forth were based on the KR and KRTT. The sidevalve engine was smaller and lighter and carried its weight lower. When the XR first got to the track, it had extra weight, too high and too far back; the extra bulk on the rear made for better traction sometimes, but the front wheel was light under power and washed out—pushed, as the stock car guys say.

Lawwill recalls that they began by cutting 1 in. out of the frame backbone, pulling the steering head back and thus putting more static weight on the front. If they'd moved the rear wheel back to get the same weight shift, the wheelbase would have been longer, he adds, and that would have made the machine even more difficult to turn. If they'd steepened the steering head rake to pull the front wheel closer, that would have cost stability at speed: again for the complete subject of chassis tuning, everything you change, changes other things as well.

The steering head was trimmed at the bottom, with the material going back onto the top, as recommended to owners. The rear springs were shortened, so the bike would be lower at both ends.

These changes got the XR so low that the lower left corner of the engine, the primary case wall and cover, dragged when the bike was fully cranked into a corner. The only way out of that was to make the case narrower and when they trimmed the case walls, the clutch hit the cover so the clutch outer hub was trimmed and six pairs of clutch plates went where seven had gone before. (When Mert said that, it solved a mystery for me. When I built my iron engine I couldn't find room for the seven pairs of plates called for by the book. That was in 1981. Not until 1990 did I know it was a factory change instead of my clumsiness.)

1971: Season of Agony

One other problem area for the iron engine and the team was that the new ownership had labor problems and the unhappy employees meant that O'Brien, rightly or not, felt he had to farm out some of the development work for the racing team. A lot of the problem chasing and machining was done at Nichels Engineering, in Indiana. The men who worked there were Ron Alexander and Walt Faulk. They did excellent work and came, as people who care about their work do under such circumstances, to care about the engine.

Meanwhile, as the engine began to become worth the effort and the chassis and suspension were sorted

out, the team was able to run the Sprint-based short track and indoor machines, and to use the XLR for the faster TTs and the KR when the XR simply wouldn't get going—but it wasn't enough.

Not to make a sad story long, the XRs broke, or faded away until it became a case of, quoting *Cycle News,* "Even more surprising, all but two of the XRs survived." Right. The Harleys broke so often during 1970 that when they didn't, it made the papers.

At the end of the 1970 season, Mert Lawwill was no longer number one. Gene Romero had taken the plate, for Triumph.

Nor was that the end. The 1971 season began with Brelsford second in the Houston short track, while Lawwill led but faded to seventh. There were no team Harleys in the TT final.

In their Daytona preview, *Cycle News* said Harley was only an outside contender because "The word is that the really good engines are another year away."

They were even further away than that. Instead, the 1971 Daytona 200 was an occasion for heroism.

The fastest qualifier was Paul Smart, on a Triumph triple that had to have at least 80 bhp. Smart's Triumph was clocked at 150 mph on the straight, and 2:09.64 for a full lap.

Cal Rayborn was second fastest for a full lap at 2:09.79. His iron XR with full fairing but no better

While the road racers and the factory did exotic tricks, or tried to, the riders soldiered on. This is Rex Beauchamp, which he and his friends pronounced "Bow-Champ," backing it into a turn at the Louisville half-mile, still with the *one carb in the right center. The half-mile needs more craft than speed, so that was the only place the iron XR could keep pace. Harley-Davidson*

This is Lawwill's 1971 mount, with a non-XR fuel tank, two carbs (not visible here of course) and changes. Note first that the steering head has had an inch trimmed off the bottom and added to the top, so the front of the bike is lower. Next, there are drains from the lower corners of the rockerboxes to the corrugated tube that drains below the magneto. The primary drive is probably narrowed, but that doesn't show. Cycle

than 68 bhp was clocked at a drawling 142 mph. How'd Calvin make up for the lack of power? Here's what *Cycle* said: "Cal Rayborn works the infield like no man alive, his weight on the footpegs, crawling all over the bike, power sliding, man-handling, turning the wheel in, bending and shaping each corner until it complies with his interpretation of it. No one else can push as hard as Calvin."

To no avail on that occasion. The factory and team had literally done everything they could do, with a special frame just for Rayborn because he sat and rode differently, with all the new engine parts and with an airbox to feed cold air to the new carbs, with oil coolers everywhere and with four-shoe Fontana brakes, still reckoned as more reliable and effective than discs in 1971.

So Cal's gearbox collapsed. The crew rebuilt it in a pit stop so long it was obvious he couldn't win, but he went back out and lapped at an incredible 2:05, winding the doomed engine to 8700 rpm, just to thrill the fans and perhaps work off what had to be rage. Brelsford meanwhile lost his rear sprocket, Roger Rei-

man's pistons disintegrated while he was in fourth place, Rex Beauchamp was top Harley finisher at thirty-sixth, with Cal forty-seventh, Dave Sehl forty-eighth (after only twenty-nine laps) and Lawwill seventieth, out after twelve laps. It was another of those days.

And so the season went. There were bright spots, like Sehl's win at Louisville, and the always-brave Brelsford ignoring the loose oil line and seizing engine to squeak past the leader at Loudon, winning by 6 in. on the last lap, for the only national road race victory the Waffle Iron managed to collect.

Rather than drone on, Cal hit a rock, his engine blew, he was thrown off and hurt; Mert's engine blew; Brelsford won Ascot on good ol' *Goliath*; and Cal got a rare dirt win when dust stopped the race early.

Item: Harley-Davidson released photos of the new XR, with alloy barrels and heads and a host of improvements, in September 1971.

Item: Dick Mann was national champion for 1971. He rode an XR early in the season but got British backing later, so the number one plate was BSA property.

Here's the right side of a late iron XR. The rubber hose at the center of the vee runs to a cooler, atop the front rockerbox, then to a junction and the rockers, at the top of the vee. The tube snaking below the front intake manifold is the drain from rockerboxes to cases, and there's a one-way valve in the giant breather hose coming out of the rear of the gearcase. Cycle

The full factory version. The former spark plug holes have been filled and the plugs moved up, to the center of the reworked combustion chamber. The cylinders are one fin lower than stock, to allow shorter connecting rods, and the separate bolts to hold barrel to cases and heads to barrels have been replaced by through bolts, from case to top of head. That's a Lowboy frame, as shown by the height of the steering head relative to the cylinder heads, but it's a factory frame because you can see the tomahawks beneath the rearset and raised left footpeg. Jim Greening

Item: Season's end standings showed Sehl fifth, Brelsford seventh, Rayborn fourteenth and Mert a dismal forty-third.

Item: At Ontario, the iron XR's last official race for the factory team, Calvin was in the hunt until a plug fouled, and visiting family, Renzo Pasolini, who rode for Aermacchi, Harley's Italian connection, was top Harley, in fourth.

Item: Late in 1971 the team did some comparison testing and the old, patched-up, strapped-together and thoroughly futile iron version was marginally faster than the new alloy version. (There will be repercussions of heroic nature, coming soon.)

Next-to-last item: According to gossip in *Cycle News*, at the end of the season "John Harley took a hammer and proceeded to knock every fin off Cal's racer, to hand out as souvenirs."

Final item: "Mert, what word comes to mind when you hear 'iron XR?'"

"Agony. That thing took ten years off my life."

Heat was the enemy. Roger Reiman's factory-backed iron XR road racer, with 18 in. wheels and full brakes, 1971. The dual carbs are housed inside a box so they can get air that hasn't been warmed by passage across the fins or through the oil cooler canted just above the right-side fork slider. The seat and 6 gal. tank date back to the KR, as does the dished rear sprocket. Jim Greening

Time for another of the few high spots, as Dave Sehl goes for the win at Louisville, 1971. No brakes, but the left-side exhaust hints this is an engine with two trailing carbs. Sehl's classic steel-shoe stance illustrates why the left-side footpeg is mounted so far back. Cycle

An odd one. Bill Werner bought and built his own iron XR, even though he worked at the factory. This is it, with his brother perched on the seat. The visible difference is the rotated air cleaner, to clear the rider's knee. But notice the two separate exhaust pipes. Someone tried to patent the idea but this photo, an actual piece of evidence, proved that Werner had done it before the patent was applied for. You can also see both the gear and rear brake levers on the right, out of the rider's way. Bill Werner

Mert Lawwill gets the past word, so we'll give him the last picture, too, proving once again that if you have the right picture, you don't need the words. Mert Lawwill

The carbs have been removed for service and so has the oil cooler that connects to the hose running from the rockerbox oil feeds. But you can see the tach drive from the top center of the gearcase, the breather at the rear of the case and the drains feeding the front and yes, this cover is a lot more compact than the first one was. Jim Greening

Calvin Wows the Limeys

The Waffle Iron's finest hour couldn't have happened in any other way in any other place or time.

Begin with Calvin Rayborn's incredible talent as a road racer. He was good on the dirt, won his share, but road racing displayed his genius. During the same time Harley-Davidson, for whose racing team Rayborn worked, wasn't in contention on pavement, not against the triples and two-strokes then in vogue and, OK, in power.

But there was honor and goodwill on all sides, so Calvin did his dutiful best on the ovals and H-D supplied the best they could on pavement and let Rayborn race other brands in the lightweight class.

Next, there's the British devotion to team competition. You'd think racing would be rider against rider but no, the English have motorcycle teams the way we have baseball teams. So a couple of English promoters got the idea of match races, a Yank team and a Brit team, racing in England for points.

The inaugural series was scheduled for early in 1972. It was entirely the wrong time, in that Harley had replaced, make that scrapped, the iron XR, but the alloy version wasn't ready for racing yet. Except that guys who work for factory teams often have their private programs as well. Jay Springsteen owns a couple of XRs, so does Bill Werner.

In late 1971 Walt Faulk, a Harley technician who'd worked with Nichels Engineering in the iron XR development program, had an iron engine on loan from the racing department. He'd borrowed it because on his own time, Faulk raced in amateur events. He'd done lots of work on the engine and he believed in it.

The match race promoters invited Rayborn, who asked Faulk to help. Harley-Davidson management didn't like the idea much, their name was on the bike after all, but they couldn't figure a good way to refuse so they said, OK guys, do your best.

They did that. And they created a legend that's still powerful.

All the English fans knew then was that Americans raced on horse tracks and chewed gum. And they'd seen the biker movies.

So they knew what to expect from the clunky old Harley and the lanky Californian with the big grin—except that the combination won three of the six races and would have won four except the poor old engine, stressed to the max and kept alive only by Faulk's wizardry, lost power in the last few laps.

Give credit here: the English are good sports. Everybody in the stands knew instantly that Cal and the Waffle Iron were going beyond what man and machine could do. He'd never seen the tracks before, didn't expect the climate and clearly the Harley wasn't a match for the factory Triumphs.

But there Calvin was, time after time, cheerful and happy and unimpressed with himself. The reporters asked about his lines through this or that corner and Rayborn said he didn't know the names of the curves, he just rode 'em.

His warmth and talent and enthusiasm and courage canceled any negatives the press and public might have harbored. Quoting Jim Greening in *Cycle,* "When it was all over they could have given him Buckingham Palace and nobody would have minded."

Against all odds, is the slogan here. Calvin Rayborn was in a new country and climate, on tracks he'd never seen, riding a bike the factory wanted to forget. So here he is, leading England's Ray Pickerell on the factory's best Triumph triple at Brands Hatch in 1972. Jim Greening

"The eyes say it all," was photographer Jim Greening's comment and indeed, they do. Waiting for the start at Oulton Park are Rayborn and Walt Faulk, who prepared the engine he borrowed from the factory and who went to England to keep it running beyond its natural life. He did that, but as their eyes say, the Waffle Iron is on its last legs. Jim Greening

Chapter 3

Aluminum Rules

Early in 1972 the Harley-Davidson Motor Company, in the person of sales manager Charles Thompson, issued a press release to the effect that the Harley-Davidson racing team wouldn't enter or attend the Daytona 200, the prestige race of the year.

Thompson was an unusual man. He later became president of the company, a job for which he was supremely qualified: he'd begun as a motorcycle en-

thusiast, a schoolteacher who liked bikes as a hobby. He enjoyed being a customer so much he became a dealer, and was so good at that he joined the company, in which he rose to the top.

No small part of Thompson's success was due to his honesty. Nobody who knew the man could doubt that the words in the press release came from the man whose name was at the bottom line: "The deadline

At a casual glance and in broad detail, there wasn't much difference between the 1970 and 1972 XR-750s. Same wheels, forks, shocks, same lovely shapes to the fiberglass tank, seat and fender, same efficient profile for the cases.

But you can't miss the two rearward-jutting carbs and now that you know what to look for, check the position of the steering head in relation to the backbone and brace. Harley-Davidson

[for getting the machines qualified] cannot be met without breaking the rules. Harley-Davidson does not choose to break the rules. . . . The moment the new XR is approved and ready, we will race. We will race to win.''

Honest, open, straightforward . . . and a surprising way to begin the saga of the world's most successful motorcycle racing engine. It was such a surprise in fact that *Cycle News* said, in nearly so many words, that there had to be something behind the scenes.

And there was. The late arrival of the alloy XR-750 began back in the mid and late 1960s, when the rules were being discussed and revised. Harley-Davidson management was in flux, and the company was in financial turmoil. Team manager Dick O'Brien was told to start on a full 750 cc racer, then told to stop and told to start again. The result, as detailed earlier, was chaos and disaster. To make things worse, after H-D was bought, actually saved, by the AMF conglomerate, there were labor struggles and feuds and O'Brien wound up farming out various projects, for instance the road-racing bikes and various aspects of design, such as frames. He was buying parts, and re-

search and time. All the parts would come together, but it wasn't nearly as easy as it looked later.

Scrap Iron and the New Alloy XR

Everybody in the team and the company and probably in racing knew the iron XR was a stopgap, too little and too late. What the outsiders only suspected was that O'Brien knew from the start that he'd need a real racing engine. He began design work when the rules were changed. He didn't have management's permission because he hadn't bothered to ask for it. Instead, he knew that by the time he was asked, he'd be behind again.

Politics and results will come later. We'll begin with the heart of the XR-750, the engine.

And that begins with some basics. The overall design was pure H-D, the inline V-twin with gearbox in unit. There are the four cavities mentioned earlier: crankcase, primary case, timing case and transmission case. The next level of detail follows the iron-barrel engine, with 45 deg. included angle, primary drive by triple-row chain, four one-lobe cam wheels with pushrods and rocker arms and two valves per cylinder, a dry clutch in a wet primary case, four for-

The new engine is even more obvious here, with the two tuned exhaust pipes high on the left. The 3 qt. oil tank now has its filler neck on the left, and the left-side footpeg bolts to a bracket on the rear frame lugs. The chrome-plated primary cover was shared with the iron XR and the KR. Harley-Davidson

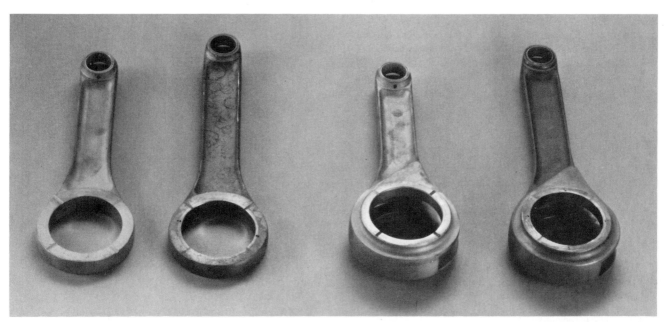

The new engine's shorter stroke (and Dick O'Brien's belief in short connecting rods) gave the new engine shorter rods. The new front rod is on the left, then the old front and the new rear and the old rear. The configuration was traditional Harley fork and blade. Harley-Davidson

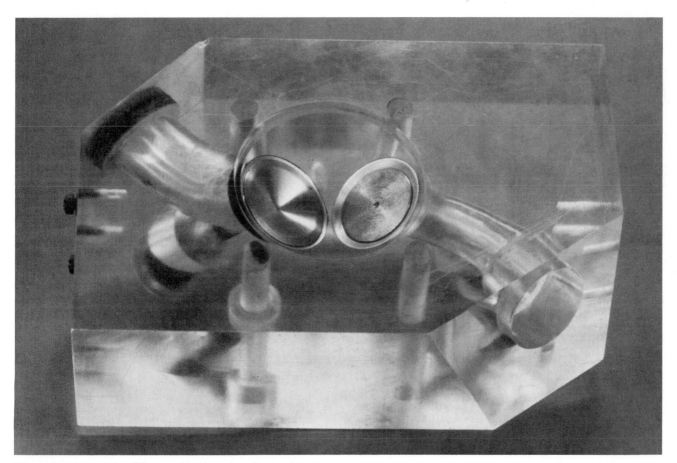

Clear plastic models of the combustion chamber and ports were made so flow efficiency could be checked. Harley-Davidson

ward speeds, a pair of flywheels joined by a crankpin and riding in ball main bearings with roller bearings for the connecting rods, the rods in fork-and-blade alignment, air cooling and so on down the line. The alloy engine was so much like the iron engine that some parts interchanged: for example the engine sprockets and primary chains, all the clutch parts, the transmission, timing cover, oil pump and breather. If you want to push this to the limit, the clutch plates were shared with the KR and K models from 1952! Harley-Davidson doesn't like to throw away parts.

Next, more of a surprise was that the later iron engines were based on what was going to become the alloy engine. When O'Brien and Pieter Zylstra began laying out the engine, late in 1969, they came up with what seemed to be the optimum valve sizes and port sizes and shapes. They knew that they wanted the exhausts in the front and the intakes at the rear and that the engine couldn't breathe or be tuned correctly unless each cylinder had its own carburetor. Thus, when the late iron engines appeared, for the team only, they had the front exhausts and the two carbs, on the right rear, that the alloy engines used and still use.

In the same way, the new flywheels were forged, not cast. They were made of 413 chromoly steel. The iron engine had used cast flywheels with the main-shafts, to the primary drive on the left and the cams, oil pump and ignition, on the right, pressed into place. These came loose, as we've seen, and had to be retro-welded. The new engine's forged flywheels were made with the shafts integral and markedly stronger for it. And the resourceful Zylstra drew the flywheels so there was extra material in the flank where the hole would be drilled for the crankpin. So early examples of the second-version flywheels could—by no accident at all—have their crankpins set farther away from the center and, by golly, the stronger flywheels went right into the late iron engines. Again, there were no part numbers for this, nor could the ordinary buyer get them.

To offset that seeming violation of the rules and principles involved, let it be noted here that there were not that many customers, especially not by late in 1971. Along about the same time the alloy engine was supposed to come out, the warehouse was still packed with close to 100 unsold iron XRs. Some were

Hard alloy valve seats are a shrink fit into the head casting. The new heads had a modified hemisphere with the spark plug offset. Cycle

The new flywheels were forged steel, with the shafts and wheels in the same forging. The short stroke put the crankpin so close to the shafts that the flywheels and pin were held together with seven tons of pressure instead of the *traditional jam nuts. The long shaft on the left is for the primary drive, the short one goes to the gearcase. Harley-Davidson*

pirated for spare parts, a handful were converted and the rest were scrapped for accounting purposes. Yes, scrapped. Companies that aren't sure of a future don't worry much about posterity.

The Alloy Advantage

The differences between the iron and aluminum XR engines were of course vital, critical, major and obvious.

First, dimensions. The Iron XR was de-stroked to make the displacement limit and still it was woefully undersquare, that is, it had more stroke than bore. The engineers had a much freer time with the real racing engine, so bore was larger than stroke:

	Bore	Stroke	Displacement Per Cylinder
Iron	3.0 in.	3.18 in.	22.467 ci
Alloy	3.125 in.	2.98 in.	22.845 ci

Nominal displacement for both was 750 cc, with some latitude allowed for the occasional overbore.

The big change was in material. The new barrels and cylinder heads were cast in an alloy called KO1A. It had a silver content of one percent, it was very expensive and it was the best material for the job, simply because it would transfer and dissipate the heat from the power needed from the engine. The cylinders were generously finned so they'd cool under full power and they were sized so they'd fit neatly in their vee. Iron liners, the material in which the pistons actually travel, were spiggoted and protrude from the

New pistons were modified to have shallow hemispheres, with cutouts for valve clearance. The first ones were made in Italy, by the folks who did the work for Aermacchi, and they gave some trouble. Cycle

Alloy cylinders were generously finned. The iron liners were topped by a shoulder that fitted between the cylinder and head—check clearance machined into combustion chamber—and the lower edge spigotted into the cases, for perfect, no-gasket sealing. Cycle

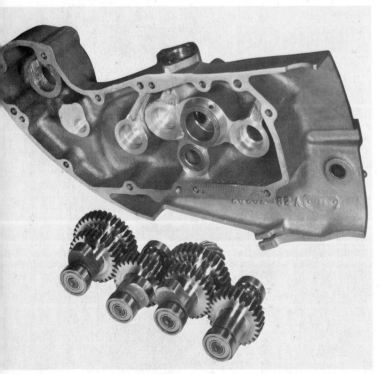

Gearcase cover—shown here with a set of cam lobes and gears—is an intricate casting. The cams and gears are driven by the right-side mainshaft and in turn drive the magneto, off the front cam, and the oil pump and tach off the third cam. Harley-Davidson

bottom of the cylinders into the crankcase. The barrels are held in place by through bolts, from the heads to the cases.

The actual cases were revisions of the originals, which in turn were descended from the XL and XLR cases. The alloy cases provide for the larger bore, and for a larger right-side main bearing.

Connecting rods for the new engine were nearly identical to those used in the later iron engines. The rods were 1 in. shorter than the originals, and with the shorter stroke of the new version, the rod-stroke ratio was 2.15:1. O'Brien would have preferred 2:1, which is the theoretical ideal in the view of those who believe in the short rod principle, but there wasn't enough room to bring the piston any closer to the flywheels. The roller bearing for the small (piston) ends of the rods rode in the rod itself, while earlier there had been an insert for the cage that carries the rollers.

The new flywheels dispensed with the cinch nuts and separate shafts on the old XL engines and the new crankpin, still of course carrying the fork-and-blade big ends of the rods, was now a press fit, seven tons' worth, instead of a taper and nut.

Pistons and the valvetrain were from Harley's Italian connection. A few years earlier, H-D had bought Aermacchi, a small and struggling firm with some excellent designs. One was a four-stroke single-cylinder engine, in 250 and 350 cc, which was used for road and racing in Europe and America. The engine had a good service record and the piston supplier was tapped for the new XR's pistons.

By this time the pure hemi was on its way out, so the new combustion chamber was a modified hemi, with the valves at an included angle of 68 deg. rather than the classic 90 deg. Valves were smaller, with 1.65 in. intakes and 1.38 in. exhaust, compared with 1.93 and 1.75 for the old engine. Not only did this improve flow, the smaller valves were lighter and allowed higher revs and lighter springs, which meant less strain on the pushrods and rockers and tappets and cams and gears. This in turn allowed a rocker ratio of 1.48:1, that is, the valve side of the rocker arm was longer than the pushrod side, which let the lift at the cam be less than at the valve. Valve clearance adjustment was provided by eccentric rocker arm spindles: Loosen the clamp, rotate the spindles until the feeler gauge says clearance is correct, then tighten. It's quick and because there's no more need for threads and locknuts on the lifters, it's lighter.

The exhaust ports were at the front left of both heads, where the hottest part of the cylinder head would be in the air stream, with the pipes carried high on the left. At first there were two pipes, turned for length and with reverse-cone megaphones that

Exhaust pipe spigots into the exhaust port of the lavishly finned new head. The large threaded holes in the rockerbox are for insertion of the gauge to check clearance, and the small holes are for the ends of the rocker shafts. Cycle

The new engine was slightly shorter than the old one while the frame's vee was more fully occupied by the finned cylinders. The exhaust pipes tuck into the head's deep recesses and are held there by the springs. The rear rockerbox has a stay to the frame backbone, and the front box has a stay to the downtube. Cycle

Thanks to a cutaway engine displayed in the factory museum, we can see the primary chain to the clutch hub and basket, the stack of fiber and metal clutch plates, the pressure plate, the keeper for the springs and retaining nuts and the alloy cover that keeps gear lube out of the dry clutch.

made the tuning extra sharp at a specific rpm. After some experiments with domestic and imported products, the team settled on slide-valve Mikuni carbs, with 36 mm venturis. There was some soul searching here, but in plain fact the Mikunis produced power and could be easily jetted and adjusted to suit the engine and the day.

Ignition was the familiar magneto, tucked below the front cylinder and driven by a train of gears from the right-side mainshaft through the cam gears, as with the iron XR. And the timing gear cover had provision to mount a magneto or a tachometer drive, again as before.

The oil system was also as before, in that there was the two-level pump driven at one-quarter engine speed, and the timed breather set to open and close off the crankcase in sequence with the rise and fall of the pistons. The problems experienced with this design in the iron engine hadn't gone unnoticed. The alloy engine got a one-way breather working off the timing case as well as a vent line to the oil tank, and there was an oil cooler sited between the pressurized return line and the tank. The tank itself was similar,

Early versions of the alloy engine were tidy and still used production parts like the countershaft-sprocket cover with provision for a kick-start lever, and the gearcase cover with flange for mounting the ignition on top rather than in front. Mikuni carbs have been used on the XR from the beginning.

a triangular aluminum canister beneath the seat and behind the engine, but with the filler on the left because the new intake system took the space on the right.

The first alloy XR-750 engine was given its first dynamometer test on June 1, 1971. It produced 69 bhp, corrected to standard air density and temperature, at 6800 rpm. After the carbs were checked and set and the timing adjusted, the engine peaked at 73 bhp. Years later Lawwill recalled that he hoped if they worked extra hard, someday they'd see a full 75 hp.

The engine was off to a good start and met the rest of the motorcycle, which was already doing fine.

XR and XRTT Frame Variations

The new model, non-working models of which were built for display, looked almost identical to the older version.

In many ways, it was identical. The production XR frames delivered in 1970 came through the good offices of Earl Widman, a racing dealer from St. Louis. He was one of O'Brien's trusted helpers and he knew design, so he and his son Ron and their crew got the contract for the XR frames. The Widmans built 250, which was more than the AMA required and twice as many as were sold with the iron engine, so the first batch of alloy engines went into the leftover frames.

It should be noted here that the team was large and loose. The racing department had four full-time and two temporary workers when Zylstra joined the company. Then there was Nichels Engineering, doing the road racers, and people like the Widmans and the Wixom brothers, who'd designed the fairings and seats for the later KR road racers and kept on with improvements. The riders were part racer, part builder. Each man on the team, that is, who'd agreed to ride for the factory, got his dirt machine plus spare parts as needed plus expenses. The road racers were prepared separately and delivered to the track. Each rider was expected to do his own work, or as much as he could. He was also expected to find help for those mechanical chores beyond his time or talent.

So it happened that the riders formed alliances, with each other or with outside—but acceptable—sponsors, as in Dudley Perkins, the San Francisco dealer who employed Jim Belland and backed him and Lawwill and Mark Brelsford.

This also meant that some of the riders, Lawwill being the most prominent, did more than their own chores. The second batch of dirt frames for the alloy XR came from Lawwill and Terry Knight, who'd later go into the frame business for himself. These frames were to factory spec, on order, with Lawwill being just another subcontractor. They were to dirt dimensions, even to the cast junctions for the rear engine mount and swing arm pivot, the twin tomahawks.

The castings were used on the earlier XRs, so on purpose the new engine slipped right into the frames

Details. This was a prototype engine. The adjustment ends of the rocker shafts are square, to fit a wrench, and the settings are fixed by the Allen bolts that hold down the slotted plate. This worked, but because there were so many parts and so much machining, the system was changed before the engines went to customers. Note also that there are two oil feed passages at the bottom of the vee, with one plugged and the second going to the rockerboxes. And at lower right there's been a breather fitting machined into the top of the mag drive and then plugged, and there's another breather on the outside face of the housing. Cycle

Cycle parts for the XRTT road racer were mostly carryover, as in fairing and tanks and the huge four-shoe drum brake that will barely fit inside the 18 in. rim. Harley-Davidson

designed for the old one, with the engine stay being almost the only change needed.

The new bike got the fiberglass fuel tank and seat-fender as used for the first XRs, and was delivered to the customer with a dished sprocket fastened directly to the rear hub, and with no brakes at all. Only a few years before this, the AMA had authorized brakes as a dirt track option; the older guys didn't like the brakes and they cost money and the accountants

More differences are visible here, for instance the reversed gearshift lever, the clip-on bars, the tach and the rear disc brake. The XRTT is wearing a flat rear sprocket bolted to a carrier, rather than the dished sprocket that went directly on the hub on the plain XR. Harley-Davidson

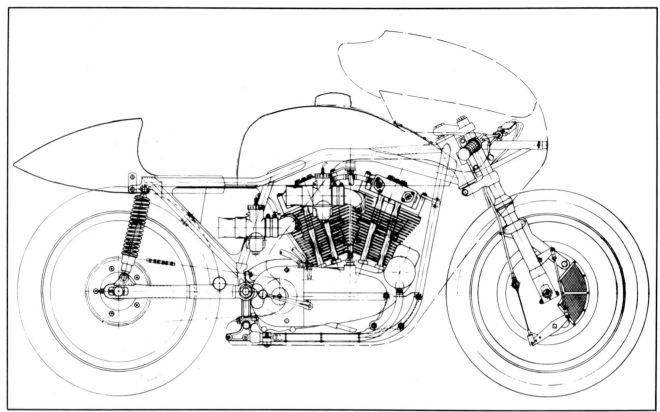

The major difference between XR and XRTT shows up best in the official blueprint. The frame backbone bends down in front, lowering the steering head and making the forks stiffer and better controlled. Racing engineer Pieter Zylstra, who drew this, jokes now that for symmetry's sake he made everything level and if the chassis had been as shown, there would have been only 1 in. or so of rear wheel compression from static. Harley-Davidson

probably couldn't see giving away parts that didn't need to be provided and could be sold.

At the time, the AMA was still requiring production motorcycles but the options had become so loose that frames and such were accepted if they came with the team.

That was useful because there were at least two XR-750 models in 1972, and you could make an argument for a total of three.

The flat-track XR, in black and orange, no brakes, was the production bike and the customer bike, the one seen in the ads.

Then there was the road-racing model, known in Harley's language as the XRTT.

First, the mechanical requirements, as in wheelbase and brakes and streamlining and seating position, were very divergent by 1972. The national championship was still one series with five types of race, so there were customer versions of both the XR-750 and the XRTT. The main parts book was for the plain XR, with XRTT parts listed when they were shared, and there was a factory supplement for bits like the fairing and tanks that came only for the XRTT.

The XRTT frames, the last of the Lowboys, were done by Nichels Engineering. There were between forty and fifty frames—the number varies with the memories of the guys who were there—and of these, seven or eight were heliarc welded, for extra strength and peace of mind. The special frames went to the team, which is why I hint that there sort of was a third version, especially because Rayborn's frames were different, done to his liking and tuned to depend on reaction times only he could muster.

But not totally. The road racers used a curved backbone wrapped around the heads, with the steering head lower to make the front suspension lower and stiffer. And the XRTT had a shorter wheelbase and swing arm mostly because that's what Rayborn, the best road racer on the team, wanted.

A larger percentage of Daytona's 200 miles are run with throttles wide open. The XRTT had a larger oil tank and fuel tank because of that, along with the full fairing and 18 in. wheels wearing a single disc brake in the back and four-shoe drum in front.

According to the factory's pamphlet, here are some specifications:

	XR-750	XRTT
Wheelbase	56.75 in.	54 in.
Seat height	31 in.	28 in.
Weight, dry	295 lb.	324 lb.

	XR-750	XRTT
Steering rake	26 deg.	24 deg.
Trail	3.44 in.	3.31 in.
Fuel capacity	2.5 gal.	6 gal.
Oil capacity	2.75 qt.	4 qt.

According to the factory's press kit, which gave the same fuel capacity and dry weight, the production engine had 10.0:1 compression ratio. There was no claimed power given and the gearing, according to Harley-Davidson's system, was twenty-five-tooth engine sprocket, fifty-nine-tooth clutch sprocket, sixteen-tooth output sprocket and forty-tooth rear sprocket. That's 25 over 59 times 16 over 40, or 5.9:1 overall.

Is that clear? For as long as memory shows, racing Harleys have come with nearly infinite choice of gearing. There are four engine sprockets, twenty, twenty-five, thirty and thirty-four, just the one clutch hub with fifty-nine teeth, ten output sprockets, fifteen through twenty-four teeth, and eleven rear wheel sprockets, thirty-six through forty-six teeth.

Not only that, there are sets of mainshaft and countershaft gears for the transmission, which multiply into ratios too numerous to list here. Stock, the XR came with first gear of 2.09, second gear 1.51, third gear 1.14 and top gear 1:1. First through third are for getting off the line in mile and half-mile races, but all the speeds are used in TT and road racing. The choice, juggling the three of the four sprockets in the driveline and the four sets in the gearbox, means you not only can gear the engine to deliver exactly the power you want when and where, but you can—as we'll learn in the tuning section—use the gearing to help the suspension and vice versa.

And yes, it's so complicated one suspects many of the people using the gears are not getting anything for their efforts.

Peak Power

More notes from the press introduction. The press kit says the engine is "re-designed," which is an understatement. The claimed weights seem light, or optimistic, but in fairness nobody outside the factory weighed an XR back then so we can't be sure. Thirty pounds for brakes and fairing and larger tanks seems close, though. The production fuel tank holds two and a small fraction gallons and the oil tank takes exactly 3 qt., this from my firsthand experience and why the brochure says 2.5 and 2.75, I can't imagine.

The factory's redline for the new engine was 8000 rpm, with peak power coming at 7600. That lines up nicely with the dyno tests from 1971, with 73 bhp at 7600, and the runs from late in 1972, when the team engines had 82 bhp from 7600 through 8000.

There are two comparisons to be made here. One was numerical, in that the alloy XR engine weighed 17 lb. less than the iron engine did, and that the alloy engine had seventy-three percent more fin, or cooling, area. That's impressive even without knowing that the conductivity ratio capacity of aluminum is much better than that of iron. Fin for fin, the new motor was bound to be better cooled.

The other comparison is pragmatic. The team did some testing at Talladega with the very first alloys and the very last and best irons, the latter being cared for by the guys who'd done the work, like Ron Alexander.

The iron engine was by then putting out at least 80 bhp, according to O'Brien. The alloy must have been close to that, on its way from the 73 bhp of 1971 to the 83 of later in 1972.

In the event, Rayborn rode both and was faster with the iron engine. Even so, there was no choice at all. The alloy engine was new and barely understood and had to be the next step, no matter what.

And no matter what, Harley-Davidson was going to look clumsy in the beginning of the season.

Part II The Racing Record

Chapter 4

The First Batch, 1972–76

Not least among Harley-Davidson's traditions is the habit of having the best times begin poorly.

So it was with the alloy XR-750. As noted earlier, while the iron version was ready in the nick of time, unveiled almost in unison with the new national rules, the alloy engine was announced well in advance of the 1972 season . . . and then missed Daytona, the biggest race of the year.

San Jose, early in 1972. Mark Brelsford and Dave Sehl giving the alloy XR-750 its baptism. They didn't win, but the lighter and more powerful engine made the handling better and the riders more secure. Cycle World

At the philosophical top, the team missed the race because the company followed the rules, to the letter. There were rumors, believed by people who should know, that the AMA let H-D management know that because Harleys were important to the sport, they'd be allowed to run on the basis of intent; that is, the AMA knew there would be 200 XR-750s built in due course so they could run before the bikes were actually built. But for reasons of honesty (and perhaps because there are people from whom one shouldn't risk accepting favors) H-D president Charles Thompson and team manager Dick O'Brien declined.

In a related move, *Cycle News* missed the point. The Harley team guys only had verbal contracts, the newspaper reported, and thus could ride for other teams if they wanted to.

Well, yes, they could have gotten away with it, in the narrow, legal sense. But in those days, a man's word was his bond and a handshake was better than a clutch of attorneys. In the 1972 Daytona 200, the best Harley finisher was privateer Larry Darr, on an iron XR, in seventeenth.

So, why weren't the new engines ready for inspection and acceptance? Mostly because of supply problems. Many, make that most, of the actual parts came from outside suppliers. O'Brien had 300 pairs of cylinder heads ready, for instance, and Lawwill and Knight were ready with the rest of the frames needed. But they didn't have 200 complete engines, ready to be stacked in the warehouse, never mind actually run, until April, a month after Daytona.

1972: The Debut

The season and the debut were saved by other AMA rules, namely the one that had various other machines eligible for the several other events, and by Mark Brelsford.

The 1972 season was also marked by the best Rookie crop in a generation. Ken Roberts, Gary Scott and Mike Kidd all got their expert licenses that year, after a year of wrestling each other as juniors, so it came as no surprise that Roberts won the Houston short track, first race of the year, or that the best a Harley could do in the Houston TT was Brelsford's

Step back in time a bit, as Mark Brelsford keeps Goliath, *his lightweight (relatively) XLR in contention with Ken Roberts on the expanded Yamaha 650, at the Houston TT, 1972. Brelsford's engine is the iron-barrel 883 cc Sportster-based engine from which the iron XR was made. It's got the two rear-right carbs, so it's the full factory version. Note the seat and tank and paint. And tip your hat, because only Brelsford could get the maximum out of this beast. Cycle World*

The four-stroke twin was still in contention and the Harley team showed up in full force for Ontario, 1972. From the left it's Mark Brelsford, Dave Sehl, Cal Rayborn, Mert Lawwill and Renzo Pasolini. The team allowed tuning freedom, which is why Brelsford, Rayborn and Pasolini's XRTTs have disc front brakes and the other two have drums. Harley-Davidson

Pasolini was a talented Italian who rode for Harley through the Italian connection, Aermacchi. He rode Ontario in part for practice, as H-D hoped to compete in the Formula 750 class in Europe. He saved the factory's honor on this occasion. Harley-Davidson

Team manager Dick O'Brien, left, and Lawwill at Ontario, with Pasolini's XRTT in front of them. This is late in the season and they've fitted the new carrier and flat sprocket to the rear wheel. Harley-Davidson

Brelsford, on his way to winning the half-mile at Salem, Oregon, in stylish fashion. Note the extreme angle he's hanging the rear wheel out, and with his feet up, yet! Harley-Davidson

fourth, bulling his big XR behind a trio of nimble Triumphs.

Then came Daytona, as cited, and Road Atlanta, for which Cal Rayborn used a wildly modified iron XR. It was a factory bike, slower than his match racer, and it lasted a handful of laps. Quoting *Cycle,* "To see Cal Rayborn apply his massive talent to a motorcycle that is vastly unworthy of him must drive the H-D brass into fits of periodic apoplexy." Which of course it did.

Help was on the way. The alloy XR-750 was duly assembled and certified by the AMA, and the team arrived with the new engine for the Colorado Springs mile, April 30, 1972. Brelsford had the top time in qualifying and was second in the main, behind Jim Rice on a BSA. The rest of the team didn't do as well. Lawwill was thirteenth in the main and Rayborn was sixteenth, while Markel crashed and was hurt badly enough to be out of action for several months. For the second highpoint, younger brother Scott Brelsford,

the only junior with an XR thanks to Mark's help, was top junior.

Big brother and big *Goliath* won the Ascot TT. Brelsford quipped the truth; when asked his secret of TT success he always said, "900 cc's," although it was also true that the other guys were free to ride the monsters but simply weren't as good at it: Rayborn was sixth and Lawwill fourteenth, on XR-750s with drum brakes. That leads to another point. The team was free to use their own judgment and equipment, which meant that Brelsford went with Belland's chassis and Honda discs and the other guys used the factory equipment with Ceriani drum brakes.

At the San Jose mile Jim Rice slammed into the fence, dislocated his shoulder and won literally with one hand. Brelsford had mechanical trouble, Rex Beauchamp put his new team XR into fourth and Lawwill was ninth.

Now we come to a historical quibble. In those days there were lots of tracks and races for flat track

49

Bart Markel, who was about to retire in 1972 but doesn't look it here. This XR still has the dished sprocket, but the intake manifolds have been extended for more push out of the turns, and the gearcase cover is trimmed to save a few ounces. Harley-Davidson

machines. Ascot had races several nights a week. Mert Lawwill won a professional half-mile there, on a new XR with front disc brake, surely a TT bike pressed into service, for the first professional win for the new engine.

Then, June 4, Brelsford took the Louisville half-mile with Harley riders Dave Sehl second, Beauchamp fourth, Doug Sehl fifth, Rayborn sixth and Lawwill ninth. Scott Brelsford won the junior race, for a new sort of double victory and for the alloy XR's first national run.

Things were going well. At the Loudon road race, Cal took the pole and was eighth in the big race, while Mark was second, right behind Gary Fisher and his incredible little Yamaha two-stroke twin. "All the Harleys had little bugs," *Cycle News* said, but the bikes were obviously competitive.

At Indianapolis, Rayborn's full factory XR had triple disc brakes and he got his fourth Indy national road race victory in a row.

Lawwill won the Columbus half-mile in the midst of two bits of news. One was that the engines, from Harley and the rivals, had become so powerful that they were shredding the real road-legal tires until then, which led to the AMA allowing the introduction by Goodyear of real racing tires for dirt track. They weren't knobbies and they could be used on pavement or public roads, but they were more aggressive and softer and stickier than road rubber.

The other news came from *Cycle News'* analysis of the previous few races and qualifying sessions: "The new alloy Harley obviously has motor on everybody."

That probably was true, but only for that time and place and not for very long. The rules had reached an odd stage; by the book all machines had to be production based, 200 of each model, with all the major components like frames and suspension and heads and cases and such either as sold to the public or as modified from produced parts. The limit was 750 cc or 45 ci, *and there was no other limit.*

There was Harley's alloy 750 cc twin, there were homologated 750 versions of the formerly 650 BSA and Triumph, and there was a racing version of Yamaha's 650 twin. Yamaha was in good shape. Roberts was a remarkable talent, and the factory's broad range

50

of models gave the American team a good spread of singles and twins, two strokes and four, to run the short-track, TT, half-mile, mile and road-race format. Nobody else had quite this breadth while those who might have, Honda for instance, didn't wish (yet) to spend the money. Kawasaki and Suzuki had triples, two-strokes and plenty of power, so they were a force in road racing but not the dirt. BSA and Triumph were in desperate financial straits at home but that hadn't shut down their American teams.

Next, there seems to have been some fudging of details. The inspectors were allowing what amounted to new, racing frames on the say-so of the factory reps, which is how the Harley racers and even more so the imports, had tailored equipment for the miles and half-miles.

Another, more subtle, factor was the increasing division between dirt and road racing. When production class racing became the national standard, even the road races were run on tracks that had dirt or sand sections and things like fairings or even low bars were banned. But streamlining and big tanks and lower frames and such became optional and even *Cycle News* noted that only the top experts could buy a road-race XR-750, production rules or not.

Meanwhile, road racing was worldwide and dirt track was an American phenomenon. The Japanese, notably Yamaha, took an interest and began drubbing the big English triples that in turn had more power than the Harley twins. This wasn't total. Calvin won, make that dominated, the Laguna Seca national, his second road-race national in a row. He did it by first, not making as many fuel stops as the more powerful Kawasaki two-stroke triple and second, he used Honda front disc brakes.

Brelsford won the Salem, Oregon, half-mile and Dave Sehl took the Atlanta mile and at that race Brelsford cinched the championship. It was a statistical win, in that only Gary Scott could overcome Brelsford's lead, so when Scott's engine let go, Brelsford had the title.

Equally, Brelsford had won three races in the 1972 season while a few of the others, Scott and Dick Mann and Rayborn, had won two each. Mark's point lead had been fairly won and he'd done well in all the various events. (Historians may note here that Mann that year was the first to win at each of the five types of national event.)

More important, it was a popular win for a popular rider. Brelsford was as cheerful and outgoing with fans as he was photogenic. He worked hard and enjoyed racing. If there was any lack, it was one shared with Cassius Clay, that is, he liked to compete and win but he really never enjoyed beating people —no killer instinct or need to crush the others.

The others in fact gave Brelsford a banquet at the end of the season. No discouraging words were heard and everybody seemed pleased that his title also brought an estimated $100,000 in purse, series and bonus money.

Cliché or not, Brelsford was photogenic and cheerful in victory, and his honest delight in the fun of racing made him, as they say, a credit to the sport. Harley-Davidson

So, all right. What about the machines?

Mert Lawwill sums up the alloy engine versus the iron one: "It was a whole new world."

Technical Review

The alloy engine was 17 lb. lighter than the iron one and because the rules required the machine be as certified rather than meet a weight limit, the new bikes were lighter. Plus, the lightness was on the top, you could say. The engine's center of gravity was lower so it could handle well with the engine higher in the frame, or the suspension set to raise the chassis: equal weight transfer for acceleration and braking, but with more ground clearance on the turns.

Reliability was vastly improved, although there were some concerns, as we'll see. Most of all, of course, was the plain and simple fact of more power.

There were some problems. The first fixed, assuming the fix to be described is one, involved the rocker arms.

The valvetrain was borrowed from Aermacchi, where it was used on a single-cylinder engine with the camshaft directly between the crank and the rockers. With the V-twin, the four one-lobe camshafts are splayed and the pushrods aren't parallel to the bores. Nor are they parallel to each other while the intake rockers have the valves inboard of their shafts and the exhausts are outboard. What we have here are dif-

It's Houston TT time again, and it's Brelsford in the air again but this time it's 1973 and he's got an XR. But because it has the old tank and seat and paint, you have to look for the Ceriani forks, the twin tomahawks and the massively finned barrels before you can be sure. Cycle World

ferent angles between the valve stems and the cam lobes.

Geometry is the word and the problem here. Unless you have the pushrod side of the rocker arm just right in relation to the valve side, the acceleration and lift of the valve won't be what it was at the cam. You can subtract or add lift, you can change the rate and you can induce stress.

None of this was apparent when the design was done. Well, some of it was and there were two castings for the rocker arms. Even so, the exhaust cams had to be redone during initial testing and later the rocker arms began breaking.

What they did then, and still do, was cast the rocker arms and then cut them into pieces and reattach the sections so with each valve closed and each pushrod relaxed, cam lobe pointed directly away from the lifter, the two ends of the rocker are at perfect right angles to the pushrod. It seems like a lot of trouble. But it worked then and still does.

There were some concerns, as opposed to pure problems, with the oil and ignition systems, and of course with the sheer strength of the engine and its parts. But because those will be dealt with later, we'll mention them later.

There were some shortcomings in the road-racing program, but the XRs were still in the hunt. At Talladega, won by Yvon DuHamel on a Kawasaki triple, Rayborn and Brelsford lost their engines, to bad pistons and ignition, respectively. Lawwill snapped the cable to his drum front brake.

That's right, drum. Discs weren't as speedily appreciated as we tend to think they should have been. Riders and tuners were allowed latitude in that area, and the team portrait at Ontario shows some bikes with drum front brakes and some with discs.

Perhaps the oddest part of this was that really effective discs weren't available until Honda began selling them—on the road-going, not-terribly-sporting CB750 four. So, as soon as the AMA dropped the rule requiring brakes from the chaps who made the engine and frame, you could buy street Honda brakes and put them on your Harley racer and that's what people did.

Kawasaki won Ontario, this time with Paul Smart riding. Concern for tire wear caused the race to be run as two heats. Brelsford was fourth on aggregate, with finishes of eleventh and third. Lawwill was sixth, with eighth and eighth. Cal was knocked down by a slower rider in the first heat, so his fiftieth and fifth kept him out of the money.

The surprise Harley star, third overall, was Italian rider Renzo Pasolini. Harley-Davidson's Italian branch, Aermacchi, was a hotbed of racing enthusiasm and knowledge. They fielded an excellent team of two-stroke twins. Pasolini was scheduled to run an XR in Formula 750 and came to practice. Obviously, he was a quick learner.

In the Race of the Year in England, for which Rayborn had the latest alloy engine and full factory support and encouragement, he dueled with Jarno Saarinen until the magneto quit and anyway, according to Jim Greening of *Cycle,* the old iron version might have handled better.

We'll deal with the magneto later. Suffice it to say that 1972 was a good year, and justified the alloy engine and the factory's investment and the willingness to play by the rules.

As a cap, by coincidence 1972 was the first year of the AMA's Manufacturer Championship, separate from the rider's championship, and the very first winner was, no prize for guessing, Harley-Davidson.

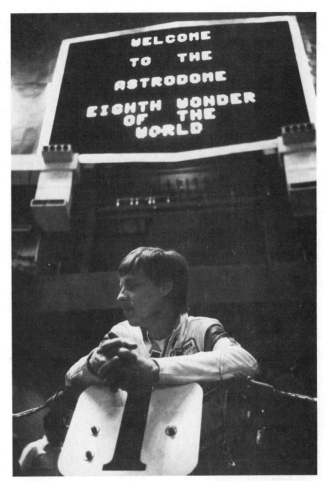

Those who believe in intuition or hunches will look at this picture of Brelsford at the start of the 1973 season and decide he knew, somehow, what was to come. Cycle

1973: The Worst Season

Begin with the rules. For 1973, admitting the obvious, the AMA no longer required approval for frames, tanks, swing arms, wheels or brakes. Instead, the engine would be the motorcycle, 200 examples were still required, but the examination would only be for safety and suitability, not production.

Short track would be for smaller engines, either 250 cc four-stroke twins or 360 cc two-stroke singles; as you'd guess, virtually every motorcycle company doing business in America had either or both of such engines, and there were several companies ready with frames and suspension to fit.

At the other end of the spectrum but just as logical, TT races were now for 750s. No more 900s. Brelsford shrugged and said he'd convert *Goliath* into a cowtrailer.

In the rumor department, Harley-Davidson was supposed to build another 200 XRs because they'd run out. They hadn't; in fact, the original supply lasted until 1974. There was supposed to be a five-speed gear cluster for the XR and there wasn't. There were several sets built and tested, but as Clyde Den-zer, O'Brien's right-hand man, pointed out, when you put five pairs of gears in a width that used to have four, you have reduced their strength by twenty percent. The gear size was dictated by type size of the cavity allowed back in 1952 for a 750 cc sidevalve engine with one third the power of a top XR. The five-speed cluster wasn't available in 1973, it hasn't been since and it probably won't be.

Cycle commented that the XR frame was archaic, presumably because it used the casting and lug system of construction at the lower rear junction of swing arm pivot and engine mount. But, added the magazine, "the Harley-Davidson racing department is the best in the business," and it probably was.

They also had the largest team, with reigning champ Brelsford, former champions Lawwill and Markel and upcoming Rayborn, Sehl, Beauchamp and Scott Brelsford, who'd been 1972's top junior.

The opposition was at least as well prepared. Yamaha was especially ready, with motocross-based short-track engines, with two-stroke road racers that already were the machines against which all others

The Harley team went overseas, to Imola, Italy, for a series of races for big, production-based machines. The XR twin wasn't quite a match for the multis or two-strokes— represented here by Kel Carruthers on the Yamaha—but Rayborn, number 44 for this occasion, managed fourth overall. Jim Greening

Rayborn's XRTT had three disc brakes, that issue having been settled by mid 1973. He also had a slick rear tire and patterned front, and the engine was fitted with what looks like an early experiment with a mini sump. Jim Greening

were compared, and with several years' work on a 750 cc twin.

This last had been something of a problem, in that at the very first, Yamaha tried to use its true 750 twin, which was big, clumsy and fragile. Later they switched to enlarging the 650, an overhead-cam vertical twin inspired so completely by British engines that it even came with electrical problems. These were overcome and the engine was lightened, tuned and certified into a viable flat-track competitor.

And of course Yamaha had Kenny Roberts. He was fourth in national standings at the end of his first year as an Expert. He had lots of raw talent, matched by hunger and by determination.

Roberts led the Houston TT, the season opener, until his engine stalled. The Astrodome TT was perfect for Triumphs and only Roberts and the Harley team weren't on the British twins. Only Brelsford, who finished second in the final and was one second per lap slower than Roberts, could make the big bike work. And the next night Roberts won the short track and the Harleys weren't even mentioned.

Then came Daytona, and disaster.

There had been change, perhaps even progress. In a preview, *Cycle*'s Kevin Cameron said, "handling, reliability, good people and good power should give Harley-Davidson a very good year."

In his race report, *Cycle* editor Cook Neilson wrote that "Harley-Davidson . . . never had a chance."

As they say, things happen. What mostly happened was the Japanese two-strokes were much more powerful, and they'd gained handling and good riders and experience. Top qualifier Paul Smart, Suzuki, clocked 101.871 around the full course, which now included a chicane on the back straight. Rayborn was best Harley, at 98.503.

The race was simply tragic. On the eleventh lap Brelsford, who qualified at 97.945 and was the only other Harley in the top twenty, came up on Larry Darr, whose XR had blown an engine and who was trying to coast to safety. Brelsford had been drafting another rider and passed him as Darr crossed his path. Darr was knocked down. Brelsford spun through the air, thrown from his machine—thank God. An exhaust pipe was wrenched loose and ignited fuel as the bike, still upright, rolled a few hundred feet, in flames, then toppled. Brelsford suffered two broken legs, a broken hand and a ground-up kneecap. He would be out for the rest of the season. So much for defending number one.

Twenty laps later, Rayborn's engine locked up. He was thrown off and landed with a broken collarbone and damaged ribs.

Jarno Saarinen won for Yamaha. Neilson wrote that at the victory banquet, Yamaha celebrated, the other factories went home early but O'Brien and John Davidson, company president, congratulated the winners and went through the ceremonies and the evening because that's how sportsmen behave.

The year didn't get any better. In the dirt, half

The strain of herding the XRTT against the lighter four-stroke multis and the nimble two-strokes had begun to show by the time Rayborn won the Indianapolis road race, in 1972. He would score one more win for the XR, later that year at Laguna Seca, then went winless through 1973, before he was killed. James F. Quinn

miles were won by Lawwill, Corky Keener (who replaced retiring Bart Markel), Jim Rice and Beauchamp. Lawwill took the Peoria TT and Indy mile as well, for the best season he'd had in years, and the best dirt results of the team.

Rayborn raced hurt. The XR wasn't quite competitive in Formula 750, an FIM class invented at least in part to keep the production four-strokes busy and the two-strokes at bay. At Imola for the Shell 200, quoting *Cycle News*, "The Harley was down on power, giving away three seconds a lap. Calvin has been making up for it." There was an oil leak and the magneto failed, "but Calvin made his point."

What they didn't know, as O'Brien admitted years later, was that Rayborn wasn't healed. At Imola, the XR "went into a full wobble. He had to put so much force into it that it separated that fracture," said O'Brien. "He rode the race with that thing."

Next, the Easter match races. Calvin was team captain. On the record, he was tenth, retired, won, then came twelfth, fourth, eighth, sixth and led the last race until the engine faded and he dropped to second.

That's the record. Here's O'Brien: "He rode the Easter series with his collarbone broken. When he came in we had to put him in the back of the truck and pull his shoulder back, the skin out and help him take his clothes off. And that's how he rode the whole series, I kid you not."

Back home on the dirt, at Louisville, Cal's XR went into a tankslapper and it looked painful. *Cycle New*'s reporter asked Rayborn's tuner, Babe DeMay, how his man was holding up and DeMay blurted, "I'm not supposed to talk about that," which was as good an answer as one could imagine.

DeMay also tuned for Rice, who won the Columbus half-mile in part because DeMay looked at the plugs and one looked funny so DeMay popped in another magneto.

Next, Yamaha was reported to be testing a 700 cc two-stroke four, two of the astonishing 350 twins side by side. The 350 was the only pure road racing machine the average guy could buy, *Cycle News* said, the rules and catalogs to the contrary. After that came the unveiling of the Yamaha 700 in Japan *and* the announcement that there would be 200 built, that is, the pure racer would be production and qualified for AMA nationals.

At Laguna Seca, quoting the newspaper again, Rayborn "was dry-gulched. He was riding the wheels off the Harley just to keep up. It's amazing how much ground he can make up in the turns. But no matter, he loses it on the straight."

Rayborn was on the front row at Pocono, and was in third place, until the clutch went. The clutch was foolproof, or so it was thought but then, so was the drive chain and Rayborn's XR broke two at the Ascot TT.

We are hearing some discouraging words. Constant replacement of magnetos was becoming a habit and even on the good days, as in Mert winning Indy, Beauchamp, Seale, Sehl and Rayborn all retired with mechanical failures. When Beauchamp won, Rice's ignition failed and when at Talladega Yamahas took the top five places, Rayborn's right-side handlebar, the clip-on, lost its grip and with it he lost his controls and trailed home nineteenth.

By the middle of September Kenny Roberts, with his strong short tracker, his working big twin and his growing skill on pavement and his hunger, had number one cinched.

Ontario was Kawasaki one-two-three in both heats. Rayborn and Lawwill both blew their engines.

Now begins the incredibly awful part.

The AMA announced the rules for 1974. First, there would be a noise limit, 92 dBA at 50 ft. from the exhaust pipe. No problem there.

Next, the four-stroke folks proposed an answer to the fuel crisis: a limit on the amount of fuel to be burned during a race. By no coincidence, the only factor still in the four-stroke's favor was fuel efficiency and if the limit had been accepted, that would have effectively gotten rid of two-strokes from then on. A straight partisan issue, that one, and the proposal lost, 32 to 23.

Then came the shocker. The production requirement was dropped from 200 examples to twenty-five, actually one complete motorcycle and twenty-four engines to be built and offered for sale.

One swift move and the AMA's production rule, in effect and effective for nearly forty years, was changed, make that eliminated, forever.

Why? Because first, all the motorcycle factories and the club had always thought small. They'd assumed that requiring 200 examples meant that no factory would offer purely racing engines with no relationship to road machines.

Second, they'd reckoned without Yamaha. That firm was ready and willing to win, in the United States and at home and around the world. Yamaha was ready to meet the rules head on, pay any price and bear any burden as they say in politics, except politicians don't mean it and Yamaha did.

The rivals weren't as willing, and they acted as if Yamaha's acceptance of the challenge was some sort of insult. They got even by dropping the limit, so they could do what they didn't let Yamaha do.

With that silly and unsporting move, they changed racing forever for the second time that meeting.

It's not quite on the subject here, but for purposes of understanding what happens in due course, let the record show that Yamaha did in fact build the 200 TZ700s they'd promised and for the next ten years the Yamaha four, which quickly became the TZ750, was the best machine a guy could buy for road racing. It was in fact what we're going to see the XR-750 become on the dirt.

Now we come to the low point of the year, perhaps of this era: on December 29, 1973, Cal Rayborn was killed. He was killed when his Suzuki GP bike rammed an embankment at a track in New Zealand.

This was beyond shock. Rayborn was a hero, an enormously popular man on and off the track. At the time of his death he held the world's motorcycle speed record, 265 mph, set in a streamliner powered by a bored-and-stroked Sportster engine. He'd set the record after the beast tipped over and rolled some thirty-five times during the week of time trials. Rayborn led every national road race he entered in 1972, then crashed at Daytona and rode hurt, as noted. He was generally accepted as the best road racer in the world, even by the Europeans.

Rayborn was Harley family. But Harley couldn't provide machinery equal to his talents. Just like the folk tales, Rayborn had to leave home to seek his fortune. He'd gone to Australia to race cars during the off season, and to negotiate. He signed with Suzuki December 26, sold the car and went to New Zealand for a series of races that would be rehearsal for the 1974 season. The bike was a good one, the machine used by the Suzuki team at Daytona that year. According to the evidence, the engine seized and Rayborn had no chance.

By some quirk of fate, Daytona winner Saarinen and H-D teammate Pasolini were killed in a collision in Italy earlier in the year.

It was a bad year, 1973, one of the worst.

1974: Less of the Same

In common with every season since racing began, 1974 was a time of change and uncertainty. Motorcycle sales were up, racing was increasingly popular and the balance was shifting. Yamaha not only had the top rider, but the 1973 maker's championship as well. In second? Triumph, edging Harley-Davidson into third.

But the British were in as much trouble as the four-strokes. Triumph-BSA-Norton had combined. Their team cut back, losing riders to Yamaha (Gene Romero) and Harley (Gary Scott).

The official H-D team was Scott and Brelsford in road races, plus Beauchamp on the dirt. Lawwill was

approaching retirement but decided on one more year, and O'Brien went along. The junior varsity, with support but not full team backing, were Gary's brother Hank Scott, Jim Rice, Dennis Palmgren, Corky Keener, Jim Maness, Dave Sehl and Greg Sassaman.

The season began with disquiet. The team missed the cut for Houston's short track, Scott was fourth and Brelsford eighth in the TT. At Daytona, cut from 200 to 180 miles as a sop to the fuel crisis, the XR-750s, make that all the four-stroke twins, were 20 mph off the pace of the two-stroke multis. Giacomo Agostini beat Roberts by 40 sec., both on Yamaha fours. Suzuki was top qualifier, Scott and Brelsford dropped out with a missing cylinder and a crankcase full of oil respectively, and fifteen of the top twenty were Yamaha.

(Overseas, in a balanced sort of partisanship, the FIM banned the XR-750 *and* the TZ700 from Formula 750 because neither was considered to come from a road-legal motorcycle.)

There was some hope, in that Aermacchi was doing well in Europe with its 250 and 350 two-stroke racing twins and now, thanks to the new rule, Harley-Davidson could certify and import enough of the small ones—and there were plans for full 500s—to keep the team on pavement.

Meanwhile, again, there were no Harley riders in the Anglo-American match races.

Greg Sassaman, a promising rookie whose family owned a Harley dealership in Georgia, joined the factory team in 1974. Cycle

Worse, when the real season opened with the San Jose mile, Roberts edged Scott by inches. It was close and fast: thirteen riders were under the old lap record and Lawwill had been top qualifier. Mert was sixth in the national, trailing Scott Brelsford and Beauchamp while Mark, coming back after those terrible injuries, was sixteenth.

In Colorado for the half-mile, Mert won, surviving, as *Cycle News* said, "a wreckage-strewn main event" with "vicious ruts, chuckholes and berms." The race was cut to fifteen laps from twenty. Scott was second, and Brelsford didn't qualify for the main.

At Road Atlanta Harley-Davidson wasn't mentioned. But at Loudon, the RR-250 had been certified and Scott won the lightweight race, leading Roberts and all those Yamahas. Except that in the big race, he was seventh, well behind Nixon and his Kawasaki.

And then, at Columbus, Mike Kidd won for Triumph, with Roberts second and Lawwill, who'd been top qualifier, in third. He was the only Harley in the top five, which may have been why the crowd booed Roberts.

Mark Brelsford crashed in the semi-final, breaking his leg, again, and putting an end to what had been a dismal season, never mind coming back after his 1973 Daytona crash. The newspapers didn't even dare guess as to when he'd be back.

The year became a contest between Roberts and Scott. The Harley man won three straight; the San Jose mile, Castle Rock TT and Ascot TT, first time in thirteen years anybody had managed a streak like that. So Roberts got three straight, Laguna Seca, the short track at Santa Fe and the Peoria TT.

Notes on that: Somebody wrote a letter remarking that the Laguna Seca road race marked the first time in living memory that no English bike had qualified for the race. Things were changing.

Next, Roberts' streak also meant that he'd become the third rider to win each of one of the five types of national championship race: he'd later miss the Ascot half mile and fail to be the only man to win all five types in one season.

At the Indy mile, won by Romero on a Yamaha, fourteen of the twenty machines in the national were XR-750s. Obversely, when Roberts blitzed the Talladega road race, Scott crashed his RR-250, plus there were twenty-four Yamahas in the lightweight race against only Scott and in the big race there were no Harleys, just two Kawasakis, two Suzukis and sixteen Yamahas.

Enough. Roberts was hot and Scott was hurt. So was Lawwill. The other guys did their best, with Hank Scott taking the Syracuse mile and Keener the Terre Haute half-mile. But well before the final race, Roberts and Yamaha had the titles sewed up again.

Technical Review

The machines in the picture then were wonderfully varied. According to the Harley team dyno charts, an average XR engine by the 1974 season was producing 84 bhp at 7800 to 8000 rpm. Yamaha's team charts show 80 bhp from the radically modified 650 into 750 vertical twin, with narrowed cases, new crankshaft and lots of work. There was a limitation imposed by the basic design of the head, which is why the Yamaha had less power and had to be wound tighter to get it.

But power wasn't everything, witness Roberts and Romero winning miles. Witness also the failure that year of a 95 bhp Honda four and a collection of Kawasaki triples to make an impression on the dirt.

Traction was the difference, evidently. *Cycle World* took a radar gun to the San Jose mile and got Lawwill at 121 mph, Roberts at 117, Gary Nixon on the Kawasaki at 118 and Rick Hocking with the Honda at 115. As *Cycle's* Gordon Jennings intoned, "multis have been tried on the dirt before . . . and all have failed." Watch this space.

At the end of its third year the alloy XR-750 engine was a marginal success, no better than a match for the competition.

Why? There were three problem areas. One was effectively cured, the second began a series of improvements that became a cure and the third would plague the engine (and the tuners) for at least another ten years.

The cure involved the main bearings. The XR engine has two flywheels joined by a press-fit crankpin. The alloy engine got a stronger pin and more pressure to hold it in place as well as mainshafts integral with the flywheels proper. The shafts ran in ball bearings, as had been done in racing engines since racing began. Ball bearings are low friction. They are also rigid. Assembled flywheels joined by crankpin are never perfectly aligned. Close, as close as measuring devices can manage. But not perfect. The rigid bearing became the classic immovable object, and the flywheels were the irresistible force: the two worked against each other and the engine came apart.

By happy chance the team engineers found the answer. A new type of bearing, known as Superblend, used rollers shaped like—sorry, there's no better description—beer kegs. They had low friction *and* allowed the bearing races and cages to self-align, making up for the tiny imperfections in the same way the computers in a supersonic airplane makes corrections faster than the pilot can know corrections are needed. The Superblend bearings were a running change and gave the XR lower end a working life as long as the longest race.

The ongoing improvements were for the oil system. When last examined, the alloy engine was using a combination of timed breather and one-way valves, sequenced to keep oil going to the bearings and internals *and* make the oil return to the tank.

Cycle News did an interview of Gary Scott late in 1974, in the course of which Gary and brother Hank were working on Hank's XR. They had plenty of power, but when they ran the engine the tank emptied and the sump contained eight or so ounces of oil. The reporter noted that the brothers knew the other guys ran with no more than two ounces in the sump (actually, the reporter said *in* the engine, indicating he didn't know much more than the Scotts did), but they didn't know why or what to do.

They called in Gary's tuner, a former not-too-talented rider named Bill Werner. The story doesn't say what Werner did, but one week later Hank Scott won the Syracuse mile, his first national win.

How they did it was typically Harley-Davidson. O'Brien knew that the timed sequences were perfect only for a given rpm, and then only when the timing was perfect.

"Even when you timed it right, one engine might sump [fill the sump with oil] and the other might not," said O'Brien. Which is what happened to Scott and Brelsford in Daytona in 1974.

Scott's engine was taken back to the team shop and instrumented, but all they could find was that when the engine had the lowest pressure and the least vacuum, it ran the driest: O'Brien said some engines would retain no more than half an ounce of oil in the sump, while even three or four cut power.

Atmospheric pressure wasn't doing the job, so first they reworked the passages and scrapers inside the crankcase and timing case. Next they developed auxiliary pumps, driven off the gears that used to drive the magneto when the ignition sat atop the case, to pull oil from the bottom of the crankcase.

Meanwhile, Bill Werner was at home in his basement shop, thinking. He cut a hole in the bottom of the cases and tacked on an aluminum box, a mini sump, baffled and passaged so oil could drain from the cases into the box.

As the team is supposed to do, Werner took his project to O'Brien. They tested and experimented and adopted the mini sump for the team and later, with the 1975 production run, for customers. This was a big improvement, although the problem wasn't gone yet.

The persistent concern was the magneto. The idea was classic. A magneto is self-contained, with generator, coil and points all in one package. No battery to fail, no wires to fray. In pre-electronic times, the magneto was what the racers and aviators used because magnetos always worked.

Except on Harley-Davidsons.

The precise nature of the problem was difficult to define. One odd fact was that the magneto fired both plugs at the same time. The points broke in the required sequence, with the rear cylinder firing 315 deg. (one revolution less the vee's included angle) after the front one but with both spark plugs getting a spark when either piston arrived at firing time. This mimicked the way the street engines had fired since the V-twin was developed. Lawwill says when he began working on his own engines he learned that they ran hotter with spark to both plugs than with spark to one at a time, and that while you couldn't prove double firing hurt, "it can't have helped."

Bill Werner theorized that the magneto didn't work right on the 45 deg. V-twin because the magnetic poles for the windings that produce the current are 90 deg. apart and the cylinders aren't, so there's always a mismatch.

More practically, the actual magnetos came from Fairbanks-Morse and were intended for four-cylinder industrial, or tractor, engines with even firing orders and less vibration. The parts were simple and the driveshaft long and flexible and the bearings few and far between, and the things broke. Lawwill remembers endless tests and random failures and hurling the things to the floor in fits of rage. Zylstra says the ignition was barely good enough to work and it was left barely good enough because the racing engineers had more important problems.

Elsewhere there was parallel progress. Lawwill became a subcontractor for the team and worked with Terry Knight producing frames to factory specs. He also began his own business, making frames for outside buyers.

Great minds don't always think alike. The factory frames used the lower rear castings, the twin tomahawks, while Lawwill's own frames were full tube. It was mostly for cost reasons, he says, and while the castings were criticized as out of date, it takes hours of fabrication to use tube and plate and replace that twenty-five cent casting.

The 1975 factory frame was different, with the steering head 1 in. higher and moved back 5/16 in., and with the top of the rear shock mount moved forward 1 in., to give a rising rate to the springs, and to deliver more wheel travel for the same shock travel. As a general rule, as the engines got more power, they needed more traction and one way to get that is to transfer weight onto the rear wheel and the way you get *that* is to raise the bike. The production run was 100 complete XR-750s.

Racing was a thriving, if small, business. The factory bought frames from C&J and Champion, which also sold privately. Dealer net for a complete 1975 XR-750 was $2,395, which sounds cheap in 1990 dollars but wasn't cheap then. It was cheaper to keep your engine and replace the frame.

Even the factory guys admit that if you bought a new engine then, you had to take it apart and check and prepare every part, never mind cutting and re-attaching the rocker arms if you wanted the engine to work right.

1975: A Turning Tide

Classic case of good news-bad news: Late in 1974 Ascot held an invitational race for juniors, pitting the new kids from all across the country against each other. Two of the entries were brothers, Ken and Jay Springsteen, from Michigan. Jay was the faster and won his heat. He looked a winner in the big race, except on the last turn he came in too fast, purely exuberant, and lost by inches, victim of his own energy.

An at-work team portrait from 1975, it's Jay Springsteen (65X, the experts who still had to wear letters made them *as tiny as they could get away with), Gary Scott (64) and Rex Beauchamp (31).*

Dick O'Brien, on the occasion of a team win. Cycle

Off the bike he was a shy kid. He'd kind of thought maybe the Harley team would invite him to join, top junior of the year and all that, but he wasn't the kind to put himself forward.

Dick O'Brien meanwhile reasoned that the best team in the league should be asked, not go recruiting. So while he'd seen the new kid, he accepted the application of Greg Sassaman to join the team, while Springsteen got a ride from a good private group, Vista-Sheen. On Harleys, of course.

The bad news was first, Mark Brelsford retired. The broken leg needed additional treatment and it would be at least another year before he could ride and anyway, he'd never been comfortable on the track since the 1973 disaster and he'd done all the racing he wanted to do.

Next, Harley-Davidson's big twins were out of road racing. The 1975 team would be Gary Scott, Lawwill, Beauchamp, Keener and Sassaman, with XRs for dirt.

Dropping the XRTT made sense, in a sad way. The machine hadn't won a race since 1972 and even then it was more the man than the machine. The four-stroke twins didn't have the power of the two-stroke threes and fours, not when they all were 750s. Rather than waste time and money, Harley-Davidson decided to develop the 250 and later 500 cc two-strokes from Italy, instead. As it happened, both were soon

History in the making, as Ken Roberts on the screaming two-stroke Yamaha four, gets inside Corky Keener at San Jose. Cycle

The villain. To be fair, the road-racing Yamaha engines were jammed into dirt-track frames by privateers, not the Yamaha factory, and Roberts straddled the beast only when all else had failed. Cycle

Ascot, 1975 and Robert is about to lose his championship. Cycle

61

No one ever said Roberts, here on the TZ700 beast at San Jose, didn't try hard. Cycle

eclipsed or underdeveloped and Harley wasn't seen in road racing for another ten years.

Some final XRTT notes: Factory records show five XRTTs were sent to Nichels Engineering and five were kept at the Milwaukee team shop. Another ten or twelve complete machines were sold or loaned to private teams. Beyond that there were stocks of parts kept in reserve or for later production which of course never took place.

Or did it? There were fifty XRTT frames produced, with a fifty-first built by hand as the prototype for the model. That first one was different in that the seat rails were lower than those specified for production. The measurements suited Rayborn, and the bike with that frame was known as the Rayborn Special around the shop. More than one collector claims to have that very XRTT, although it would be difficult to prove.

Beyond that, the parts runs varied with price and estimated need. There were fifty fuel tanks and fairing bubbles, but other pieces totaled as many as 200. Then, when the road racer was in full eclipse, the leftovers were trashed so they could be written off for accounting purposes. Twenty years after that shameful practice there are outside firms ready to build ex-

Greg Sassaman has won the San Jose mile, with Gary Scott second, and O'Brien doesn't mind one bit. Cycle

Straight from Bill Werner's basement, the cure for oil problems. Werner used XL cases, which were cheaper and easier to get, and he made a collector box, shown at lower right. Bill Werner

Werner cut a hole in the bottom of the sump and installed baffles in the collector box and routed the scavenge side of the dual oil pump to the bottom of the box. At last, the oil had some place to go instead of collecting on the flywheels. The machine face with the small hole next to the sump is where the oil pump bolts on. Bill Werner

act replicas of the XRTT frame and swing arm. The rest can be bought or adapted and if vintage racing becomes even more popular, someday there may be more surviving XRTTs than there were built in the first place.

Not that things were formal then. Lawwill, Champion, C&J and Trackmaster offered alternative frames for the XR-750 engine, using different specifications and, Lawwill's for one, lighter than the stock version. Or you could do what Vista-Sheen's builder did and lower the engine and stretch the wheelbase, putting the engine farther aft and gaining traction with selective additions to the downtubes and backbone.

Things were informal, is the word. Springsteen and Scott and Beauchamp all used outside suspension components while the factory offered Girling and Ceriani. When the race shop and test cells were closed by a strike late in 1974, Werner and Scott went to Werner's basement shop to prepare for the season.

For reasons science can't quite explain, an engine often works better (or worse) on the track than on the test bench. Werner and Scott's final testing was done drag racing, engine versus engine, and because Scott was lighter than Werner, he did his racing with flywheels piled in his lap.

The official 1975 season began at Houston, with Roberts winning the TT. Scott came second, Lawwill seventh and Springsteen fourteenth.

None of the big names did well in the short-track race. Daytona only matters here because Gene Romero won for Yamaha and Roberts didn't.

The real reason began at the San Jose mile. Sassaman won, in his second mile race with a 750, using an engine that showed 88 bhp on the team dyno. Scott was second and Beauchamp third, after turning the fastest qualifying time. Roberts was fifth and Springsteen crashed, unhurt but out of contention.

The next race was Louisville, a half-mile of slick limestone base. "With the aplomb of a seasoned veteran," raved *Cycle News*, Springsteen won going away, 14 sec. under the old race record. He was the youngest national winner ever, two weeks past his eighteenth birthday and just through with his junior year of high school. He was a bit behind in school, having taken time to go racing and perhaps more significant, he had a bone disease when younger. Jay wasn't supposed to walk, so his dad cut down a minicycle and for more than a year, a motorcycle was Jay's legs.

He earned the title Super Rookie at the next race, the half-mile at Harrington, Delaware, winning after being fast qualifier and taking the fastest heat. He was followed by Beauchamp and Scott, with Roberts fourth. Scott's better finish put him ahead of defending champ Roberts in points, while Springsteen vaulted into third.

Then Scott won at Columbus, followed by Keener and Springsteen and four more Harleys. Roberts dropped out with ignition failure: reading the record always shows that when you work from behind, things break; Roberts in 1975 was a lot like Rayborn in 1973.

Meanwhile, Scott Brelsford had switched from Harley to Kawasaki and teamed up with Erv Kanemoto, a brilliant tuner from San Jose and a man destined to partner riders like world champions Freddie Spencer and Eddie Lawson. Kanemoto built a miler powered—as in 105 bhp—by a 750 two-stroke triple. Brelsford won a regional championship race on the Stockton half-mile, first ever dirt win with a two-stroke multi.

Then the past returned, with Triumphs one-two-three in the Castle Rock TT. Scott was fifth, Jay ninth and Roberts was knocked cold in a crash.

When Mert Lawwill finally got fed up with magneto failures, he engineered this cure, a distributor that popped into the mounting base for the Sportster mag. It used a constant-loss battery and a coil. It gave spark to one cylinder at a time, and it didn't fail. Lawwill ignitions are still in service fifteen years later. Cycle

The team at speed, 1975, with Scott, Keener, Springsteen, a guy who's poked into the line-up, and Rex Beauchamp (31). The engines have been fitted with mini sumps and with oil filters, another useful way to protect the engine, add capacity and cool the oil. Harley-Davidson

By September the papers were talking about the "Harley Freight Train." Scott won the Sacramento mile with Beauchamp second. The difference between a mile engine, with big carbs, long cams and power, and a TT engine, with small carbs, short cams, lots of torque and instant response, was such that when Springsteen's mile engine lost a piston he had to use his TT engine, and couldn't qualify for the main event.

Scott won the Ascot TT, Roberts won Laguna Seca, and it was Keener at Syracuse and Toledo, Beauchamp at San Jose.

Yamaha had problems, mostly not enough horsepower. Romero hadn't done well since Daytona and

The rival. Roberts' Yamaha 750 was about as close to the street 650 twin as the XR was to the XL; that is, it looked like it until you got close. They wound up with new heads, obviously narrowed side covers, new cranks but not quite enough power or traction to do the job, not even with the formidable Roberts. Cycle

said he might "rather switch than fight." (For the record, a Harley dealer offered him a ride, which was politely declined.)

Roberts meanwhile was asked his feeling about the two-stroke multis. Sounds odd in light of his later achievements, but Roberts, who subsequently would refer to four-stroke production-derived race bikes as "stupidbikes" and "diesels," said, "I'm not anxious to see the two-strokes come in. I think they could ruin mile racing like they have road racing."

On the other hand, Yamaha was 10 or 15 hp down while poor Norton-Triumph quit national racing in midseason.

The Indy mile has short straights and wide turns, just the place for having more power than you can stick to the ground. Private builders with factory help had built six mile machines with TZ750 engines, call it 125 bhp in a 350 lb. sack. Five of the beasts were hauled to Indy, for which Springsteen had been appointed to the factory team because Sassaman had broken an arm.

Roberts literally and poetically had his hands full. He wrestled the TZ into sixth-fastest qualifying time, lost control in the heat and fought into the national final by winning the semi.

The big race was Springer and Keener, neck and neck back and forth while Roberts bucked and leaped

and crossed up in the marbles, working his way from the back.

On the last lap Keener and Springsteen were side by side heading for the flag and then, Keener stammered later, "I heard that screaming SOB and I knew it was all over."

As it in fact was, in several ways. Roberts calculated to the inch; slid wide through the apex of the third turn, hooked the rear wheel to the ground, climbed onto the front wheel, whacked the throttles full open and hung on. He howled past the two Harleys, won the race and managed to slew sideways in time to keep off the wall.

In the press box Roberts said, "They don't pay me enough to ride the thing."

Then he paused, and added, "I didn't ride it anyway. It rode me."

Things got back to normal. Keener won at Syracuse, followed by Beauchamp, Springsteen and Lawwill. Keener won again at Toledo, with Scott second and Roberts well back in sixth.

The San Jose mile track is long and thin, not as easy to overpower. It was, *Cycle* said, "A futile, last-ditch stand . . . for Roberts . . . to retain his crown."

To have a mathematical chance, Roberts needed to finish ahead of Scott, in fifth or better. He rolled out the missile for another shot. He won his heat but the soft tire that let him do it chunked so badly he knew it couldn't last the race and besides, he'd been slammed into the wall hard enough to rip off the right-side footpeg and brake lever. He picked a road race tire and, quoting *Cycle* again, "courageously hung on to the flailing, writhing monster machine until he couldn't stand it any longer . . . the great little man simply motored into the pits. The race for the national championship was finished."

At the race finish it was Beauchamp and Springsteen with brother Hank Scott, on a Yamaha, in third.

Fair is fair and later that night Springsteen said, "I'm sure glad Roberts doesn't have a Harley. Nobody would get a smell of him anywhere."

He may well have been right. But Yamaha rider Roberts won the Ascot half-mile and the Ontario road race. He did the grand slam, all five types of event in one season. Roberts won six races and mostly because of road-racing sweeps, Yamaha repeated for the manufacturer's title.

But Gary Scott, with only two wins, was the new national champion. When he didn't win, he was close. When Roberts didn't it was most often because he broke or crashed, and didn't get points.

As midseason's nonsurprise, Springsteen joined the Harley team.

As midseason's shocker, Gary Scott quit the team. And when he left he took his XRs with him, an act that can still make veins bulge in some quarters.

One factor had to be money. Yamaha had one rider, Roberts. Harley had less money and, counting Scott, six riders who had to share. Scott thought he should get as much as Roberts because he'd done what Roberts did, that is, win the title. H-D management and O'Brien didn't see it that way.

There was another factor. At the Santa Fe short track in 1975, Scott was a factory rider and had three machines, based on the road bike 250 cc four-stroke single, the motocross 250 two-stroke single and the road race 250 two-stroke twin. Springsteen was on a private team so he had his XR-750 for the big tracks and a two-stroke Bultaco for short track. Springsteen beat Scott.

It was Scott's view that because Harley-Davidson didn't have a complete set of machines, he'd have to work harder, which was another reason to want more money.

Returning to lack of surprise, shortly after the TZ750's dirt win and loss, the AMA instituted a new regulation limiting dirt track engines to two cylinders. Same displacement, same choice of valve system and so forth. Because this was considered a limitation and not a new rule, it took effect immediately. Not even the guys who built the two-stroke and four-stroke threes and fours had much to say in their defense.

1976: Springer

Cylinder limits aside, this was a time of marked diversity. Three of the big Japanese four were contesting the road races and there was a flock of motocrossers from East and West in short track, while new big singles from Yamaha replaced the light vertical twins from England as the alternate TT mount.

Harley-Davidson was hard at work in the middle.

One of the problems addressed was ignition. The racing department first added second and third bushings to the shaft of the old magneto, in hopes the shaft could be kept straight despite increased engine speeds. Along with that came a new system of wiring and firing, with single-cylinder firing instead of the old paired system with its spark just as the intake sequence began. But the rotor broke and the department, which had sold some of the new magnetos to private customers, had to offer conversion kits back to the old way. For the time being they settled for improving wiring and shielding the sparks from outside interference.

An alternate came from Mert Lawwill, who found himself less keen on just riding and more in-

Time for a demonstration. Alex Jorgensen, who is no slouch and who will win this event on this Norton two years later, leads The Springer down the back straight at Ascot, 1976.

One lap later, Jay leads into the third turn . . .

. . . And here he's pulling away. He did this sort of thing all the time. Cycle

Not only that, but Springsteen, here doing what one does with the trophy girl, was so happy and exuberant when he won that not even the guys he'd just whipped could resist cheering right along with everybody else. (Notes: The head at left is the late Roxy Rockwood, dean of dirt-track announcers; the white hat on the right is worn by J. C. Aga-janian, easily the best promoter and enthusiast ever and the man behind the success of Ascot; and the woman in the middle is Lynn Griffiths, Miss Camel Pro and a lovely person who genuinely liked racing. The hat being held over her head is because Camel always insists that you wear the sponsor's hat for all public occasions.) Cycle

terested in the technical and development sides of racing.

Came the day he put three different magnetos on the same engine, on test. Each mag checked out identically, but the engine ran differently when he changed mags: "In a fit of rage I threw them all on the floor. I never ran a magneto again," said Lawwill.

Instead, Lawwill came up with a distributor, using a small constant-loss battery and a separate coil. The points cam was ground to allow for the Harley's odd firing order and there was a rotor so each cylinder got just the one spark, when it was due. Spark advance was fixed so the system was simple and easy to tune. There are still Lawwill ignitions in service fifteen years later.

The clearest benefit of the 1975–1976 development programs came from valve and porting experiments. When the alloy XR was designed it used valves and ports based on certain theories, for instance, that exhaust flow should be a percentage of intake flow. After the first heads were built and raced, it was learned that there was an imbalance, that the heads were letting in more mixture than they'd let out and that this pressure was passing heat into the head around the exhaust port.

The 1972 heads came with intake valves of 45 mm diameter and exhaust valves with 35 mm. The 1976 version, which was developed and put into team use during the 1975 season, had 44 mm intakes and 36 mm exhausts, one down and one up, you could say. The ports were revised to work with the valves and power went up, witness the 88 bhp for Sassaman's mile engine, as heat went down.

The 1976 season began poorly for the team, mostly because of the diversity mentioned earlier. The Houston short track finished Bultaco, Yamaha, Yamaha, Yamaha, Yamaha, Bultaco. Springsteen was the only Harley rider who made the national and he missed the start with the gearbox jammed. The TT went to a Yamaha single and no team riders made the show. Ditto for the Daytona road race and the Dallas short track.

Then, not too soon, it was the San Jose mile.

There had been a lot of escalation. The XRs could up compression ratio, from 10.0:1 to 10.8:1 because of the better flow and cooling. They were using bigger Mikuni carbs, 38 mm venturis from 36, and the claim was 85 bhp at the rear wheel, this despite the boom box, a bulky muffler fitted because the track and pro-

Nobody who saw Jay Springsteen in his prime ever doubted for one instant that he was the greatest natural rider the sport has ever produced. Cycle

moter and the AMA had all agreed to placate owners of houses near the track. The big boxes absorbed sound without restricting flow nearly as much as a more tidy muffler would have done.

The Yamaha twin meanwhile had benefited from having the home factory send cylinder heads that were blank castings, the better for American tuners to port and shape. The basic engine had been converted with narrower cases and a stronger crank to take the gains in power.

The power could be used. Motorcycle racing had a new tire supplier, Carlisle, and Goodyear replied to that with a new tire, called DT II because it was the second generation of dirt-track racing tire.

It was also a treaded version of the road-racing tire, with a compound that would transmit the extra power and hold up for the twenty or twenty-five miles of a national race.

The new tire was wide. The motorcycle people were a bit behind the car people in proving that the more tire, the more grip, in contrast to what the physics books had misunderstood. Road racing had proven the benefit of fat tires, so the new DT was wide and used wider rims. And the rims were cast alloy,

more precise and less flexible than the laced-up traditional wire wheel.

The DT was rare. Goodyear wasn't sure yet how the new tire would work or if the racers would take to them, so only the top guys, Roberts and Springsteen for two, got sets in time for practice and the race.

Finally, the tires had such traction and the dirt, sort of, track surface was so firm and compacted that the tires squealed and chirped when the fast guys put the power down. Honest.

Not to make a good story long, Roberts looked good in practice but lost the combination and then his ignition. In the race Springsteen led but his mag came loose and Beauchamp got past and won, with tenacious Gary Scott third.

Not to make a good season long, Scott and the team had an ugly feud for most of the year, Goodyear had to withdraw the new tire until there were enough to go around, Carlisle tires proved competitive and twelve different riders won the first twelve national races.

Springsteen was the twelfth man. He also won the thirteenth and five of the remaining fifteen nationals. It was about time for a new era.

And some days the bear eats you. Just as classically Spring-steen was this mishap at San Jose. Chasing Gary Scott, *Springer keeps the gas on too long and the rear too far out, so he lowsides.*

Rear wheel and feet first he slides at a good clip until . . .

Whump! Into the bales, arms and legs flying.

But the bales and Springsteen's strength have done their work. He gets up, dusts himself off and gets ready to see if the bike fared as well as he did. As they used to say at Indy, Into the Field, or Into the Fence. Cycle

A team portrait, with Lawwill, Springsteen and Scott tucked in, in the paint as the racers would say, as they fly down the straight. Mert Lawwill

An experiment, from the fertile brain of Mert Lawwill. This is the engine mount and swing-arm pivot for one of his early frames. It's fabricated rather than cast. Mert Lawwill

He's moved the frame tubes and right side of the swing-arm outboard of the chain. The purpose was to give a wider and thus stiffer brace to counter torque fed from the wheel into the frame. Its result was to offset said force, which twisted the frame and made the steering, um, odd. But that, says the modest Lawwill, is how you learn. Mert Lawwill

Lawwill was still racing, as sort of a team associate. The frame looks stock but the gas tank is smaller and the exhaust pipes are longer, indicating a half-mile. Mert Lawwill

Beasts That Never Were

On the outside, Harley-Davidson has done well in racing and in business by sticking to what the company does and has done well, namely the classic V-twins with overhead valves and cams in the block.

On the inside, the engineers in the racing department (and in the engineering department for the entire motor company) have never lost sight of the rest of the world, nor of the other ways to reach whatever goal is in mind.

Here are two previously secret projects to illustrate just how carefully this watch was kept. Both date from the mid 1970s, and each covers its own ground and looks the competition straight in the eye.

XR 50 Deg. V-Twin

First, there were plans to meet Yamaha head on. The Japanese giant followed AMA rules just as Harley did, with a racing conversion of the maker's road-going sports twin. In the Yamaha case this was an overhead-cam vertical twin, bored from 650 cc to 750 cc and with its own (narrower) cases, a crankshaft with the two throws side by side for evenly staggered pulses and what amounts to a bigger hammer, and with cylinder heads cast to be converted to full race. By late in Yamaha's program, 1975–1976, the racing Yamahas had 95 bhp and were safely revving to 9600 rpm.

The machines couldn't get traction and the frustration drove Roberts overseas, but that didn't mean the engine wasn't worth looking at—especially when the XR was breaking rockers and bending pushrods and peaking at 90 bhp.

Harley's racing department, in the person of Pieter Zylstra with O'Brien looking over his shoulder, drew up what amounts to a radical conversion of the XR-750.

Radical because bore and stroke would have been changed to 3.3125 and 2.65 in., bigger bore and shorter stroke. Radical because the vee's included angle would

have been 50 deg., not so much wider as to not look like a Harley, but enough to give more room for carbs and pipes between the cylinders and perhaps to make the engine's inherent imbalance a little less so.

The new heads would have one camshaft each, working one intake and exhaust valve per cylinder, 45 and 38 mm in respective diameters. Thanks to having room for four cams in the gearcase, there would have been room for two sprockets driven off the right-side mainshaft and driving the cams by chain. The combustion chamber would have been bathtub shaped, with the valves' included angle of 66 deg.

Modern, is what this engine would have been. Incredible, too, because Zylstra says they could have revised the cases and used the current flywheels, gearbox, primary drive and so forth. And Mallory, the racing ignition folks, were ready with a magneto designed for racing motorcycles rather than agricultural implements.

All the drawings for the conversion were completed and there were some castings and forgings made for the heads, pistons, rods and cylinders. None of the parts were finished, though, and the engine was never built.

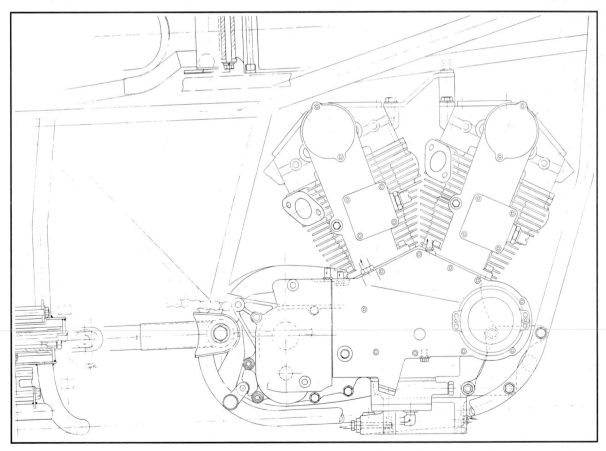

Engine: *Blueprint from designer Pieter Zylstra's files show the engine conversion to have been notable on two opposing points: First, the basic profile would have remained the same and second, the overhead cams and wider angle of the vee would have made it so different.* Harley-Davidson

RR-750 Two-Stroke

The second project covered the other side.

It was a complete motorcycle, a four-cylinder 750 cc two-stroke. And it was virtually all-new.

For background, recall that Yamaha produced its 750 two-stroke racer, with the four cylinders upright and across the frame; two twins side by side. The rule was changed from 200 examples to one machine and twenty-four engines, mostly to get even with Yamaha for upping the ante.

But the TZ750 ruled road racing, the XR-750 was hopelessly outclassed on pavement and at the time everybody reckoned you had to run all the races to win the title.

So Harley-Davidson bought a TZ750, dismantled it, measured and weighed every piece and sat down to make some improvements.

The racing department was qualified to do the job. Harley-Davidson had gone into the two-stroke business back in 1949, with the little 125 cc single that was supposed to lure kids into the Harley habitat. O'Brien made his name tuning the two-strokes, in fact, and then came the motocross team and the Italian team that won the world 250 and 350 cc classes with their two-stroke twins.

In 1976, O'Brien, Zylstra and Greg Sassaman, the team rider with the most interest in road racing, went to Italy to consult and inspect. At the time the AMA displacement limit was 750 cc and the FIM backed, with some reluctance, a 750 class for road racing. Harley's Italian partner Aermacchi was doing well in the smaller classes but the 500 cc twin wasn't enough for the big leagues—the Americans came home inspired and ready to tackle Yamaha and the others head to head.

Zylstra began not exactly with a clean sheet of paper, but with no specific limits and with some ideas he'd been mulling over since the department had analyzed their competition.

He decided the inline Yamaha was too wide and Suzuki's upright square four was too tall. So he drew up

plans for what amounts to four single cylinders, laid on their sides in a square. Each cylinder had its own crankshaft. Bore and stroke was 66 × 54 mm, nicely oversquare.

The engine was of course a two-stroke and was laid out that way because two-strokes use pressurized, sealed crankcases. The four cranks were geared to an idler gear in the center of the square, and the drive went from there to a long jackshaft to the clutch on the right, the water pump and other accessories on the left. The upper and lower pairs rotated in opposite directions, so balance was virtually perfect. Induction was with disc valves rotating outboard of each cylinder, and carburetors outside the discs. The exhaust pipes and expansion chambers routed above and below the barrels.

The engine was so low and compact that the frame backbone ran direct from steering head to swing-arm pivot, just what the book calls for.

There were some deft touches in Zylstra's design, notably the oval frame sections and the tapered swing-arm legs. (Right, arms don't have legs. But you know what I mean.) The rest of the machine was conventional, state of the art in the true sense of that phrase, with water cooling, disc brakes and cast wheels. And there are a few items, for instance the spindly stanchion tubes, that look out of date fifteen years later.

But those are quibbles. The RR-750 would have been at least equal in design in 1977 or whenever they could have put the bike on the track. Because Aermacchi won world titles in the 250 and 350 classes, and Sassaman and Springsteen were at least a match for the Yamahas on dirt, we can extrapolate and say the Harley road racers would have been competitive.

So, what happened? What you see here is as far as the project got. Three months after he began, Zylstra was told to stop. The accountants, villains as always in these epics, said the expenditure wouldn't be returned in sales or prestige and true, Harley-Davidson didn't have the money in 1975 to spend on racing when the government had its demands. Beyond that, the basic product, the road-going twins, needed help too.

But if you keep pondering, it's hard to not decide that what really killed the program was success. Springsteen proved you could win the rider and the maker championships without going road racing or even building a new engine.

Not for nothing do people say the Harley-Davidson motto has always been, If it ain't broke, don't fix it.

But that's not fair either. As a French philosopher said, The tragedy of life is that everyone has reasons for what they do. No doubt management's reasons were good ones.

All the projects amounted to are some extraordinary glimpses of neo-history, what might have been. These drawings have been in the racing department's archives for fifteen years. They are made public only because I argued and thundered and yes, whimpered and begged, to let people know what the guys involved could have done.

Next time somebody says Harley-Davidson can't innovate, show 'em these drawings.

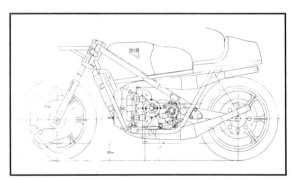

Bike: Zylstra spent several months doing the inclusive preliminary work for the road-racing 750. It was truly different, with the stack of four horizontal cylinders in a square, with the four cranks connecting to the central jackshaft and with carbs neatly on the side and exhaust pipes top and bottom. The engine was a departure while the frame and suspension and brakes were much more conventional. Harley-Davidson

Chapter 5

Willy and Jay, 1977–79

One of racing's most enduring questions is also the most basic: How do they do it?

It's basic because nobody has completely answered the question.

This attempt begins with Bill Werner, known around the pits as Willy unless, another thing nobody can explain, it's one of those days when everybody on the Harley team will call everybody else on the team, Jimmy.

Bill Werner was a hobby racer and a self-taught scientist. He tuned for riders better than himself and got a job in the Harley racing shop, as a line mechanic mostly. He's a good and active union man, which caused some trouble because his work in the shop was so good that the riders, Gary Scott first, asked to have Werner as tuner on his own time. This was awkward because of the rules and (not always openly) because management never really liked giving extra money and time to the union guys.

But the race team and department and management as well wanted to win. So Scott got Werner for a tuner and won back the number-one plate, and then Scott quit and Werner was assigned the new kid, aka the Teen-Age Lightning Bolt, eighteen-year-old Jay Springsteen.

Werner is several people in the same package. He's a family man with wife and two daughters, to whom he's devoted while he spends months each year on the road. He's modest and affable and fiercely competitive. Werner is interested in just about any subject you can name, and knows about what interests him while spending weekdays in the race shop, weekends on the tracks and evenings down in his basement where he keeps his own, as opposed to the factory's, XR-750.

Springsteen is also several men at once. Basically, he is an honest, affable man's man from a closely knit blue-collar family from Flint, Michigan, the very definition of a blue-collar town. He was in-

stantly at home with racing fans and in some chemical way they took to Springsteen and his clean and visible enthusiasm, as soon as he began racing.

A second facet was his will to win. He simply wouldn't tolerate having anybody in front of him and he'd go to any length, ride any line, to be in front. Early in his career he sailed past a veteran who until that instant thought he'd been going as fast as the corner could be taken. In the pits he said Jay was nuts, to which the Super Rookie replied, "No I'm not . . . 'cause I can get away with it."

The team, Willy and Jay, grinning in unison on the occasion of another win. Cycle

As he could. And did, except that in those days he'd either set top time or throw the bike into the haybales trying.

The third part, which nobody knew until later, was that he was a small town kid who'd never been exposed to the big world beyond racing. He liked his pals and he liked the fans, but the public and more so the glib and never-satisfied press made him nervous.

Willy and Jay became a team to a degree most managers can only dream of. They were truly parallel in that both wanted to win and enjoyed winning *and* the sport at the same time. They were complementary in that Werner appreciated Springsteen's talent as only a lesser talent can, while Springsteen had done enough of his own tuning to know how extraordinary Werner's skill was.

Plus, they liked each other. Jay moved into Bill's spare room and became one of the family, with Mrs. Werner and the girls taking equally to him.

The 1976 season came down to one of those mathematical finishes, at Ascot. If Springsteen and Roberts came to dismal finishes Mike Kidd could win, likewise for Roberts if Kidd tripped on his own tongue. All Springsteen had to do to take the title, meanwhile, was finish the national in seventh or better, even if the others came in one-two.

So, doing what not even Hollywood would dare to do, during practice Springer was close behind Beauchamp when the lead man got sideways and Springsteen T-boned him and went down. The only visible damage was a dislocated finger. Werner had coached wrestling, so he grabbed the digit and snapped it back into place. Springsteen then quipped that if you don't crash, you aren't trying hard enough.

He then went on to win, the first non-Californian to take a national at Ascot. He wasn't teaching anybody any lessons, nor being reckless. It was just that winning races was why he was there and surely, in some subconscious way, that basic honesty was why the fans went wild every time he rode.

1977: Might Beats Money

Harley-Davidson had the manufacturer's title again, along with the plate not just for the brand but in the team, so management did the practical thing and made full members of Springsteen, Keener and new kid Ted Boody. Sassaman and Beauchamp were

The other side of the sport is called Race Face, here at the Santa Fe TT in 1977. The choice of equipment is practical, as in the cast front wheel and laced-wire rear. There's just one front brake disc, to balance brake power versus weight.

Brake and shift pedals are both on the right and the gearcase has been trimmed back. The intake hoses look extra long, for mid-range torque off the turns. Harley-Davidson

cut back to support riders while Lawwill, who'd missed part of the 1976 season and didn't himself ride early in 1977 because of problems with his inner ear (the part affecting balance, which is something no motorcycle racer can do without), became an independent, tuning an XR for Kidd and going into the frame and parts business for himself.

This turned into another one of those happy accidents. There have never been more than a few hundred expert or junior professional racers and even then, at this time no more than 400 XR-750s had been sold, in iron or alloy versions. I mention the iron ones here because it's possible to put the alloy engine in the iron engine's frame. Thus the market for parts or improvements is small.

Except that a small improvement means winning races or titles and money, so the guys with the brains and drive found it worthwhile to compete for the racers' business.

The factory and team were on the same side as the outside Harley racers, while competing against them.

This is as delicate and fraught with emotional overload as you'd expect. Inside, guys like Werner and Carroll Resweber, who tuned for Keener, and Steve Storz, lured away from the fading English camp to team with Boody, were on the same team except each wanted to win. The outside Harley guys expected to know what the factory knew, while keeping their own secrets. . . . What we had here was sibling rivalry. O'Brien didn't invent this friendly competition but he did manage to manage it, and keep the information flowing among the rivals while not, make that seldom, infringing on individual rights.

This limited freedom, if one can contradict like that, along with casual rules freely interpreted, gave rise to the infinitely adjustable XR-750.

The factory-specified frame of the second batch of complete XRs was revised to cope with more power from the engine and traction from the track and tires. Next came swing arms that had multiple mounting points for the shocks, with different spring rates for front and rear, and a choice of viscosities for shock and fork damping fluid, hard and soft compound tires, wider or narrower rims and so forth. This put a premium on the rider who could interpret the bike's behavior, and on the tuner who could take that input and use it to adjust. The rider who didn't understand the dynamics and the tuner who wasn't able to translate were equally able to dial themselves out of the main event.

Springsteen and Werner were clearly the best at understanding what the bike and the track were doing with each other. They began the season with sixth in the Houston TT, best XR in a field of Triumphs and BSAs. Then Jay won the short track with an MX-based 250 single, the first Harley-Davidson win there in that class in seven years.

Time for money versus might. Springsteen's 1977 retainer from the factory was $30,000, twice

At the close of the 1977 season, the team let Cycle World *inspect and ride the winning XR. It was dusty but dazzling. Shown here, the distributor that provided the main sparks, the oil filter used for insurance and a better look at the cut-down gearcase.* Cycle World

what he'd been paid in 1976. He, Keener and Boody collectively were paid less than the $80,000 Roberts got from Yamaha, while *Cycle News* calculated that Roberts had collected an even million dollars during his five years as an expert.

Roberts was also his own boss, building his own frames for the Yamaha engines and with the help of engine wizards who in turn were getting blank cylinder heads from Yamaha, so they could port and shape and improve. No, that wasn't exactly what the

On the other side of the Werner-Springsteen engine was the magneto, the second ignition. It's grounding out on the cap for the rocker shaft but if the battery-powered distributor *failed, or if the team wanted to check its operation, they merely had to pull one set of plug wires off and pop the others on the plugs. Not elegant, but it worked.* Cycle World

AMA had in mind, but it wasn't much different from Harley practice either.

Yamaha once again won Daytona but Roberts didn't. Instead he won the road race at Charlotte, North Carolina. The dirt season began at San Jose, with a win by Scott on his private XR, while Springsteen blew an engine, something that never happened, and Roberts also lost a motor, which happened a lot.

(Side technical point here. Steve Eklund, a new expert with tuning by a college professor in mathematics, introduced an electronic ignition, saying that the magneto guys were gonna turn green. The battery came loose and the electronics failed. But don't go away.)

Springsteen won, then Scott, then Boody, all on XRs of course. Roberts couldn't get traction, then he was hurt in a fun race and ran with his hand taped to the grip, honest. As if to make up for it, Roberts won the Loudon road race and Scott's Yamaha broke.

Racing luck is even more fickle than regular luck. At the Santa Fe TT, Springsteen's magneto failed in the heat. But he coasted to a finish and there were so few entries that he qualified for a semi, won it, got

into the national and won that. Roberts lost a sprocket and got no points, while Springer took over the points lead.

At the Columbus half-mile Kidd won, with Springsteen second; his rear brake faded and his XR slipped out of the groove. Roberts was eleventh. His new monoshock-suspended Yamaha was too heavy in the rear, an imbalance done for traction.

Kidd won the San Jose mile, followed by Boody and Springsteen, another Harley one-two-three. Roberts was sixth, no traction still. But he did win Sears Point's road race.

Scott played his best card at the Ascot TT, riding a Triumph to the win. Springsteen was fourth and Roberts' Yamaha lost its battery, for a dismal fourteenth.

Springer won the DuQuoin mile along with the fastest heat and the best qualifying time. Boody and Roberts were out of points again. Kidd's ignition, the distributor Lawwill devised, let them down. Roberts was the only non-Harley in the field and by no coincidence there was talk he'd go to Europe next season. Road racing, not dirt, and to back that up Roberts

Two mainstays. Those are the 35 mm Ceriani forks with which dirt and road racers prospered for a generation, and if you look closely you'll see the tire is the Pirelli MT-53, introduced in the 1950s and still used on some half-mile tracks in 1990. The hub of the front wheel has a pattern of mounting holes so a front brake disc can be used if required. Cycle World

The surprise here is that the rear wheel of the XR, fresh from winning at Ascot, also had the Pirelli MT-53, which looks awfully narrow by 1990 standards. You can see the steps from the rear hub to the carrier to the bolt-on sprocket so it lines up with the chain. Plus, the right shock is mounted upside down. Werner said there was no reason for it. None of the magazine crew believed him, but we never could figure why he did it. Cycle World

plucked the Pocono road race, his fourth straight such event in 1977 and his twenty-fourth national win.

But Springsteen was much the same on dirt. At the double Indianapolis miles, he was in the lead until it was stopped. Spilled oil made them stop the race again, Springer in front. The other riders said they hadn't had a chance, so Springsteen shrugged and beat the field for the third time.

Of course the next day, the Sunday mile, he got so exuberant he crashed and was lucky to finish eleventh. Boody won, while Roberts' battery failed again and he was twelfth.

And so 1977 went, with Springsteen, Boody, Scott and Kidd doing most of the winning. Roberts went to another two-shock chassis, to no avail. There was his Yamaha team and another Yamaha team with some help, run by Shell Thuet, who was getting at least as much power. The Yamaha was overhead cam,

with special head and crank and narrowed cases and covers and five speeds. Everything that could be done, they did.

At one point Roberts wished he could persuade Yamaha to begin again, from scratch. "I just know we could build a bike that would blow the Harleys into the weeds . . . the Harley people are starting to get kind of cocky," said Roberts.

Shifting focus again, to Riverside, where Roberts does what you'd think. The surprise was that the Harley team built one more XRTT, out of storage is more likely, and rented the track to see what they could get from the machine and their man.

They decided it wasn't quite enough, so rather than risk Springsteen going too hard in a lost cause, John Davidson, president of the firm his family founded, stepped in and said no, they'd run where they had the best chance.

A private entry at San Jose, 1977. Longer intake tracts promote mid-range power, so this tuner has added another piece of hose to the distance between port and carburetor. There's a tachometer drive, rare on dirt, and this is a good look at how the sprocket and gearcase covers are cut back wherever possible. The brake and gearshift levers are on the right, where they won't foul the rider's left, balancing, leg. Cycle

Scott took Ascot again, fifth straight on his old Triumph. Jay was sixth, and picked up the points that ensured his second championship. And racing luck played a part, as Roberts was top qualifier except his gearbox popped out of gear and when he tried to ride with foot jamming the lever the box locked up.

In the pits somebody asked about Yamaha's 1978 dirt-track program, and Roberts grinned and said, "What dirt track program?"

There was another kind of luck here. Springsteen's magneto went bad. He reached over and flipped a switch and boom! the second ignition saved the day.

Werner had been at work. While the official team policy had been to use magnetos by the boxful, Werner had tapped the heads for a second set of plugs and had built a second ignition, using battery and black box. The second ignition was independent of the first, either/or rather than parallel. It didn't add power or smooth the engine or break engineering ground. All it did was save the day—and it forced the team designers to begin wondering if just perhaps there was a better way than the old tractor mags.

This is an elusive success story. At the close of the 1977 season Roberts confirmed the talk. His new contract "paid enough not to race dirt or think about it."

Few people knew how hard he'd worked. Those who did, the managers at Yamaha's American branch, understood. They gave him a reward, enough money and parts to go to Europe, where all he had to do was whip the world-class European riders and Japanese factories.

We'll hear from Ken Roberts again but for now, the record shows that American Yamaha backed him because Yamaha Headquarters wouldn't. That was because the Japanese took their cues from Europe and the Europeans, exemplified by Barry Sheene, knew that Americans were cowboys and weren't smart enough to race against the polished chaps from the old world, that is, himself.

Roberts whipped 'em. He rubbed it in their faces, modestly but firmly, and literally raised the level of international racing by several great leaps. Again literally, they hadn't known what real competition was. In Europe you could race whatever Dad could buy. In dirt track, you had to earn that expert license against racers just as young and hungry as yourself. It's no accident that the majority of AMA champions have come from northern California, southern Michigan or Texas.

Enough digression. One reason Harley's XR drove the Yamahas out of contention was that Harley-Davidson wasn't cocky. Check the nearby box for two examples of that.

Next, O'Brien's extended family. When the race department drew up plans for a new frame to go with the proposed major engine revision, independent contractor Lawwill got to see it. And take pictures. And when Lawwill went into the frame business, O'Brien was one of his first customers. When Werner made his back-up ignition, he showed it to the department and the rest of the team. He was allowed to sell copies to privateers, and the team was allowed to use it *and* to effect a cure for the problems.

1978: Third Time Jinx

This is probably a good place to inject a touch of witchcraft or wishful thinking: pragmatic tuners who

The 1977 team, from left, Ted Boody, Jay Springsteen and Corky Keener, a mixture of youth and age. The bike is remarkably unchanged from 1972, at least outwardly. Still the cast twin tomahawks and the small Cerianis. The brakes mean TT and that also explains the two-into-one exhaust pipe, which limits top end but adds punch at lower rpm. Harley-Davidson

skipped the theory of physics like to say that the real reason for the XR's success is that the narrow angle of the vee gives a staggered beat and power pulse, which it does, and that this irregular delivery of power becomes a staccato pounding that digs the tire into the dirt, like a cog railway or a knobby tire.

Graduates of high school physics laugh. Calculate how many pulses per minute and it's impossible for the dirt or the tire to know the timing. Even so, we'll return to this again. Suffice it to say that the Harley V-twin had just driven the vertical twins from Yamaha, BSA and Norton out of contention.

What's left is the easy answer, that Bill Werner had built the best XR, the most adjustable and reliable and powerful. Partner Jay Springsteen was the sharpest, quickest, bravest and most determined and he could tell Werner what the bike was doing, which made Werner's job all the more easy.

Mother Nature is a good sport and feels about easy wins the way she feels about a vacuum, that is, she's against them. The 1978 season opened with Eklund, the new guy with the professor behind him, winning both Houston races on Yamahas. Springsteen was third in the TT, after turning the best qualifying time, and second in the short track. There was an ominous note in *Cycle News*: "Springsteen was sick after each night's races and had to skip the postrace press conference."

AMA rules then required a road-racing license no matter what the rider had done elsewhere, so Springsteen ran the old RR-250 in the lightweight race, sixth behind a flock of Yamahas. In the 200, Roberts got even by lapping the entire field.

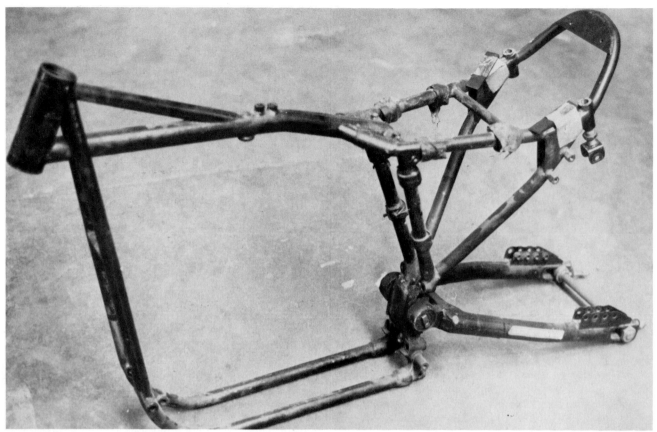

Secret stuff. In the mid 1970s, Werner went to the extremes of chassis tuning, as much to find out what worked as to win a given race. This frame is one of the results. It's scruffy because this inquisitive reporter spotted it under a bench in the back of the race shop and dragged it out for these photos. From here you can see the two bosses in the middle of the backbone, to put the tank where its weight works best, and the four mounting locations on the swing arm for the rear shocks.

Werner has bridged the two triangles at the rear of the frame, for torsional stiffness, and he's installed an adjustable top shock mount so the length of the rear shocks can be varied while leaving position and spring preload alone.

Another era was being formed. On the one hand, only the Norton fielded by master builder Ron Wood could stay with the swarms of XR-750s. On the other hand, the Harley tuners themselves were as competitive as they would have been with a choice of nameplates. Boody and tuner Steve Storz had their own frame and picked motocross-style front forks; for instance, Lawwill's XR had so much power that rider Garth Brow won the San Jose mile despite jumping the gun (OK, the flag) and being moved back to the penalty line.

Alex Jorgensen won the Ascot TT, followed by Skip Aksland and Brow, with Jay fourth. He had a new kind of ignition problem. A wire had come loose and while the engine ran fine, every time Springsteen tucked his right leg against the tank, he got zapped.

Then came some dirty business. Springer won the Denver half-mile and Gary Scott claimed his XR.

This requires a recap. Back in the 1930s, when Class C was instituted, there was the fear that the mighty factories would buy all the wins with machines the little guy couldn't afford. To prevent this the AMA came up with a claiming rule: a competitor could post money and claim the winner's machine.

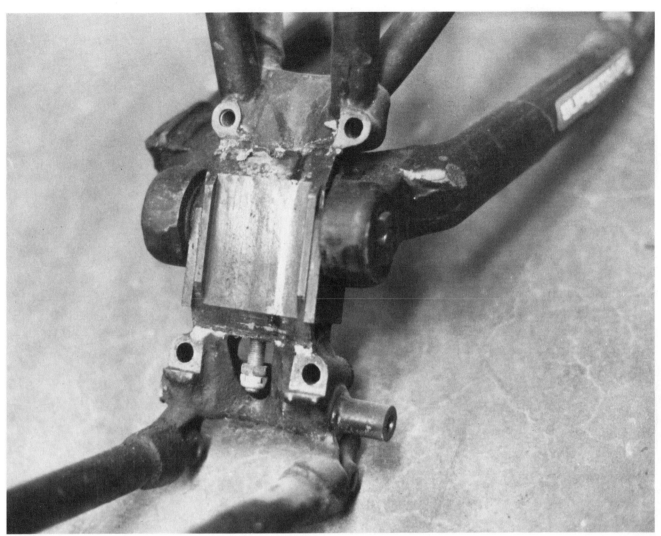

Remarkable. The old frame casting is there but the swing-arm pivot has been cut loose and fitted on a grooved track, with a bolt for adjustment. Move the pivot up and down and you change weight transfer and the effect of engine torque on the suspension, which is to say you can tune the *chassis for whatever traction is out there. Werner used this frame in TTs, mostly, because that's where traction varies the most. When he learned what setting worked best, though, he no longer needed such devices.*

One can empathize with the feelings behind this. But it hasn't ever worked the way its backers hoped. Instead, think about anything you ever made, never mind how good it was. Would you like it if some bozo or even a rival could take your work away? Neither did the tuners.

But after the Denver win, Gary Scott filed for Springsteen's bike. Not for spite, he said, but because he couldn't buy normal replacement parts. Four other riders, Springsteen's friends and teammates, filed claims right behind Scott. Randy Goss, a new Michigan racer riding for former national champ Bart Markel, won the draw and handed the XR back to the team.

Springsteen won the Louisville half-mile, with Eklund second and Boody third. Scott claimed again and this time won the draw and for $6,500 got the

machine. He also protested Springsteen on a claim of illegal use of intoxicants or stimulants, forcing the AMA to withhold the prize money and the points. To nobody's surprise, the tests were negative.

Springsteen won the Harrington half-mile, with Boody second and Keener, the third full team member, third. Eklund was top qualifier.

Eklund was a privateer, and like Scott and Aksland, was free to pick the horse for the course, as in a Yamaha 750 for road racing, a 250 single for short track and a 500 single (or Triumph twin in Scott's case) for the TTs.

The points race was tight, so for Loudon Springsteen got an XRTT with a new mile-spec, as in big carbs and hot cams and all top end power, engine. Alas, it blew in practice before the race, which was won by Aksland on the inevitable TZ750.

Sour grapes? Look down the line at San Jose, 1978, and there are several tanks with the factory's logo on the sides.

But nowhere on Gary Scott's XR (5) does the maker's name appear. Cycle World

Just as tough but much cooler about it was Steve Eklund, shown here at San Jose in 1979. He was tuned and spon- *sored by a university-level mathematician who simply liked racing and machines.* Cycle

In what may also have been a hint of the future, the 1978 rules required restrictors in the carburetors of the 750 cc fours in road races. There were two reasons: first, to limit speeds because the tire people were worried, and second, to reduce power to let the engine last longer and make racing cheaper. Or so it was claimed. Opponents said then and still say that what artificial restrictions mostly do is give an advantage to the tuners with money, time and skill to design around the limiters, which they usually manage to do.

Eklund won the Santa Fe TT with his Yamaha 500, Scott was second on his Triumph and Springsteen followed on the big, relatively anyway, XR.

Eklund went back to his XR and won the Columbus half-mile, again followed by Scott on his XR and then Keener and Springsteen. Eklund did his three in a row with the San Jose half-mile, getting past Brow on a last-lap bit of daring. And the lab sent back

results of urine tests done, without warning, on all fourteen finishers of the Columbus race. Clean, every one. Seems there were rumors, which presumably were defeated by the surprise tests.

The Scott-Harley feud ended, officially, with the news that Scott now had all the parts he could use, thanks to John Davidson working with Scott's sponsor and an Ohio H-D dealer. One of the problems had been that the racing department can't sell direct, but must deal with an authorized dealership. It does sound like the sort of thing that could have been handled with better manners.

Willy and Jay pulled a surprise and won the Castle Rock TT, which for all history had been the province of local talent and light bikes. They did it the clever way, by using a hard-compound tire that didn't work until the rest of the field, on soft compounds, had their traction go away.

Eklund was as determined as he looks here. Not a natural rider, he was determined and he never quit. Cycle

Sears Point was a Yamaha festival except that Aksland and Eklund both crashed and Scott wasn't ready in time. For some reason even the guys with road-racing equipment never managed to do well with both at the same time.

Jorgensen won the Ascot TT on a BSA "somewhere between 25 and 50 years old," or so he said.

Last we saw Hank Scott he was bravely riding a Yamaha in midpack. He joined brother Gary's former tuner Carl Patrick and cylinder-head wizard Jerry Branch and went the XR route and won the Sacramento mile. The team next won the DuQuoin mile, and with a lap of 35.956 sec., the first 100 mph dirt-track mile ever recorded. Not to take away from that, but rain shortened the event from twenty to sixteen laps, catching Springer, who'd done the late-blooming tire trick again, in second. Sometimes you win, he said, and sometimes not.

It was Eklund at the Santa Fe short track, after tuner Tom Hasler warmed the rear tire with a blowtorch, no kidding. The twenty-minute wait for the start after the barbeque surely cooled the tire back

down, but it did give the guys something to think about.

Gary Scott took the Des Moines half-mile, Brow and Hank Scott split the Indy double miles and Springsteen, who was seventh in his heat and missed the main event, could only say, "I rode as hard and fast as I could. What can I say?"

Concerning that, the teenage lightning bolt was coming up against some sad facts of life. Springsteen's natural talent and his joy in exercising that talent made his riding look easier than it was, so winning came to look the same way. People began to expect a record every lap.

In real life, Werner was building the most reliable XR engines and was at least equal in chassis skill. But Lawwill, Carl Patrick, Tex Peel and Jim Belland were spending as much time, perhaps even more, because they didn't have real jobs, while C. R. Axtell, Jerry Branch and Ron Alexander, the man who made the Waffle Iron cook, were doing ports and cams and exhausts of their own. On more than one occasion Hank Scott's Patrick-tuned XR "clearly had the ponies," quoting *Cycle News*.

There were other choices. The AMA considered banning the Goodyear DT II, also known as the gumball tire, because it was stickier than the other, road-based tires. But Carlisle could keep even and the top riders, including those on the Harley team, were free to swap compounds and even brands, depending on what looked to work on the day.

What the AMA finally did was accept the soft compounds while putting a limit, 3.5 in., on rim width. Much easier to police, they said, and as good a way to limit tire contact patch and thus speed.

The closeness of the points race was such that again for Loudon, the tightest and thus slowest of the road races on the schedule, the Harley team dragged out an XRTT "of Cal Rayborn vintage," as *Cycle News* put it, for Springsteen.

The combination was in midpack when three crashes brought out the red flag and the tech crew gave the old XR a careful inspection, in case it was leaking oil and had caused the spills. All they could find was a fine mist from the breather. But O'Brien pulled Springsteen out of the restart. "The engine was slowing," O'Brien said, "and we didn't want to chance Jay getting hurt. We had no oil problems."

Eklund had been in ninth at the stop, and he also scratched from the restart, on grounds it was too risky for the points he could collect. As we'll see, it was a poor move.

More racing luck. Jay won the Syracuse mile, with Morehead second and Hank Scott, top qualifier, in third. Eklund missed the national and the points because he swapped engines and it looked like rain, so they ran the national early and he missed getting to the line by seconds.

Morehead won at Meadowlands, a harness-racing half-mile south of Pittsburgh. Springsteen did the hard-compound number and came from last at the start to sixth, with Eklund eighth.

At San Jose's mile Brow had top time on Lawwill's XR and won, trailed by Morehead and Hank Scott, privateers all. Eklund was fifth and Springer ninth; no traction, he said later. The two top riders went into the final one point apart.

The cover for *Cycle News* of October 11, 1978, had no words. None were needed. All there was, was a photo of Miss Camel and Jay Springsteen, arms in the air and grins ear to ear, while one step below stood a pensive Steve Eklund.

The Springer had done it again.

By 20 ft.

And five points.

It was a classic finish. In front of a sold-out, standing-room-only crowd the flamboyant and flashy Springer took the lead and rode beyond human potential, flinging the bike beyond the limit time and again, catching it when all was lost as the quiet, contained and scientific Eklund grimly trailed. All he could do was wait for Springer to make a mistake, which the leader did, except that he got away with it.

It was Werner's fourth straight title. What was his secret? Werner told the reporter, "I've got a hell of a rider."

It was so popular a win in fact that eighteen leading experts, including Eklund and the only non-Harley man at the top, Alex Jorgensen, took out a two-page ad in *Cycle News* to congratulate Springsteen.

In a practical sense, the victory—Harley-Davidson repeated as winning manufacturer, of course—the series and the finish challenged the view that if you only had one brand, you had no contest. So it made sense that O'Brien announced the 1979 team would be Springsteen and Morehead as full members, tuned by Werner and Storz, respectively. Keener would get factory support but no mechanic, and Boody was offered bikes and parts but decided to go independent and did some riding for a tuner named Kennedy, who was building an Americanized version of the vertical Triumph twin.

Technical Review

Speaking of parts, an outfit called Harley-Davidson West, an aggressive dealership that did a good business selling Harleys to Japan, was also in the racing game and advertised any and all the XR parts in the book, right off the shelf. They meant it; in fact, they supplied a number of the parts I needed for my own XR.

There was evolution going on. The dynamometer tests from the time show a broadening of the curve rather than sheer power, with 90 bhp at the top and 85 or so on average. The factory's exhaust systems began including mufflers in 1977, because everybody knew tests and limits were on the way. So even when there were two pipes instead of the boom box, the engines were quieter and made power anyway.

The real difference was between the best and the rest. Mike Kidd was a rookie expert in 1972, along with Gary Scott and Ken Roberts. He didn't do as well and during 1978, with more money going out than he could win, he had to build his own engines. At one race he took the lead and got his pipes blown off as the top guys thundered past. He couldn't figure why until C. R. Axtell put the engine on the dyno and it showed 76 bhp, ten or fifteen less than needed. Axtell went to work on Kidd's XR heads and Kidd won a sponsorship from the army, of all people. But this was a strange era, culturally and politically, and Kidd was careful to say he didn't endorse the army and they didn't sponsor him. Rather, he'd sold them advertising space on his bikes and suits and truck.

The secret wasn't so much a secret as it was combinations. The original camshaft timings had been based on what worked for the old flathead and iron engines, so new experiments from new people, Sig Erson for example, gave new settings for miles, with lots of overlap for top end, and for the half-miles, with more mid-range. Erson's cams went into the parts book, with the logical designation of "E" for Erson. The exhaust pipe diameters and lengths and the taper of the cones for megaphones were arrived at by tests on the dyno and the track. The early engines worked best with pipes of $1\frac{5}{8}$ in. diameter, but when the new valves and ports came along, the better breathing meant the pipes had to grow to $1\frac{3}{4}$ in. Tuning the intakes was easier. The 36 mm Mikunis were best on half-miles, the 38s won the miles, and thanks to metal stubs and rubber hoses between the stubs, you could lengthen and shorten the intake tract until it worked with the cams and carbs. At this time a length of 10.5 in. from carb mouth to port was optimum for the mile.

The 35 mm exhaust valve was supplemented by an optional 37 mm valve, and there were three intake port sizes, 1.5 in., the stock 1.375 in. and one of 1.19 in., calculated to improve the velocity of the intake mixture. The shape of the combustion chamber and the dome of the piston required to fill the chamber and give a high compression ratio was also a compromise, with a ratio between 10.0:1 and 10.5:1 working the best at the end of 1978. The first 90 bhp engine was built in 1975, and the peak stayed there for the next few years while team and private tuners worked on fattening the curve.

The Harley-Davidson XR was easily the best machine for the big ovals. That doesn't mean overconfidence. First, note that the aborted effort at Loudon was the final official team use of the XRTT, the road racer, in AMA national competition. Plus, the factory had been working on a purely road-race machine all along, but had been forced to abandon the effort in its planning stages.

And just because the pushrod XR engine had beaten the ohc Yamaha didn't mean the Harley engineers hadn't read the textbooks. Once again, the limit came from the accountants.

And there was no lack of challenge, internal and external.

But there were also customers. In 1978 there was a production run of XR-750s. The run began with another batch of frames, done to the factory's specifications and subcontracted through Lawwill, with the work done by Terry Knight's shop. The records show eighty-three actual machines built and/or sold to dealers, who presumably had racing customers waiting for them: Harley-Davidson has for generations refused to build more motorcycles than the dealers were willing to order in advance.

1979: Charm Becomes Jinx

Despite the fantastic finish to Springsteen's 1978 season and his third straight title, there were chilling portents.

One was that he was booed by the crowds.

This sounds worse than odd. The papers said it was because he'd been accused of using drugs, but that doesn't make sense. There had been no proof of drug use. The charge was brought by a personal rival known for vindictive behavior, and Springer had been found clean, twice. Heroes who are cleared of false charges don't get booed.

My own feeling here is that Springsteen was the victim of his own natural talent. He rode so hard, with such flair, that it looked easy and the fans counted on a new record every time. But the other guys were good and their machines had as much power and they were hungry, too. There were days when Springsteen did his best, as noted, and managed second or third and was asked why he hadn't won.

By 1979 the magneto was outmoded but the replacement was still subject to cut and try. This XR's electric power came from as big a battery as the tuner could install, witness the shelf bolted to the gearcase cover. Above the battery is a second-generation rockerbox. Valve clearance is adjusted by setting the eccentrics that carry the rocker-arm shafts. You move the setting with the slots in the shaft, then tighten the Allen bolts. Cycle

Same time, same place, other variations. There's a rotor driven off the front of the gearcase and a coil between the rotor and the tach drive. The bundled plug wires indicate multiple plugs. Note that this engine has its rocker-shaft adjustment on the other side of the box. See the notches in the end of the shaft and on the box itself? They indicate where the eccentrics are set, and the range within the settings must fall. If they don't, you have to change the length of the pushrod. Cycle

Springsteen at DuQuoin, 1979. Still using the spindly Ceriani forks and what looks like a stock frame, but the fuel tank is now aluminum, the fiberglass version having fallen prey to the corrosive strength of racing gas. The seat, with no snaps visible, came from an aftermarket outfit called Grand Prix Plastics, which furnished them for less than the factory charged. Even champions mind their budgets. Bill Werner

He's not an introspective man, but Springsteen is human and the strain showed, to the point of shouting at Werner in public.

The 1979 season began poorly. Honda, of all people, had become interested in dirt track, mostly because they had some good, large four-stroke singles. Mickey Fay, a TT specialist, won the Houston TT on a Honda. Jay was T-boned in his heat and felt bad, so they scratched so he could rest for the short track . . . but he was sick the next night and missed that race, too. Best XR in the TT was ridden by a new guy Randy Goss, to third, while the short-track win went to none other than Ted Boody, on a two-stroke Yamaha.

The Sacramento mile went to Kidd, with a new and obviously competitive XR engine by Storme Winters. Eklund was second with Springsteen third, having overcome "stomach problems, nausea and a second row start," as *Cycle News* put it.

Eklund took the mile at San Jose, with new kid Ricky Graham second and old guy Gary Scott third. Springsteen was in the hospital, sick to his stomach again.

Then begins Werner's slogan, When He's Well, He's Hell. Springer took three straight half-miles, Ascot, Laurel, Maryland, and Louisville. He did it with another one of Werner's all-nighters, an XR tuned to fire both cylinders on the same revolution (45 deg. apart, of course). Theory here was to give a great big staggered bang, then a pause. Such an engine is known as a twingle, for obvious reasons. The idea had been around since some of the Norton guys did it, and it does seem to give more traction. Werner is one of the few who's won with the idea. He says it's easy to make the engine fire that way, but that there's one little thing you have to do and he's never told anybody what that is.

Ron Wood, motorcycle racing's Silver Fox, astride his very different XR-750. Wood has had an amiable (mostly) feud with Harley-Davidson for years, but that didn't keep him from using the XR-750 engine in his own frame. Cycle

Wood's frame was smaller and tighter than the factory's design, with the cradle wrapped around the engine and with a large, curved backbone. Cycle

Rookie expert Scott Parker, a seventeen-year-old from Flint, Michigan, and the youngest rider to earn his expert license, had engine help from one Tex Peel, a huge and jovial employee of Buick's Flint plant. The joke was that Buick sponsored Tex's equipment because so many guys in the tool rooms helped with this part or that machine tool operation. Parker did what the best do, that is, shot into the lead at Ascot and then fired himself and machine into the haybales.

And there was the sort of racing luck you make yourself. Doug Sehl, whom we met as a rider, had been hurt and become a tuner. He designed a monoshock frame for his XR and got Corky Keener, the former H-D teamster, to ride it. It didn't work. Keener said they couldn't get traction and he went back to riding his own machines, with two shocks. An aggressive Texan named Terry Poovey was breaking

his own machines, meanwhile, and volunteered to ride Sehl's equipment.

Now we get into politics. The Brits were gone, while the miles and half-miles were virtually all XR. Yamaha and Honda began hinting that they surely would like to take part in AMA championship racing if only the races were for bikes they made, namely 500 cc singles. Somebody came up with an equalizer, that if you restricted the 750 twins, they could race against the 500 singles: The old sidevalve-overhead valve gambit, sort of in reverse.

There was the usual acrimonious debate, with Tex Peel saying that a Lawwill XR had 90 bhp now and couldn't do better than 65 bhp with 28 mm restrictors, against 80 bhp for a full-race 500. Proponents of the plan argued that you could at least buy a Honda or Yamaha engine while the XRs were in short supply. Anyway, late in the season the AMA rules committee recommended the 750s be fitted with 27 mm plates. Gary Scott, the rider representative on the committee, was quick to let people know he was opposed, as of course was O'Brien, who said simply that Honda and Yamaha were free to build engines that met the rules, just as Harley-Davidson had done.

In the actual racing, Parker won the DuQuoin mile, youngest rider to win a national. Springsteen took the Santa Fe TT, with his XR now wearing an alloy fuel tank, a Moto-Plat electronic ignition devised by Werner, and one front disc brake, because one was enough and lighter than two.

Then came wins by Goss, Kidd, Parker again and Kidd again, as tuners Peel and Lawwill and Winter showed their skills. Springsteen was in and out of the hospital, while Eklund picked up points in the middle of the pack.

Randy Goss, shown here on the occasion of his first national win at Middletown, New York, in 1979, was tough and energetic and a self-taught, rather than a natural rider.
Cycle World

Scott Parker—tucked in with the lead while Jay Springsteen (9) hugs the inside—was a flamboyant natural who had to learn control before he could consistently win.
Harley-Davidson

Poovey proved Sehl's merits, and persistence, by winning at the Meadowlands, New Jersey. Sehl had stuck with the monoshock idea, originally drawn by New England enduro master Joe Bolger, and had moved the engine up and down, back and forth, until he and Poovey could make it work.

Equally revolutionary in that race was O'Brien stepping in and taking Morehead's XR from him and giving it to Springer, on the grounds that Morehead's bike was faster and Jay needed the points more. Things then reverted to normal Harley-Davidson practice: Morehead beat Springsteen anyway.

The points race came down to San Jose, where Springsteen had to win and Eklund had to get no points, if Jay was to keep his plate.

Eklund tuned his suspension out of contention and had so little traction he didn't qualify for the main, that is, no points.

Springsteen struggled into the main, finished seventh and threw up.

In the final race of the year, Ascot's half-mile, Goss won. Springsteen had flown home for more tests. Eklund was fifth and collected his plate. Steve Storz, Morehead's tuner on the factory team, decided to go home to California and go into business for himself. O'Brien decided to let Morehead go and hire Goss, with support for Rookie of the Year Parker.

As what had to be a consolation prize, Harley-Davidson dominated the manufacturer's contest, winning with 420 points to 178 for Yamaha and 78 for Honda.

Before one can say, That won't last, the AMA trustees voted to reject the contest board's recommendation. Instead, the expert nationals would be run as before, 750 twins period for the big tracks and 250 singles for short track. And if you wanted to run a 650 twin or 500 single in TT, you could do so. At the same time, the problem of policing tire compound was avoided by instead limiting rim width to 3 in., while junior riders were given the choice of restricted 750 twin or open 500 single. Not to be judgmental here, but for the past ten years the rule for juniors has worked quite well.

Mike Kidd was another canny racer, so sharp he persuaded the US Army to sponsor him. He's shown here in his private

Harley days, with pursuers including Hank Scott (14) and Randy Goss (13). Cycle News

Chapter 6

The Rivals Return, 1980–83

Now that the AMA trustees had retained the rules that Harley-Davidson used best, and the brand was winning most of the races and there were complaints that some racers were more equal than other racers, what was going on in the shop?

Technical Preview

First, a generous portion of what was going on, was going on outside the shop. There were half a dozen good smaller outfits making frames, some better than what you'd get from the factory parts book,

This radical Honda beggars description: it was the 500 cc cross-mount twin turned one quarter turn, then converted from shaft to chain drive. It was nearly hopeless, so how'd it get the number-one plate? By having Honda hire Mike Kidd to race with the title he'd won on a Harley with Yamaha's money. Cycle

Kidd was tough and overcame injuries and never gave up, and it paid off finally with the national title and a factory ride. When that ended, he went on to another career as a racing promoter. Cycle World

some maybe not as good. But in either case, they'd be as different as Sehl's monoshock, which was made by the Canadian shop called Panther, or they'd be all-steel tube and no casting, like Lawwill's, or they'd have the engine in a different location. Whichever, frames were easy to find.

Ditto for cams and ignitions and suspension. Girling and Ceriani supplied the parts for the stock machines, but Red Wing and later Marzocchi had components that were at least as good. The team used them, which surely proves that.

There was some evolution. When the alloy XR was built out of parts left over from the iron XR, the new bikes used some bits, the rear hub for one, that went back to the KR of 1952. The rear wheel was a steel hub laced to a 19 in. rim and as narrow as it could be, the better to fit within the swing arm of the rear subframe—no suspension or brakes, then, don't forget.

The outer faces of this hub carried short splines and fine threads. There was a sprocket, steel or even iron, dished so its inner-radius splines slipped over the splines on the hub, but the outer radius, the one with the teeth, lined up with the engine's output shaft. Come to think, the hub was so much narrower than the XR, which had the same external dimensions as the KR, that the hub might have come from the even older WR.

Yamaha's entry, or re-entry, for the national arena was more conventional than Honda's, but even less successful. The road engine was converted to chain from shaft drive, which caused the engine to rotate counter to the wheels, while all other racers have always spun with the wheels.

The Yamaha never had traction or handling and years later, the team guys said one major factor was their failure to tune the suspension to work with the counterrotation. Cycle

Anyway, the dished rear sprocket was held on the splines by a nut that fitted over the fine threads, and which was made tight by fitting a wrench with little nubs matching the notches on the nut, and with wings, to be hit by a soft hammer. This was the design originally used by the factory and later done by Barnes, which became supplier to most everybody.

There were some changes. The dished sprocket was fine with 50 or 60 bhp from the KR. The leverage, with the force from the engine outboard of the mounting face of the sprocket and hub, was too much when the XR went to 70 and then 90 bhp.

The first running change was an adapter, an aluminum casting that went over the hub's splines and to which a flat sprocket, also aluminum, could be bolted. The ring nut was still there, but the casting was stronger than the dished hub. As another protection, the aluminum splines wore before the steel splines, so the adapter could be replaced periodically and the hub, which cost much more, would last.

Except that the factory went to aluminum hubs, which were lighter but not nearly as strong. They weren't strong enough for the job, and they broke and before you knew it, all the racers were using hubs and wheels from outside.

The outsiders did it differently. They began with wider hubs, and taller faces on the hubs, machined to accept a choice of bolt patterns. Then came adapters, all this in alloy by the way, and with spacers and even a variety of axle diameters. The tuner measures his frame and swing arm, decides how wide or thick, then orders the blanks from Storz or Kozman and does the final machining or—this is how mine was done—farms out the delicate parts. From all these pieces come spool front wheels, for miles and half-miles, and rear wheels set up for disc on the left, sprocket on the right, or fronts with one or two discs and so forth. This isn't exactly production parts. The current wheel doesn't come off the shelf. Instead, the tuner-builder-racer gets precisely what's needed.

One more odd note here is that the factory hubs, made for the racing department and listed in the parts books, aren't up to the job. Rather than use time and budget, though, the shop and the team get their parts from the outside.

The principle appears through the parts book. The fiberglass fuel tank was easy and economic to make in lots of 200, but the later alloy tank, same capacity, was stronger and safer and could be supplied for less money when the numbers dropped. That lithe seat and fender with snap-on pad cost $400 out of the official parts channel, but you can get the same thing except with a pad whose base bolts to the seat, for $100 and change from Grand Prix Plastics, with an option of turned-up tail.

This idea has been working since the first XRs. As noted, there were leftover 1970 frames on hand for the 1972 production run. There were replacement cases made even in years when there was no official production of XRs.

Next, we need to remember that official H-D policy has been and still is to sell racing parts to and through the regular dealer group. Every Harley dealership has—or should have. Some don't bother and some even throw the things away—an up-to-date parts book for the XR-750. All the parts are on the computer and when the parts man punches in the right number he'll know in minutes if the racing department has the part in stock. And if so, the piece will be in the regular weekly shipment from the factory to the dealership.

There have always been a few hundred riders with expert licenses, no more and no fewer. Most of the experts are local experts, that is, they are good enough to earn the white plate but they don't make a living on the track. Rather, there are twenty or thirty guys who do the full circuit and the rest of the field makes a few races each year.

What that means, and meant more strongly when the old Triumphs and BSAs and Yamahas were competitive, is that only a few score racers, make it 100 on the outside, *need* to own XR-750s. There are another score or two of experts or juniors or even hopeless amateurs like yours truly who *want* an XR, never mind being able to justify the beast.

This is as true in 1990 as it was in 1975 or whenever there was the flap about how you couldn't buy an XR unless you had influence.

I mention this here because we are about to arrive at a milestone.

1980 Version XR-750s

At one of the 1979 nationals, only thirty-seven experts showed up to try for the forty-eight places in the four preliminary heats. There have been races with 100 experts entered, and we in 1990 tend to think the old days were graced with larger fields but they weren't, not every time.

We know there were 200 iron XR-750s assembled and parked and counted before the new model was allowed to race. We know that something close to half those Waffle Irons sat unsold until they were scrapped or parted out.

In 1972 there was the required full production run of 200 dirt-version XR-750s, the alloy-top-engined XR. Add the ten XRTTs made for the team and the other fifteen (an estimate, I admit) assembled and sold to private parties.

Assume the sad truth that nobody could make an iron engine even useful, never mind competitive, by 1972 and subtract that 100 and we have 225 dirt and road XRs. Then came the second run, another 100 all dirt style and the third run, the eighty-three to fill orders, and there are 408 XR-750s in public hands.

That's thoroughly unofficial, admittedly. The factory records show 383 by the end of 1978 and nobody can really know how many guys got one of the older 1970 frames or a Champion or Knight frame and a set of replacement cases and put together a legal XR that the factory never saw.

Further, the system for stamping and numbering the cases has been irregular since the days when each rider had to own his engine. It's possible to find cases stamped H3 or H6, standing for 1973 and 1976, even though no XRs were supposed to have been made in those years.

To sum up the facts so far, and the ads in the papers back this up, it was never impossible to buy an XR-750. Difficult, probably. Your local dealer might have taken a dislike to you, or the shop might have been busy with the team bikes and not gotten around to yours. But you could have found one and if you didn't like the wheels or the cams or the ignition or the shocks, you could have found replacements at less than factory prices.

Here's where we arrive at the milestone:

In 1980 there was another revision for the factory-sold frames. This version was called the TT frame, because it was higher and because TTs have jumps and need extra ground clearance so when you set up for a TT you have the static ride height higher than you would for a mile. In this example, though, the frame was higher because the engine had more power and the rule there is that the higher center of gravity will transfer more weight to the rear (driving) wheel and you can transmit more power with more traction.

The TT frame got this height by using rear shocks that were 14 in. long. XRs are never discussed in terms of seat height, as in motocross. Rather, the comparisons are 14 in., or 13.5, or 12.4 rear shocks.

To compensate, or perhaps it's better to say take advantage of and balance this change, the front of the engine was 1 in. lower in the cradle. Yes, the front. Weight and center of gravity are factors, but so is the height of the output sprocket and the swing arm pivot. Tipping the engine lets you adjust one and leave the others alone.

Another major change was the front suspension. The angle of the steering head was pulled back, that is, made steeper, with a nominal value of 24 deg. from vertical. The next change was use of Marzocchi forks instead of Cerianis, which were undergoing business problems. The Harley designers used a trick borrowed from Aermacchi and had the triple clamps and stanchion tubes slightly angled to the steering head and stem. That's why I said nominal value: the *steering* wasn't as steep as the steering head. The engineers did this because they were afraid the steering would be too heavy if all the components were aligned. A few years later, having noticed that nobody noticed, the angularity was eliminated.

The 1980 XR engine was mostly as it had been, or rather as it had become, except that the stock exhaust system was separate pipes from the cylinder joining into one megaphone and muffler. The two-into-one system is lighter, takes up less space and gives a broader power band at the expense of peak power. And the stock valves were larger, the optimal

sizes from before. Better porting meant more flow *and* good velocity.

Racing department records show 160 1980 version XR-750s were produced. That's carefully worded because they weren't all done at the same time. O'Brien said the first forty had been delivered by January 1980, with another eighty or ninety due out by Daytona, which of course had nothing to do with the dirt program but was a date everybody knew.

Minor point here is, the racing department built as many XRs as they guessed they could sell, or had orders for, and it was less than the traditional 200.

Major point here is that the 1980 production run was the final run of complete XR-750s, complete meaning the frame, engine, suspension and so forth, needing in theory only fluids and a push to be race-ready. By 1980 there were so many people making replacement parts and good-as-stock parts that there was no need, or even enough business, in selling complete racing machines.

And while we're on that subject the racing department could, or so they say, have assembled and sold complete XRs until 1989, the year during which the last factory-spec frames were sold out of the racks in the racing department.

There were shortages, there had been when the complaints began and were for years to come, but they were for the more demanding and precise parts, sets of connecting rods, for instance, which require truly expert machining and preparation. That task has been beyond anything the aftermarket people have been willing to commit to, and the factory is stuck making sure they have a supplier.

1980: Return of Yamaha

The 1980 season was an odd one. Begin with the announcement that Mert Lawwill had been hired by Yamaha to build TT and short-track bikes for Roberts, rookie Jim Filice and TT expert Rick Hocking. Racers know better than to swear lifelong fealty to a brand but even so, it came as a surprise. Not only that, Kawasaki had submitted forms for AMA approval and had built twenty-six short-track engines, all the rules required by then, in hopes of making the show at Houston. There was news that some eastern tuner was working on a Ducati 750 cc twin for dirt, and an even stronger rumor, stoutly denied, that Honda was about to convert its water-cooled 500 cc V-twin, the CX500, into a dirt racer despite shaft drive and having the vee crossways in the frame.

As fact, the Harley team would be Springsteen and Randy Goss, accurately described as not a natural talent but tough, hungry and the hardest worker around. As it happened, Goss was so accustomed to doing his own work that the hardest thing team tuner Brent Thompson had to do was make Goss go home at quitting time.

Things still looked workable for all-round riders. Eklund planned to defend his title with two XRs, Ya-

Brave as two tigers, Ricky Graham hurls his XR into the outside, back wheel way beyond what any of the others, here Alex Jorgensen (44) and Randy Goss (6) will try. Cycle

maha 250 and 500 singles for TT and short track, and Triumph and Yamaha 750 twins for back-up or just in case.

It was old reliables at first. Roberts won the Houston TT on a Yamaha 500 single, and was third in the short track. Ronnie Jones won the short track for Yamaha, with Mickey Fay and Honda second. No Kawasakis made the final.

Springsteen was sick. He was fourth in the TT, got sick immediately and missed the short track. He'd been to the Mayo Clinic and been diagnosed time and again. In the end, Springsteen would miss most of the 1980 season, making the fans so upset that the promoters had to offer refunds when they announced Springer's absence.

Once again, the record has only facts and we're left wondering, why are some riders hot and others not? Hank Scott won Sacramento, trailed by Kidd and Ricky Graham, who was riding for Tex Peel. It was so much a Harley show that even Ron Wood, the Norton devotee, had an XR. And that denied version of the Honda showed up and practiced, even though it wasn't fast enough to qualify for a heat.

Hank Scott won again at San Jose, with Springsteen back in action temporarily. Sportsmanship fans will want to know that when Jay was sick, dismissed

Graham was hungry and always willing to try whatever he could come up with to win, or crash. Cycle World

teammate Morehead used his bike, and when the Harley team needed engine parts, who'd they borrow them from but Ron Wood, whose denunciations of Harley-Davidson engineering are works of art.

It was Billy Labrie, Graham and Parker at Ascot, while Eklund was sixth and got a point, first the defending champion had won in six races.

Hank got his third at Louisville, chased by Morehead and Gary Scott, another former champion who'd faded for no visible reason. At Harrington, Delaware, it was Morehead, Hank Scott and Labrie, with Parker fast qualifier and with all the leaders' soft-compound tires worn to the cords by the finish. Gary Scott was rider representative on the AMA contest board and complained about the tires, saying that everybody knew the soft ones wouldn't last a full race but that nobody was willing to run hard compounds because they'd go slower in the early laps. He also said he was the only member of the board willing to go public with the problem, which seems to have been the case. The DuQuoin mile was cut from twenty-five to twenty laps because of tire wear.

Weaving in and out of the record are some trends. The Honda and Yamaha 500s were the machines best suited to the TTs, with Mike Kidd winning Ascot, first 500 cc single win in that TT in seventeen years. Harley-Davidson still had a viable short-track bike, witness Parker winning Santa Fe on Springsteen's 250.

Soft tires and more power were obvious. Graham won the Indy mile at an average of 100.467 mph, first 100+ race in AMA dirt-track history. It was Tex Peel's first national win in seven years of trying. Fast qualifier was Hank Scott, at 102.032 mph, tuned by Tex' brother Gary.

Late in the season a new record was narrowly averted. While Hank Scott had won the most races, he was locked in a points battle with Goss, who hadn't won any but had earned points every time. Never since the series began had anyone won the title without winning a race, although it obviously could be done. Then Goss won San Jose, with Hank second. The final race went to Labrie, with Eklund second, Scott third and Goss fifth. The points tallies were 207 for Goss, 206 for Hank Scott and 175 for Graham. Harley-Davidson's team had the title back.

So did the Harley-Davidson factory, with 365 points against 216 for Yamaha and 83 for Honda.

More on that: Honda was obviously interested in AMA dirt track. The Winston (alternately Camel) Pro series was the last major venue in motorcycle racing, including the European titles pretentiously labeled world championships, that Honda hadn't won. They were doing well with the 250 and 500 singles and during 1980 sponsored a series for junior-class races, 500 cc limit, on the program with the nationals. In fairness, all brands were eligible and Yamaha won as many as Honda did. But Big Red clearly wished to do more, never mind that the official types said once

again at the end of the 1980 season that they weren't going to build racers out of the CX500.

On the other side of the triangle, the Yellow and Black had a different approach to the same goal.

This had to be read carefully, because it was announced with surgical precision: Yamaha had hired Roberts and Lawwill to form a racing team, for Winston/Camel Pro. Yamaha would design and produce and certify racing engines based on the Virago, which was a 750 cc V-twin, cylinders fore and aft and not side to side. The road motorcycle had shaft drive, so Yamaha changed the gearbox and output shafts to get an output sprocket to match the conventional rear-wheel sprocket.

Here's the precision part. Yamaha would pay the Roberts-Lawwill team to test and develop this engine in racing applications. This was not, repeat not, a factory racing team. Yamaha hoped their dealers would pick up the flag, once the development crew had found the winning combination. Meanwhile, Lawwill-Roberts would field machines for established contender Mike Kidd and rookie expert Jim Filice.

This made sense. Kidd had done well with his backing from the army, but it wasn't a factory ride and that's what he'd hoped to earn. But O'Brien's choice was Springsteen and Goss for the 1981 team, with maybe some outside help for Graham, who'd ride for Wood, and for Parker and his new tuner, Tex Peel. Kidd was sharp and knew when to pick up his cards. Filice, who was so shy then that he raced for a year with "Felice" on his leathers because he didn't want to hurt the feelings of the people who made the suit, was a natural talent and had been spotted by Roberts and Lawwill before he was expensive.

Late in 1980 there was a television event called Superbikers. It pitted the best riders from motocross, road racing, dirt track and speedway, and let them use 500s or 750s, two strokes or four, with Camel Pro tires for racing on dirt and pavement. It was a good idea, and fun for the riders and did fairly well in the ratings for the first few years.

It's mentioned here because for one thing, the big XRs weren't a match for the cut-down motocross two-strokes, and second, there was technical inspection and Goss' XR-750, set up for TT with triple disc brakes and not much fuel, weighed 320 lb. on a certified scale. That's close to what the factory claimed, but it's also the first impartial weighing we've seen.

On the subject of machines, Goss was interviewed in *Cycle News* and said yes, now that you mention it, he'd really like it if Harley-Davidson had a 500 single like the others had. He added, in a good description of his quiet nature, that "I'm not really jazzed about standing up and talking."

1981: Three, Count 'em Three, Vees

The season began the old-fashioned way: Springsteen won the short-track national, riding what

And sometimes talent isn't enough. This is Tulsa, 1981 and Ricky Graham has just parted company with Ron Wood's XR. Graham was a skilled and adaptive rider. Wood built top machines, but for reasons never deciphered by science, Graham never did well on Wood's Harleys. David Edwards

Werner said was the old nail, the motocross-engined short tracker built several years earlier, used in 1980 and untouched since then. They replaced the spark plug, poured in fresh fuel and checked the tires, Werner said, and even if that wasn't strictly true, it was close. Springsteen was beaming, up to fighting weight and "hadn't felt this good in years."

He lost the TT to Eklund, big XR versus agile Yamaha 500, with Filice on another Yamaha single in third. The big twins weren't the best for tight and tacky Houston and Ron Wood read the winds right and began certifying a 500 single from the Austrian firm of Rotax, which in turn was owned by Canadian conglomerate Bombardier's motorcycle division, Can-Am. (There is a reason for all this detail, coming in a few years.)

The XR-750 wasn't much changed from 1980. Replacement cases were being made that year, and most years since, but in 1981 the case material was changed from the KO1 alloy to another mixture, with less silver content and different procedures for heat treatment, and for less money. The new alloy, still in use as of 1990, is numbered 206.

The Marzocchi forks used on the stock XRs came with a choice of two axle diameters, three sets of clamps and three steering stems. The tuners could adjust trail, the distance between the tire's contact patch and the steering axis, and thus tune steering speed and feel, without changing the steering head's rake. Careful and experienced construction of the lower end had allowed some tuners, notably Peel, to wind the XR to 9400 rpm, which O'Brien said was why there were never enough connecting rods.

Then came the rivals. Honda admitted in March that they'd been busy making the national contender, and had made the twenty-five required for certification.

It was an amazing machine. The starting point was the CX500, an 80 deg. V-twin with shaft drive, water cooling and with four-valve heads operated by a camshaft in the block. The racing version got larger bore and stroke, and a conversion to chain drive that also meant turning the engine one-quarter turn so the cylinders were fore and aft, with intakes on one side and exhausts on the other. The intakes had been splayed 22 deg. outward and that remained. The engine was set in a conventional tube frame but it looked awkward and strange. The numbers, though, less than 300 lb. ready to race and with 85 bhp in the early stages, were more impressive. Other numbers, for comparison purposes, were wheelbase between 52.5 and 55 in., steering rake of 26 deg. and 3 in. of trail, all of which were close to what the XRs used.

The Yamaha, introduced two months later at the beginning of the full dirt schedule, was less conventional than it looked.

The initial conversion was easier because while the American version of the 90 deg. V-twin, fore and aft cylinders as noted, was shaft drive, the domestic version used a chain, so chain drive for the racer was easily assembled. There was one small detail, though. Changing from shaft to chain drive and keeping the primary drive and gearbox, meant the engine had to run the other way, counter to wheel rotation rather than with it.

Now then. The engine, like the wheels, is in some degree a gyroscope, a rotating mass that resists movement or encourages the object in which it spins to maintain an attitude. Best illustration is motocross, where the rider whacks the throttle to rev the engine and keep the front wheel up over a jump.

The XR-750 and the Honda and the Triumphs and BSAs and Nortons and even the Indians, all ran their engines forward. When I asked, back in 1981 I hasten to say, Lawwill and Ken Clark, Yamaha's racing manager, if this wasn't something to allow for, they said no, or that they'd already allowed for it.

The second oddity was the frame, a massive stamped backbone running between steering head and swing arm pivot, with the engine suspended below the backbone with a network of smaller tubes. The engine wasn't surrounded by the frame, cradled as they say, again in contrast to Harley and Honda.

The Yamaha engine began life with a wide vee and with the intakes in the center, so the racing engine had the rear carburetor facing forward on the left, the front carb trailing back on the right, by coincidence just like the mid-project iron-head XRs had theirs. Yamaha had a routing problem with the exhaust because the ports were at the outsides of the vee. The front pipe ran down the right side and the rear pipe went to the left and then under and around, so they'd be the same length when they got to the boom box. Yamaha gave a wheelbase in the mid fifties and claimed a weight of 300 lb. and power of 80 bhp when the program began.

In short, according to all we've seen so far, the Honda and Yamaha should have been competitive.

They weren't.

The 1981 Winston Pro season had two parallel themes. In the mainstream it was defending champion Goss, the hard worker and team player, against Hank Scott, loosely wrapped and ready for whatever came next, with Springsteen getting well and giving 'em hell one week and back in the hospital the next, then back with a new diagnosis, over and over again.

Next to that, or rather well to the rear, came Freddie Spencer on the Honda. He was an astonishing racer. Those who saw him in his later years, feebly defending his world titles, cannot imagine the ferocity of his scramble to the top. I watched him on the Superbikes at Daytona, full on the power as the chassis wound itself into a knot, unwound, bounced over cracks in the pavement and wound back up again, all in a full crouch. Not even I could believe the way he climbed onto the front wheel of the clumsy, bucking

miler, doing all in his power to make the beast handle . . . and failing. At the end of those early tries Spencer would have barely made the program and the Honda team would be slumped in their chairs, literally knowing they'd done all they could and it hadn't been enough. This from Big Red, the team that had conquered the world.

Yamaha's Team Roberts-Lawwill had still another way to go.

Even now, it's hard to believe. But Lawwill had a backer, Yamaha's American branch, and he had some sponsors and—write this down—Lawwill wasn't running a factory team.

So they kept the name in front of the public and they (ostensibly anyway) prepared for the day when the Yamahas worked, by letting Kidd and Filice ride—yes!—Lawwill's old XR-750s.

The parallels became Goss and Scott and Springer and then Kidd, who'd always been a good racer but probably hadn't known just how good until he teamed with a tuner like Lawwill. The better Kidd did, the more he rode the Harley and let young Filice, who in justice was the junior member and thus got the short end, work on the Yamaha.

To no avail. Two-time national champion Dick Mann had been hired as a consultant. Somebody watched a team meeting and figured that Filice was being advised by Lawwill, Roberts and Mann, a total of five number-one plates and seventy-five national race wins. And he still couldn't get the Yamaha into the field.

Honda didn't say much. Spencer was always amiable, but had nothing to say, which left reporters guessing in the dark, as it were.

In contrast, Yamaha had Ken Clark, a former racer as voluble as he was astute. Every week Clark barked that they'd found the flaw, in the suspension or the cams or something, and that next week the new frame, a full cradle this time, would save the day. And every week we reporters would listen and take notes and nudge each other and sure as taxes, the fix didn't fix.

Week after week, the miles and half-miles were all XR for the final, with the Yamahas in the truck and a Honda running in the middle of the pack for the Trophy dash, which in truth was the consolation race.

There was some political stirring of the mix. Somebody came up with an idea for restricting the carbs, again, for the 750s and letting the 500s run free. As a side to that, because the proposal only mentioned four-strokes, the two-strokes would have been banned. An accident, some said. It was announced that for 1982 the rules would allow restricted 750 cc four-stroke twins, unrestricted 500 cc four-stroke twins or singles, and 500 cc two-stroke singles. Meanwhile, the Honda NS750 went on sale for a list price of $13,500. There weren't many takers. The price was about twice what you'd pay for an XR-750 and if you had to rebuild the Harley before you could race it, at least it would make the main.

And so it went. Spencer got fourth in his heat in the Indy mile, "riding for all he was worth . . . and then some," as *Cycle News* put it, and the Honda team pulled out to regroup. Lawwill said it was Kidd's turn in the barrel—I mean to ride the Yamaha—and Kidd said he didn't see why, not when he could win the title. Lawwill prevailed at the Smokey Mountain, Tennessee, half-mile but Kidd pulled out of his heat. "I could ride it," he said, "but I really couldn't *race* it."

The crew reworked the new frame so the engine was so low it dragged, and then they got new cases that were tighter. It still didn't work.

And then, in July, the restrictor rules for 1982 were withdrawn, canceled, not to be heard from again until the next battle of the factories.

Honda did more thinking. Remember the twingle, what you get when you reset the ignition and cam timing so both cylinders fire on the same revolution, then coast through the next, then fire together again? Honda set the NS up that way, and gained 4 bhp on the dyno. First time out, though, Spencer retired with a cooked engine and the team stayed home for another couple races.

We could go on. Asked why Kidd was on the XR and he was on the Yamaha, Filice said, "Number One Fever has struck the camp." Then he worked his way as high as fifth in his heat and the ignition failed.

From off-stage, Spencer said he thought next year, he'd go to Europe and win himself a world title or something. Something easier than what he was doing at the time. As if to illustrate that, Bill Hearndon won the junior invitational at San Jose, first actual race win for the Honda NS750. Ted Boody led his heat on an NS until an oil line blew, and Spencer's engine coughed off one carb.

The actual season came down to the last race, the Ascot half-mile. Goss won it, and he whooped it up until he looked back and saw second place was Kidd, who thus topped the points race and got the title.

This occasioned one of racing's great T-shirts. Yes, I still have mine and no, it's not for sale. It says:

Harley-Davidson
First Choice of the
Yamaha Racing Team

Upon reflection I realize that the 1981 season wasn't much XR and it was a lot of Honda and Yamaha. Why? Because, also upon reflection, that's as powerful a tribute as one can imagine. Once we see how much talent and money were brought to bear against the XR, to no avail, we can see how good the XR is.

Back to history and politics. The new champion was interviewed after his win and he thanked Clark and Lawwill for going along with the use of the XRs to capture the title. "If the Yamaha had been working," Kidd said, "that's what I would have ridden."

The reporter asked if it wasn't true that Roberts had laid down the law in midseason and ordered all the effort to go toward the Yamaha.

Yes, said Kidd, but the sponsors had rights too, so the team's definition of all the effort was that Filice would ride the Yamaha every race.

In one of those odd little notes that makes this a sport, Kidd threw in that far from being enemies, he and the Harley team were pals. In fact, he'd finished second on a tire loaned by Bill Werner, the very same model and compound used by Goss to win that final race.

Oh my word, I can hear you exclaim, you mean that if Werner hadn't volunteered the tire and Kidd had used the wrong compound, he might have finished, say, fourth, and Goss would have won the title? Yup. But the Harley team has never wanted to win on the basis of the other guy's misfortune.

One month later came the shocker.

Kidd signed to ride for Honda.

That might sound worse than it was. There was no hope he'd ever join the Harley team, OB and crew being perfectly happy with Springsteen and Goss. Yamaha was, underneath a show of sport, furious. The head men didn't understand how this could have happened. Yamaha decided to take the program in-house, with Filice as the rider and the factory paying the bills and doing the hiring direct.

Honda had of course suffered at least as much as Yamaha. Loss of face, as they say over there. Kidd had only one place he could go and Honda had a way to look good, so they did the deal.

Kidd in his usual polished manner said that Honda had wanted him to use his old national number, 72, because if he raced with the number-one plate, that might look as if Honda had hired him for just that. No, Kidd offered, he insisted on the plate because he'd earned it.

Honda's righteousness might have been easier to believe if Honda hadn't taken out national ads showing the plate and mentioning their sports model, called the Ascot, which was a V-twin but which had nothing to do with anything Honda raced, never mind racing at Ascot or even winning.

At any rate, Honda had Kidd and the championship number plate and rookie expert Bill Hearndon, who'd been the only winner on the NS750 so far.

1982: Team Privateer

The 1982 season could have begun on a new and different note. Harley, Honda and Yamaha had established teams, while Kawasaki, number three of the Big Four, was working on machines for short track and TT, which was easy because their 250 and 500 cc motocross bikes were readily adapted to the smoother tracks of Winston Pro. And they had riders like Eddie Lawson and Wayne Rainey, future world champions in road racing.

As another switch, the formerly restrictive licensing rules had been opened and at least one pro-

And then . . . magic. Here Ricky Graham is on his way to being the only man to win the Houston TT on the big XR, 1982. Not only that, he'd broken some ribs, and the ma- *chine is a 1972 frame reworked in 1975. Guts and torque, is how he did it—with emphasis on guts.* Cycle World

fessional motocrosser, Steve Wise, entered Houston with a pure motocross model and on his motocross license. He hadn't ridden flat track or raced as a junior and there were those who resented his entrance, those who hoped he'd fall on his face and those who hoped he'd prove that motocross racers were the best.

With all that said, Houston was a surprise in entirely the other direction.

In 1981, Jay Springsteen won with his old Aermacchi-powered machine. For 1982, Werner fitted a new piston for luck and Jay won the short track again, his twenty-ninth national win, which tied him with Roberts.

Now comes one of those odd racing quirks. Ricky Graham had been riding for Ron Wood, who builds good machines but the team didn't click. Tex Peel had Scott Parker, an extraordinary talent but they didn't win much, either. So for 1982, Graham teamed with Peel. For the Houston TT, they used Tex' old XR-750, a 1972 frame modified in 1975 by the Vista-Sheen guys, who'd introduced Springsteen to national wins.

Graham crashed in the short track and broke three ribs. No XR had ever won at Houston, in case you're taking notes.

To put it dramatically, this reporter has seen two great TT rides in his career, and Graham at Houston 1982 was one of them.

He had a big old bike, he was in pain and while the 500 singles and the motocross two-strokes battled and swapped and leapt through the air and shook fists at each other, Graham motored away, smooth and calm, using all the track and getting traction for all that power.

It was an epic and I still don't know how they did it. Heck, *they* don't know how they did, except that on some days everything works.

More to the overall point, in the short track, two-strokes all, were engines from Harley, Honda, Can-Am, Yamaha and Kawasaki. In the TT it was Harley, Honda four-stroke, then Wise on the two-stroke Honda, then Rod Spencer on a Maico motocrosser, followed by another Harley, two Can-Ams, a Yamaha and two Hondas. That's the largest number of makes per entry ever, and one can only say it's too bad such variety never happened again.

Before the TT, when he was in the grip of hope and fear, Tex grumbled that Houston doesn't mean anything in terms of the rest of the season.

Vintage Scotty Parker, vintage in the sense that he's got the back wheel so loose he's nearly backing into the turn. Parker was honed on the cushion tracks and no-quarter-given traditions of Michigan. The dual outboard ignition developed by Bill Werner and shared by the team has come into use and this is the later, higher frame, not that you can tell by looking. Harley-Davidson

He was wrong. Alex Jorgensen won the Ascot TT with Graham close behind, on the Houston winner and with the comment that "This thing is fun to ride."

Honda arrived for the Sacramento mile with four riders and five bikes, no two alike. There were single-shock and dual-shock frames, offset-leg and straight-leg forks, Cerianis and Marzocchis. The only thing in common was that all five were tuned to run as twingles.

Yamaha had former Harley teamster Corky Keener to help Filice with development. And they had a new frame with variable wheelbase, rake and trail, swing-arm-pivot height; every factor in the chassis could be adjusted.

So in the race it was Springer for his thirtieth, with Graham 2 ft. behind, then Terry Poovey and then Parker, who'd been signed as the third full member of the Harley team. The national race was an all-XR show except for the lone Honda of Kidd, who squeaked into the field by winning the last-chance qualifier.

Competition takes many forms. The 1982 XR-750 wasn't much changed. The team was using electronic ignition and experimenting with shields and baffles for cooling, a notion of Werner's that went away as quietly as it appeared.

But he was getting more power, through hard work and experiments, while Peel was getting more power because he had Ron Alexander doing his cylinder heads and because Peel would lean more heavily on the engine, blowing up being to him no worse than not winning.

In a parallel context, stock car racing legend Junior Johnson once didn't rehire a driver because the man was too used to not winning. He'd begun with a team that couldn't win, Johnson said, so he accepted less than what he could do.

That can work in the other direction. Peel and Graham had never got used to not winning. Their near misses had shown them that if they just got that little extra. . . . And then, they had it and their success made them go faster, unleashed the potential. Nor did it hurt that Peel and Graham were friendly rivals with Werner and Springsteen, with each team pushing the other beyond their previous limits.

Compressing the season here, Springer won five nationals, Graham won four, with Goss and Jorgensen taking two each and the others going to guys like Parker and Poovey and Bubba Shobert, a Texan about to graduate from bikes his dad built and prepared. And one win went to Scott Pearson on a Honda—at Louisville, that demanding limestone half-mile, which probably meant it was more Pearson's riding than the Honda's power or handling. Although the team said their 1982 machine would keep up with their benchmark, a stock Harley XR, while the first Hondas lost even in a straight line.

You might have noticed some changes in the names. Another theory here. The Scott brothers and Eklund, for example, were still racing, but they were no longer racing for wins—well, Eklund was doing better than the Scotts but he wasn't in contention for the title. My own guess, which applies to all forms of racing, is that when racing is as close and demanding as it was here, it takes more than normal concentration and energy and dedication to win, which means even the best guys can't run near the front for more than a few seasons. Springer? The exception that proves the rule.

For tech notes, Werner and Peel had different tricks. Werner had constructed a truly dual ignition, with two plugs per cylinder, one on each side of the head, both battery powered, electronically fired and firing at the same time.

Peel was doing heads with special porting and flow patterns, plus connecting rods with less length. Not less stroke, mind you, but with the piston closer to the crankpin.

Werner's thinking, aside from improving reliability, was that setting fire to the mixture in two places at once got the mixture burned quicker. Peel in turn knew that the shorter the rod, the less time the piston spends sitting still at the top and bottom of the stroke, so short rods allow the expansion of the charge to get under way sooner. In other words, the two different modifications did sort of the same thing, in different ways.

Creativity and willingness to take a chance, are what this means.

Back in the season, Graham's TT luck ran out at Peoria. He crashed and was hurt, ribs and vertebra. While he was out, Springer narrowed the gap and once again it came down to Ascot's half-mile, the season final.

Goss won, again, with Springsteen sixth and Graham eighth but because Jay had been four points back, the gain of two didn't do enough and Rick was the new champ. And Harley-Davidson took the factory title for the sixth year in a row.

That gets us to a semi postmortem. Yamaha quit, having been unable to come to grips with either their own machine or with the level of competition required in AMA nationals. Ten years later, the pressure having been gone for some time, Mert Lawwill said first, what nobody knew at the time was that the Yamaha engine was 30 lb. heavier than either the Harley or the Honda engine. Making up for that made the rest of the package weak, and making the frame and suspension strong obviously turned the Yamaha into a porker. Second, Lawwill said, they never did manage to decipher making the suspension work with the engine running the wrong direction. (I have to say here I was interested to hear my worry confirmed, but because the team was fair and open, I can't say I was glad.)

Honda sort of quit, in that the NS750 had led heats and been in the front pack, but Kidd crashed and broke his leg and the other guys didn't learn fast enough, so Honda didn't attend the final race. At Ascot, ironically note.

1983: Back to the Factory

Late in 1982, *Cycle News* did a piece on TT bikes. Graham's XR, the old reworked one, had 5 in. of rear wheel travel from S&W shocks, 6 in. of front wheel travel with 35 mm Cerianis, and weighed 320 lb. with triple disc brakes and battery. Power output was variable, except in another interview Springsteen, also on an XR of course, said that it used to be they tuned for low-end grunt and control but now, with competition from the 500 cc singles and motocross-based chassis, they needed all the power they could get. His TT bike, Springer said, had evolved into a half-mile machine with front brakes.

By way of comparison and confirmation, the other TT racers were the Honda four-stroke XR, 260 lb.; Honda two-stroke CR, 198 lb.; Triumph 750 twin, 285 lb.; and Yamaha and Can-Am four-stroke 500s, 260 lb. Tire rules at the time allowed any DOT-legal, that is, road-model, tire, plus each maker could offer no more than three racing tires, with limits on size and pattern of the tread, which meant no knobbies. Wheel travel was a compromise, with the Harleys raised and the motocrossers lowered to balance weight transfer with ease of control.

What this meant mostly was that the big XR wasn't the best TT machine. The two-strokes didn't have enough punch, while the 500 singles were a good approach for riders of less than Graham's or Springsteen's ability—and that wasn't going to last much longer.

During the midseason break, Honda came back hard. They'd hired former national champion Gene Romero, and he in turn said first, they'd field Kidd and Poovey for the full year, with Hank Scott on a race-to-race basis.

Next, the team would have new machines.

This is one of the great racing stories. Remember the Honda team's mule, the stock Harley XR? Honda did with it what Harley did with the TZ750, that is, they took it home and took it apart and figured what was good and what could be improved, then did the improvements.

By another happy chance, Honda had just introduced a 750 cc road bike, the Shadow. The new engine was water cooled and had shaft drive. It had bore and stroke of 79.5 × 75.5 mm. If you check your conversion chart you'll see that is mighty close to the 3.125 × 2.98 in. of the Harley XR-750. But the Honda engine had a one-piece crank with plain bearings using copious rather than calculated oil delivery, and it had overhead cams and four valves per cylinder instead of two valves per with pushrods. By still more

Honda's second try at Camel Pro was much more conventional, being in broad outline an improved version of the Harley XR. Legally, it was an air-cooled version of the Honda Shadow, fitted with the European chain drive instead of the shaft given the American model. By no chance or mistake, this engine rotated with the wheels. Cycle World

The two exhaust pipes on the left front are matched by the two carbs on the right rear. The Honda had overhead cams and four valves per cylinder, though, and made more power than the Harleys. This is the early, made-in-Japan frame with single rear shock. Cycle World

Speaking of team efforts, this is the Harley team, 1982, at the Indy mile: Werner is cutting a tire tread and Springer is keeping a bike on its stand. There are two bikes, both fresh. One will be prepped for what Werner expects, the other for conditions that may develop. Note the mix of new tank and cast rear wheels, with old seat and spoked fronts. Cycle World

good luck Honda had the parts to switch to chain drive and air cooling, which took less space even if it wasn't any lighter than water jackets and radiators.

Then Kawasaki won the Superbike title and quit racing. One of their secrets was an engine builder and tuner named Rob Muzzy. Romero scooped him up and Honda finally had the technical and practical minds to go with the money and riding talent that had done so poorly on the old sidewinder NS750s.

Not that anybody knew it at the time.

The season kicked off conventionally, Poovey winning the Houston short track on a Honda two-stroke and Eklund doing the same for TT, this time with a Can-Am 500 four-stroke instead of the old Yamaha.

There had been some format changes. The series reverted to the name Camel Pro, instead of Winston Pro, as RJR decided the Camel brand was worth investment and the Winston Man was doing the job for that label.

Admitting the established, the AMA assigned separate numbers to the dirt and road crews, in fact juggled enough to say that there would now be a national dirt title and a national road-racing title, ending a fine tradition while reducing the strain on the contestants. (And, to be fair, keeping Harley-Davidson from having to deal with Honda's formidable road racers along with the new dirt bike.)

Daytona was back the other way. For the first time in thirteen years a Harley-Davidson won a major race during Speed Week and never mind if it wasn't *the* race.

For there on, 1983 becomes another set of parallels. Looking at the year, the contenders were Harley mounted. There was defending champ Graham, former champs Springsteen and Goss, upcoming Parker and Shobert and even Jim Filice, who'd been released when Yamaha quit and picked up help from the Harley Owners Group. Better add here that while Graham won the title opposing the factory team and thus was almost sure to never be hired by O'Brien, who preferred finding talent before it was obvious, the better Graham did, the closer he parked to the Harley team in the pits.

So while the Can-Ams outnumbered the XRs in TT and the motocross engines took short track, at Sacramento it was Shobert, Springsteen and Graham; Ascot was Springer, Goss and Parker; Springfield was Graham, Goss and Hank Scott on the new Honda! Then Graham and Springer swapped the lead at the

San Jose mile thirty-nine times, Graham getting the nod. Parker was top qualifier there, and at Louisville and then Harrington, a record for that skill, while Springer won both of the latter two races. Then he won Knoxville with Goss, and a different kind of history was made when Tammy Kirk got third in her heat and became the first woman to qualify for a dirt national.

The 500 singles were one-two-three at the Santa Fe TT, with the Harley race finishing Jay, Rick and Randy, four-five-six. Something had to be done.

Indy was almost a summation, as Springsteen took top time and got sick. The race went to Shobert, on an XR tuned by top man Paul Chmiel, followed by Graham and Parker.

On the other side of the scale Honda had filled the stands with brass from home . . . and the new bike wouldn't even start! (Later, with the titles in his pocket, Romero said that was the low point of his career.)

The Syracuse mile was Shobert, Graham and Parker, as Shobert went into that wonderful level of getting better as he learned how good he was. Hagerstown was Goss, Steve Morehead and Springer, the winner having gambled on a soft-compound rear tire and the third-place man having played it safe with a tire that would last.

And then—the Honda team having pitched the frame that came from their factory and hired C&J to do one right—at DuQuoin, a slippery track that called for craft and skill, Hank Scott slipped past Shobert, Doug Chandler and Springsteen on the last lap and

More experiments, as Werner had fitted an air scoop, to learn if cooler air on the cylinders will make any difference: it didn't. The battery is sturdily mounted. Less visible below and behind it is a cut-down gearcase with the old magneto mounting case removed. Cycle World

What's in a name? This is a Harley-Davidson, by act of The Motor Company and the AMA, although the 500 cc engine came from Rotax and Ron Wood built the frames and supplied tanks and seats. This was a legal way to keep Harley in contention on the short tracks and TTs, and it worked. Cycle World

Randy Goss regained his title at the end of the 1983 season. Here he shows his usual joy at being interviewed. Much more outgoing is wife Vickie, who was an ice racer before Janice was born. The world's smallest leathers were made by Randy's mother-in-law and Janice's doting grandmother, who makes racing suits under the business name Dee, as in D's Leathers. Indeed, racing is a family sport. Cycle World

the new Honda, the Honda team and the factory, were winners at last.

There are the patterns. In brief, though, Springer was winning and getting sick, while Graham was winning or crashing or blowing up. Racing luck is like that, and while in 1982 all Graham's breaks came at good times, the engine letting go as he crossed the line, in 1983 the blow-ups came early.

Pause for the next mechanical news. There hasn't been much XR technical data this season because not a lot of work was done. There were other projects under way.

In what had to be politically influenced, the AMA decided to allow 500 cc singles in short track as well as TT. The good excuse was that the guys would only need two bikes, a 500 for short track and TT, a 750 for half-miles and miles.

The benefit for Harley-Davidson was that they did a deal with Rotax, the subsidiary of Can-Am, and arranged for a version of the Rotax-Can-Am ohc single to be sold through Harley dealers and called the Harley-Davidson 500-R. All according to the rules, all fair. Ron Wood was hired to build complete machines for the team. Nineteen engines were to be sold through dealers, and six were kept for team use.

The new, so-called Harley debuted at the Silverdome, last race of the season.

High drama here. While Shobert and Filice were keeping the other guys honest, Graham, Goss and Springsteen were in a battle for the lead. Springer got sick, Graham got hurt and Goss piled up points. He earned points in every race he entered. So it happened that Goss won two races, against five for Springer and Graham, but coming into the last race, Goss led Graham by twenty points.

Winning pays twenty points. All Graham had to do was win the final race of the year, while Goss got no points, and the tie would go to the man with the most wins.

I mentioned earlier two great TT rides. Graham at the Silverdome, 1983, was the second.

He was magnificent. Using a Rotax Tex had built in preparation for the day it would be called a Harley, Graham took top qualifier, and won the fast heat. In the final he not only won, he lapped the back half of the field.

Now a stroke of fate, or luck. Goss was having an off night. He was in the back of his heat race, until three guys in front of him fell down. That got him into the national. The points system is set up so the last guy in the national doesn't get a point. One rider retired early, Goss couldn't finish last, he had at least one point.

Goss was champion again, never mind just barely not getting lapped by Graham. That's racing.

In the standings it was Goss, Graham, Springsteen, Shobert and Parker. In the factory contest, Harley got the win for the seventh straight year, 474 points for Honda's 392. None of the other makes were in contention. As a historical side, one tuner built a dirt machine with Ducati 750 power but the 90 deg. V-twin, always a winner on pavement, never qualified for a dirt national.

Lucifer's Hammer

This story illustrates a reverse cliché, proving that breeding improves the race.

No sooner did the Japanese multis, two strokes or four, begin to dominate road racing than fans of the other types, the western twins one could say, began working toward a road-racing class for twins. They got their wish, a series called Battle of the Twins or BOTT for short, which began as a support class for national road races in 1983. It was dominated from the beginning by the legendary Ducati, a 900 cc dohc, 90 deg. twin. Tuner of the best Ducati was Reno Leoni, and the champion rider was James Adamo. It was a very good team.

By happy coincidence, just about the time BOTT became popular, the executives who'd bought Harley-Davidson from AMF realized they'd never done much with the brand's racing traditions. For several years there'd been an underground effort to market a street version of the XR-750. But tests had shown that when you got the alloy-and-ball-bearing engine tamed to meet federal noise and emissions regulations, there wasn't much power left. Harley's marketeers assumed that the reason people would buy a race-inspired bike was performance, so the officially street-legal XR-750 (to distinguish between the factory version and the XRs some of us put on the street by ourselves) never got beyond the prototype stage.

Also, there was a new version of the Sportster, a low-buck stripper called the XLX. Solo seat, gray paint and no extras, it was an introductory model and it sold well.

Somebody got a natural idea, and made a high-performance Harley, the first in two decades, by simply putting the alloy, dual-carb heads and high pipes on the 1000 cc XLX.

No, it wasn't as easily done as said. The project was handed to O'Brien and the racing department and they did the job in less than one year. The engine met all requirements and produced 70 bhp, which did the job.

Thing was, and this is another story, the public wasn't willing to pay for the extra engine, not when the machine itself didn't look like anything different or special. Hard to believe, seeing as Harley-Davidson has a fine record of knowing what people will like before they see it. But this one bombed.

The BOTT rules were a lot like the AMA's full Class C Camel Pro rules—with a displacement limit and a production requirement; after that, do what you please.

What it pleased H-D to do was get back into road racing. Meeting the rules was easy. A BOTT team was cheaper than a full road-race division. Mrs. O'Brien was a novelist with a supply of folklore, so they called the bike *Lucifer's Hammer,* from a legendary Celtic scourge of the bad guys.

The actual machine was as much like an XR-1000 as a NASCAR racer is like your father's Oldsmobile.

The beginning was O'Brien's reluctance to throw anything away. Remember how Springsteen won the Houston short track on the old nail? It was there in large degree because when Harley went out of the motocross business years earlier, OB salted away motocross engines, just in case. In the same manner the XRTT that threw Brelsford down and caught fire at Daytona in 1973, was hauled back to Milwaukee, stripped, and slung under a bench in the back.

When management authorized O'Brien to build the BOTT racer as promotion for the XR-1000, Carroll Resweber dragged out the frame and reworked it. The frame was originally built by Babe DeMay to factory specs. But Resweber gave it a shorter wheelbase, in the low 50s, with a steeper steering-head rake, as per Cal Rayborn. Resweber says he figured Rayborn knew best and that Springsteen, who had drawn the long straw and had the ride, would be able to handle the quick chassis that Rayborn liked.

The top of the engine loop got two more tubes, there was extra bracing for the swing-arm pivot and the swing arm was replaced with one that was wider and stiffer. The last two changes were to accommodate the wider rear tire of 1983, much wider than in 1973, and to resist the added chassis loading transmitted by the tires. Wheels were 18 in. at first, but the front was later changed to a 16, for quicker steering and the best selection of racing rubber. There were three disc brakes, Moto-X Fox shocks, from the motocross arena, and beefy Marzocchi forks fitted with anti-dive first developed for the road-model FXRT, speaking of reversed direction of innovation.

The engine was barely even a nominal XR-1000. It began with the 1000's bore and stroke of 81 × 98.6 mm, but the Superblend-bearing flywheels went (with some work) into XL cases. The cylinders were iron, but a special sort of iron. The heads were even more special, in sequence one of two pairs of special castings with small valves and optimum ports: O'Brien had been saving the heads for several years, knowing that this day would come. Engine builder Don Habermehl used XR camshafts, a pair of monstrous 40 mm Mikuni carbs and XR-style exhaust pipes tuned for drive off the turns. Officially the *Hammer* weighed 350 lb., although O'Brien grinned that it would more likely be 385 ready to race. The engine cranked out 106 bhp at 7500 rpm when tested early in 1983, and gained a few more each year for its four-year tour of duty. **Next page**

111

The *Hammer*'s debut and surely finest hour was Daytona, 1983. I was lucky enough to be standing in the infield for practice the day before the race. Adamo on his Ducati and Springsteen on *Lucifer's Hammer* came through the infield hairpin together, as Adamo hunched down and gave 'er, as Kirk tells Scotty, all she's got.

Springer looked down and I'd swear he grinned as he did the same, full sidearm windup.

The Harley fairly leapt forward and pulled away and I thought, Ah, the psychology of racing.

Sure as Freud took notes, in the actual race Springer waltzed off by a second or two each lap. Adamo later said only Jay's dirt-track experience enabled him to throw the bike around the way he did.

Perhaps that was part of it. But the *Hammer* was the act of the class. The engine was as new as it could be. The suspension was as new as it needed to be, and over the package was fitted one of the old XRTT fairings, along with the big old tank and bulky tail and seat. It was distinctive and did warm the hearts of the true believers, which was the main point.

In technical terms the engine used a full wet sump, a long and thin tank below the crankcases. This lowered the center of gravity and aided transfer of oil from the cases to the tank; no more over-filled cases here, by golly. And it provided space for frame bracing and the carbs and pipes that came in handy. The low tank was another of O'Brien's flights of invention and it was tried on the dirt bikes, notably Goss' XR. But the riders didn't like the lowered weight, said it slowed transfer of weight and thus the shifting of traction, so it was abandoned.

Springsteen's Daytona triumph was one high point. Then the program fell victim to one of The Motor Company's economy drives. I hasten to say here I don't claim economy wasn't needed. It's just that the timing was terrible.

By sleight of budget the program was transferred to the protection of the Harley Owners Group. Tuner became North Carolina dealer Don Tilley and the rider was Gene Church, a dirt expert who got the assignment in part, O'Brien said, because "he didn't have any bad habits to unlearn."

Tilley and Church won the BOTT title three straight years, 1983 through 1985. By then the machine was beyond being dated. Tilley retired it to the back of his shop, where it's been since.

The team's surprise return to road racing was inspired by the wish to get some ink for the new XR-1000, and it was made feasible by the strength of the XR-750 engine and its interchangeable parts and the fact that Brelsford's old XRTT frame hadn't made it to the dumpster. They redid the frame and reworked the fiberglass and used modern brakes and forks and shocks and won. Visible here is another of O'Brien's pets, the long, low oil tank-sump below the cases. The dirt guys didn't like where it put that weight, but rider Gene Church didn't mind. Harley-Davidson

There was enough interest to produce *Lucifer's Hammer II,* with space frame and leading-edge suspension by Eric Buell, a racing engineer who builds exotic road bikes with Harley power.

Church led the pack into the first turn at Daytona with the new bike, but it suffered mechanical failure and never won a BOTT race. Tilley says it was built too light, another of those issues about which good men may differ. Worse, the money stopped, in large part because the factory's engineering department wanted to build their road-racing engine and didn't want the racing department's help, why I can't imagine.

Lucifer's II was farmed out to Robison's Harley-Davidson in Daytona Beach, where it was raced in club and local events until the end of 1990. That was the last, Conway said, mostly because all the parts were hand-made and one of a kind and the results were no longer worth the effort.

Church had dirt-track experience but not so much that he wasn't able to adapt to modern road-racing style, as in dragging one's knee to determine just how far you've cranked the bike over. Lucifer's Hammer wasn't a technical breakthrough, but it put Harley in the winner's circle and it got some publicity for the formal sponsor, the factory-backed owner's group. Harley-Davidson

Chapter 7

The Big Red Ones, 1984–87

We're dealing with partisan history here, no pretense, so it's fair to say we're about to begin the sad part.

The sad part begins with a shocker. Late in November 1983, Honda team honcho Gene Romero announced his riders for the 1984 season.

Skipping ahead to the end of the 1984 season, it's obvious that Ricky Graham has just won back the number-one plate and that Jay Springsteen roots for Harley-Davidson. Behind the grin, though, is courage; Graham was knocked down and banged up but he got back in the race and managed to finish, which got him the title, by one point. Never give up, as Winston Churchill used to say. The actual winner of the race, on a Honda, was Ted Boody, shown here enwreathed. Cycle

He'd have Ricky Graham and Bubba Shobert.

This made hard business sense. Kidd hadn't done well with the new machines, even though he tried hard, and then he was hurt and, effectively speaking, retired. Poovey was a top talent and all guts but he was disheartened by the mechanical problems the Hondas had. Worse, from the Japanese view, Poovey expressed his displeasure and the men who signed the checks didn't forget.

At any rate, Honda needed new guys. The Harley team was out of reach, even though they obviously were the best riders.

But Shobert was better than the rides he could afford and he had plans.

Graham and Peel had won the title as privateers. That, they knew how to do. What they didn't know how to do was *use* what they had won. The money didn't fall into their laps and when the tide turned, they learned that blood and toil, tears and sweat, aren't always enough.

Tex Peel said, "I told Ricky he couldn't turn it down," and as usual, Tex was right.

The 1984 Harley effort began with a short, semi-production run, twenty-five sets of cases. They were only slightly changed, with modifications to allow use of two Superblend bearings, now known as a Doublewide, on each mainshaft. The cases were used for new engines, list price $5,695 for the engine alone although, as noted, you could still get a frame from the racing department if you persisted. To make the engine into one that could be raced hard and well would cost another $3,000 in parts and labor, and then came frame, brakes, suspension, tank and so on.

1984: The Once and Future Champ

The season began with an odd sort of standoff. Randy Goss, with his Rotax-Harley punched out to 580 cc, won the short track at Houston with Graham fourth. Next night Graham, using the Honda 600 cc single, won the TT. Goss was fourth. So the two

Randy Goss did his usual business best to defend his title.
Here he's in a lovely foot-up slide on a cushion track, the
Harrington, Delaware, half-mile. Cycle World

Mike Kidd rode out his contract for Honda, then retired. Honda meanwhile went to a C&J frame and with engine builder Rob Muzzy and manager Gene Romero, put to-gether a working blend of technical progress and empirical know-how. Cycle

former champions, who'd deposed each other, finished the first meet in a tie.

That was nearly the high point, from the Harley point of view, of the year.

Machines were a major reason. The Honda single was right on the edge, four valves disposed radially around the bore. Honda had been working on the design and while the Rotax will catch up later in this account, in 1984 the Honda was the best, on paper. That meant Honda would have a good shot at the short-track and TT races.

At the other end, there was some talk about fielding a race-prepped XR-1000 (as distinct from *Lucifer's Hammer,* an XR-1000 only by courtesy) in the Superbike class. But Superbikes didn't earn points in Camel Pro then, and money was tight so it never happened.

Honda, though, had a complete road-racing team, along with the motocross team and the Camel Pro teams, with good machines already certified. It

wasn't difficult for Honda to throw a couple more machines in the truck and fly Shobert, Graham and Chandler to the pavement events that didn't interfere with the dirt events.

In the miles and half-miles, the RS750 had overhead cams and four valves per cylinder. The engine could be wound to 9500 all day—the team said the average engine developed 93 bhp, by the way—and the two-throw crankshaft had the throws 45 deg. apart. This, to go with the 45 deg. cylinder angle, put the pistons 90 deg. apart. They were in balance, which made the engine smoother, in turn making less wear and higher redline.

The new C&J monoshock frames were designed with dirt-track experience behind them and equipped by suspension tuners who'd learned from motocross. Ditto the brakes and other parts.

The Honda was more compact, which didn't hurt. Graham has always been an exuberant rider, flinging the bike into the corners at impossible angles.

The Battles of 1984 were between Ricky Graham (3) and Bubba Shobert (67), as shown here on the Springfield mile.

The Hondas had the horsepower and ruled the miles, although they cost more to run than the XRs. Cycle

On the half-miles, the makes were more equal. So were the riders, as illustrated here by Scott Parker (11) and Graham. Parker took this one. Cycle World

Randy Goss pursued by Gary Scott at the Peoria TT, 1984, proof that there is such a thing as an old, bold motorcycle racer. Goss is on an XR, Scott has a lighter and more nimble Triumph; Goss won, obviously because he wanted to win more than Scott did. This was one of the last wins for the big twin as a TT bike. Cycle

The Harleys had to be jacked up so they wouldn't ground the cases, he said in a midseason interview, while the Hondas had the clearance he needed. And, he said, suspension and engine tuning was easier and more extensive. "It makes them a pleasure to ride," Graham said, "they're just better bikes."

This isn't to take away from Harley's efforts. Work was being done, for instance Lawwill made an aluminum frame and the team engines went with Supertrapps, tunable muffler-megaphones, when tests showed they added power. Goss hung on grimly, Parker was still finding his style and Springsteen was still sick or the best, you never knew week to week.

There was something of an equalizer in that Goodyear had quit the motorcycle-racing business and the Carlisles certified for AMA racing were too soft for the abrasive tracks and longer races. The tough events were cut from twenty-five laps to twenty or even to sixteen at the Hawthorne, Illinois, horse track.

Wait. You can't call it an equalizer because Goss was leading at Syracuse, on a street-legal Pirelli rear

tire and lost the tread. He backed off and finished eleventh. That hurt.

The season hurt. Not to dwell on it, but there were eight races for the singles and Honda won four, to one for Can-Am and three for Harley. Honda won six of the road races: Shobert took one, while Chandler scored points and Graham didn't like the whole idea. When it was twin versus twin, Honda won nine miles, to H-D's two. In the half-miles the score was Honda zip, Harley six. Only when craft and control were more important than power to weight, did the old firm acquit itself.

In the rider series Graham and Goss were tied at midseason. Goss and Chandler crashed at San Jose, putting Goss out for the rest of the year and when it came down to the final event, the two men in contention were Graham and Shobert.

It gets worse. We're going to talk money. A Honda engine sold for $8,500. Next you needed the frame and body parts, $1,200 from C&J, except that the price didn't include the elaborate linkage for the single rear shock, another $1,000, and you still needed forks,

Parker quickly proved to be the factory's in-house hope, economy drives and outright firings notwithstanding. This is an interesting configuration, a Tex Peel engine with the *front of the gearcase lopped off, an electronic ignition driven off the gearcase center and with the engine pushed forward in the frame. Cycle*

brakes and so forth. Putting a complete, competitive Honda into time trials cost $12,000 or so. An XR new cost less than $10,000 ready to go and you could save money if you were a good wrench *and* you could buy used parts for less, an option denied the Honda riders.

What this meant at the end of 1984 was that you had a better chance of winning as a privateer with a Honda, but you'd have a harder time paying for the bike.

This is said now because the final race of the season, the Springfield, Illinois, mile, was won by Ted Boody, the former Harley team member, on a private Honda. He knew which way the wind was blowing.

Shobert was second, Springsteen third and Graham, who was crashed by another rider but picked the bike up despite an injured hand, struggled in thirteenth.

And won the number-one plate by one point over Shobert.

The factory battle was much less close: Honda 583 points, Harley-Davidson 418, nobody else in sight.

Honda promptly confirmed they'd cut back, by dropping Doug Chandler and Jerry Griffith, who'd been their early team tuner. Graham and Shobert were kept for the second year of their two-year contracts, with at least $100,000 each plus generous bonus plus prize and sponsorship monies.

1985: The Year of the Ax

It gets even worse. Late in December 1984, on a day still known in some circles as Black Monday, the Harley-Davidson Racing Team was dismantled. The staff of twenty was reduced to four: manager Clyde Denzer, who replaced long-time boss Dick O'Brien when OB retired the previous year; Pieter Zylstra, the department's engineer; Jerry Reidel, who did rebuilts of team equipment; and resident wizard Bill Werner.

Randy Goss was let go and promptly signed with Honda privateer Jerry Griffith, a victim of *that* team's economy drive. Parker and Springsteen were given their equipment and advised to find their own sponsors and tuners.

Why? To a degree, it depends on whom you ask. The team's annual budget was $750,000, a lot of money when H-D was short of cash and had tackled projects with a better and more visible return. In the year Harley lost the title, the bargain-price Sportster gave the company one of its best years in a decade. Sometimes a good product is better than a win poster.

There had been problems with the union, which objected to the crew of the department being exempt from certain rules. The layoffs and transfers took care of that.

And perhaps Harley-Davidson didn't want to be seen losing, which could have happened no matter what the budget.

There was a technical possibility. O'Brien called it Stage Three and it included plans for a new engine, with a wider vee between the barrels, overhead cams and four-valve heads. On paper the new engine would have matched the Honda. And O'Brien's plans were for the engine to be modular, as in one version for 350 or 500 cc, a larger one with 750 or 1000 cc. Jerry Long, chief engineer at the time, drew up some plans and some of the parts were prototyped but that's as far as the project went.

Thus, Harley could spend money that wasn't there, with no certainty that the new engine would work.

Or, they could spend the same money on the same equipment, knowing that they weren't winning that way already.

Jay Springsteen still had the talent and the drive, when he was in good health, and he's never hesitated when it comes to throwing the bike into the corner with the power full on. The closing of the race shop put him on his own, with help from outside sponsors which is why his leathers have gained some writing here. He got his fortieth national win in 1985, on the Syracuse mile.

Yes, you read that number right! It's Ken Roberts (2) on an XR at the Springfield mile, 1985, with Jim Filice (17) and Springer right there with him. Roberts did it mostly for the fun, but also to tweak Honda. His only regret was that the engine failed before the main event. Obviously, his hands had lost none of their skill. Cycle World

The race is getting closer, as Parker on the XR leads Doug Chandler on his RS at Middletown, New York. This is Werner's work, with the dual single-fire ignition and a ·frame with the lower right tube kinked to clear the oil pump for service. Bill Werner

Or, they could pull in their necks and let somebody else lose for them.

That's harsh, I know. And I hasten to say that none of the people in the racing department backed management's action, nor were they as dismayed, at least not in public, as I was.

We can get back to the bright side, though, with thanks to the engineering department's Don Valentine, who made sure the racing shop was at least kept intact, and to Bill Werner, who made sure the lights weren't turned off.

And to be fair, early in the 1985 season the company *did* come through with money and help for Springsteen and Parker, whether because of public outrage, sporting instincts or loyalty, I can't say.

In any case, there was plenty of bad news to go around. Carlisle was the only maker of racing tires, as opposed to street-legal tires used for racing, so there was that worry. The AMA announced that the championships would be split in 1986, a dirt title and a pavement title, which was bound to take away from racing: the more champions you have, the smaller each one looks. But it does make sponsors happy and each factory has a better chance.

The worst luck was with Graham. He broke a leg play riding with Ken Roberts and missed the early

Louisville has always been Harley country, double so after the years of Honda winning the title. So when Parker came home first in 1986, the fans went as wild as the winner did. Bill Werner

part of the season. Parker, Shobert, Springsteen and Boody were the early winners, with a new record being set at Ascot's half-mile: It was Boody, Chandler and Pearson one-two-three, first time private Hondas had swept the field.

There were sprinkles of hope. Mert Lawwill had a new frame and some ideas, and Springsteen rode a Lawwill frame with Öhlins motocross shocks and with a two-into-one exhaust, for a broader power band. Graham was top qualifier at Springfield and Shobert won, trailed by Boody and Parker. Scotty wasn't bothered: "If I can get three more horses, the Hondas are going to be in trouble."

There was lots of talk like that. Honda wasn't a popular team. Graham and Shobert were well liked, but their rides were held against them. And promoters learned that while Harley fans wouldn't pay to watch their guys lose, the Honda owner wasn't interested in seeing his brand win. In other words, crowds dropped off.

Anecdotal evidence sure, but Ken Roberts got bored looking at his trophies and bought a couple of XRs, in partnership with old pal Lawwill. Roberts had always ridden for Yamaha and against Harley, but when he came to the second Springfield mile, he was second fastest in time trials and got a standing ovation. Sorry to say the engine lost power in the heat and tied up in the semi-main, so Roberts' Harley debut wasn't a success. But he was there and he wanted to whip the Hondas and the crowd was with him.

And you should have seen the crowd at Syracuse, when Springer rode the smartest race of his life, or so he said later, beating Hank Scott and Shobert, both on Hondas, by 6 in. It was Springsteen's fortieth national win, a record that still stands.

There had been another major change. Springsteen and Werner had been close friends and partners for nine years. The closing of the shop stopped that. But when the money began to trickle back, Springer went with Paul Chmiel, one of the best engine builders, and Werner stayed in the engineering department.

Then the factory gave Parker a budget. He was told to hire whomever he pleased, except that the factory had to be sure the guy knew his stuff.

Parker offered the work to Werner. The factory said no, union rules and all that. What management couldn't say was that Werner wasn't qualified. Werner in turn liked the younger rider, and was willing to put in the extra time, so after a talk with Parker's attorneys, management agreed to Werner tuning for Parker on his own time.

Parker ground away his tires at Syracuse.

He was second at San Jose, behind Graham. In third was Shobert, whose finish nonetheless earned him the championship.

And at the Sacramento mile, last race of the year, Parker won. The Hondas weren't exactly in trouble but Parker had his horsepower.

Even so, Shobert had the plate, followed by Ted Boody, a Honda guy, then Parker, then Honda rider Chandler and then Graham. (As history here, Graham missed the first third of the season. In the final six weeks of 1985, he scored four wins, one second and one third. But he finished the year out of the top three and Honda, who is all business even in sport, didn't pick up his option.)

With riders finishing that way, Honda naturally took the manufacturer's title, for the third straight year. *Cycle News* interviewed Denzer, who said the losses didn't make anybody happy back in Milwaukee but that they'd pull through. Three weeks later, Denzer was fired, by engineering vice president Mark Tuttle, who took over the operation of the team, such as it was, himself.

Once more, why? Once more, there are several sides. The team had been disbanded, the riders hadn't won but it didn't look as if Denzer did it. On the other hand, he wasn't the forceful leader OB was. Suffice it to say that there was bitterness and that Denzer was a victim of politics.

1986: On the Comeback Trail

Just prior to the 1986 season, Parker said they'd been working on the XR engine, mostly in the valve, port and cam areas, and they'd picked up enough power to stay in the Hondas' draft, while the previous year the red bikes could break clear. The Harleys had the traction, Parker said, so things were looking up.

There were other factors. The 1986 consensus was that a race-ready XR-750 cost $12,000, against the $18,000 for an equally prepped Honda. The money was important. Next, Goodyear was getting back into the motorcycle racing game, so Carlisle (and Pirelli, with the evergreen MT-53 front tire) would have competition.

But not just yet. The official season began with Eklund winning at Houston, but those bikes were the singles. The *real* dirt year began at Sacramento, at which Parker edged Shobert and Hank Scott, both on Hondas. Tires were what did it. Scotty had saved his, the others had worn their rears out of grip.

Shobert matched a record by winning the Phoenix half-mile, giving him wins in each of the five types of race. But Chris Carr, Rookie of the Year in 1985, was top qualifier on a Lawwill-prepared XR with factory backing. Then Goss, back on an XR with Harley dealer group support, won the half-mile at Ascot. Then it was Graham on a private Honda at Springfield, winning with a 103.06 mph average, fastest mile race ever. Shobert was right behind him and Carr a few feet back *and* all their tires, Goodyears, held up to the record pace. With the better tires came more traction or the ability to use power, and that beats power you can't transmit.

But power tells. Miles are where power counts most. In 1986, there were eleven miles. Honda won ten of them. Parker's Louisville win in late May was the last of the year for Harley, and the only race after

An informal team portrait, with Parker (11) on the house bike, Springsteen (9) on the backed-but-outside bike, and *privateer Terry Poovey (18) back in the H-D fold. Bill Werner*

that that Honda didn't get was the Peoria TT, with winner Carr riding a Ron Wood Rotax; his deal gave him a Harley for only the 750 races.

In sum, Shobert won the rider title again, nearly 100 points ahead of Parker, 313 to 217, the widest gap since the system was adopted ten years earlier. In 1986 there were the two titles, road and dirt. Honda won both rider contests and Shobert, who'd come to see road racing as the next step, took the Camel prize for best in both.

So, why was there hope? In degree because the XR was a stronger engine. Cosworth, the English racing engineering company best known for Formula One engines, was in the United States and in the motorcycle business, supplying pistons for the XR. They were the best pistons in the world and the first that would hold up to the power now being extracted. Steve Storz, the former factory tuner who'd gone into business for himself in California, developed a crankpin that fit the stock flywheels and which he guaranteed unbreakable. The pin kept the engine together, literally. The factory did a deal with Storz' supplier, to his annoyance. Even so, what with Storz and Lawwill and Patrick and Peel competing with each other and the factory, the object of their attention was the better for it.

1987: The Factories Wave the Rules

The unequal finishes of 1986 didn't go unnoticed.

This sounds unlikely, but about the middle of 1985 or so, various chaps not far from the AMA's offices began asking questions, as in, How would you rewrite the Camel Pro rules to make Harley and Honda equal, if you had the chance?

The search for balance began with Continental tire. They wanted into Camel Pro and submitted a racing tire. Because Honda would help in development, the new rear tire turned out to fit a stock RS750 but not an XR or Wood-Rotax, which had narrower swing arms. There was some debate over who had helped whom, settled when the Continental tire, fully 5.975 in. wide despite its nominal size of 4.00 × 19, was accepted but only on a wheel rim 3 in. wide. The tire (and the RS) had been built for a 3.5 in. rim. The thinner rim shaped the tire tread into a higher, narrower pattern and cost traction, that is, you couldn't count on getting anything for your extra power. The RS did have that, as we'll see.

The heart-warming secret about all this is that Harley, Honda, the AMA, the promoters and the sponsors *all* wanted a fair way to make the two brands equal again. But some of them couldn't admit it. OK,

By midyear 1987—this is one of DuQuoin's notorious square corners—there was a balance of power. It's Chris Carr (20) for Harley, Doug Chandler (10) and Ricky Graham (3) for Honda, and Parker (11) for Harley. But Bubba Shobert will win this one. Bill Werner

none of them could admit it. All they could demand in public was a fair shake.

Except that if Harley designed a new or improved engine, Honda would have to reply in kind. Loss of face, as they say. Honda had already backed off to just one dirt-team member. To withdraw would be unfair to the guys who'd bought the expensive engines in good faith. Equally, the AMA and RJR, owners of the Camel brand, had to be fair.

Collectively, they came out with part of the truth.

Racing is expensive. But Camel Pro, the classic dirt venue, had gotten into trouble. If you wanted to race on pavement you could buy a stock bike from the showroom and race it. If you liked motocross you could buy a competitive motocrosser out of the crate.

But dirt track was more specialized—and more expensive and labor intensive. Thus, the AMA announced in late 1986 that their experts were studying "performance of a variety of single and twin cylinder engines currently in use." Restrictions were being contemplated, the announcement went on, and the reason for the concern was to keep costs down.

Tex Peel wasn't impressed: "Why should they [the AMA] inflict Harley's problem on Honda's privateers?"

He added that once restrictors were installed it would cost $2,000 to test airflow and improve the porting so as to make up for the restriction. Lawwill meanwhile offered to do a conversion kit for the XR,

four valves per cylinder, an estimated cost of $3,500 per engine.

Against that were some claims that the rods and main bearings were the Harley's weak points, and that if they breathed better, they'd blow up more.

The AMA hired Jerry Branch, the dean and guidance counselor for anybody who wants to know how engines breathe, to study the problem. To begin with, the reporters were told, restrictors mean less air, which equals less power and less heat and less strain. Both the XR and RS "can be made to breathe beyond their mechanical limits."

Further, because the engines can be used up, they must be overhauled frequently. Branch said that maintenance for an XR averaged $4,000 to $7,000 annually. The RS, which had more parts and higher prices, cost $7,000 to $11,000 for a season.

Branch had the cooperation of all involved parties. He'd been loaned engines and reported the following:

Honda and Wood-Rotax 600 cc singles:	60 bhp
Stock Honda RS750:	92 bhp
Prepared XR-750 (there were no stock engines for sale then):	92 bhp
RS750 prepped by Hank Scott:	107 bhp
XR-750 prepped by Bill Werner:	100 bhp

Interesting, eh? It's possible that, say, Rob Muzzy could have built a more powerful Honda than Scott's,

The power behind the power? Werner pauses on his way to technical inspection at Ascot. That's a Grand Prix Plastics seat, with the exhaust boom box visible behind it, and with the huge forks made viable by the motocross guys. As usual, there are miles of hoses, showing how much care Werner takes with the oil supply.

or that Peel or Lawwill could have done the same with Werner's XR. But the test engines were a fair sample.

Branch countered some of the objections to restrictions. He said first, that even if you limited the intake capacity of the engines, the best, Scott's and Werner's, still outperformed the average engines. And, he said, the cams and pipes and porting that work best unhampered, also work best restricted. Or so it was on his dynamometer.

To no one's surprise, the AMA decreed that for 1987 all 750 twins in Camel Pro would run with restrictors, actually tubes between carburetor and intake port, with an internal diameter of 33 mm.

The odds were equaled another notch when Harley-Davidson got back into the racing-team business. Bob Conway, a racing fan and occasional participant who also, of equal importance, knew how to work with the new management structure, was named team and department head. The fabricators and builders were hired back and Werner was allowed to prepare and maintain Parker's machines on company time.

At that point (early May) the AMA said the restrictor tubes would stay for at least the rest of the season.

So of course at the next event, Springfield's mile, Parker won, at the slowest speed in years. Nobody could do a 100 mph lap, and they all said it was those tubes. But Shobert was top qualifier and eight of the top-ten finishers were Hondas, so once again, there did seem to be a balance—at the top. If we're to conclude anything, it has to be that just as Branch said, the best guys handled the limits better than the average guys did.

Shobert was the only racer with Honda backing. He'd begun with a plan to win the Camel Pro title, which in 1987 meant some of the dirt and some of the road races, but not the full AMA series. The dirt championship became Grand National, and the road races were Superbikes.

Parker and Carr and Chandler began the season strongly, while Shobert coasted. Then he woke up, won a road race and three dirt races in a row, taking the lead in both Camel Pro and Grand National. Just about the time he looked sure to win both, which he did, Honda announced the corporation was pulling out of the dirt-track series. Shobert would be given his machines and parts, while the factory would continue to supply parts for both the RS750 and the RS600, the short-track and TT singles. In the same press release, the racing department said they had four TT bikes, ready to go, make an offer.

Parker and Springsteen were full Harley team members. Chris Carr was a full (sort of) team member, on the payroll and using Harleys for all events, but with Lawwill as tuner. By agreement, Lawwill worked in his own shop. Have I mentioned that the inside and outside tuners never quite trust each other?

We can compress the season, in large part because when we began, the XR was run in all Camel Pro races. But now, with road racing separated and with short track and TT for the smaller singles, our concern is the miles and half-miles.

The 1987 season opened, for our purposes, at Sacramento. Carr was top qualifier and won after leading flag to flag. Shobert was second, then Parker, who'd worn out his tire. The racers didn't like the restrictors. Lawwill contradicted Branch, saying that he'd spent $7,000 tuning and testing with the manifolds. Graham, a distant fourth, said he'd spent $7 buying the tubes from the AMA and that the difference between first and fourth was the difference between $7,000 and $7.

Doug Chandler won the Ascot half-mile, followed by Ron Jones and Ted Boody, all Honda equipped. Chandler repeated at San Jose, with Shobert second and Graham third, another Honda sweep. Plus, it was the fastest San Jose mile ever, tubes or not. Parker was fourth in that one, having traded places with Shobert fifty-three times. The fans at least were getting something for those $7 tubes.

Both factories got sweeps, both had their guys as fast qualifier. Shobert's late drive got him the dirt title and the combined title well before the final race. But the racing wasn't as bad as that sounds. On the oc-

casion of Shobert wrapping up the Grand National title, Parker beat him in the actual race and said later, "I'm happy with the year. Those Hondas are not slow motorcycles."

And in the final race of 1987, the Sacramento mile, Parker edged Shobert and Chandler, so what Scotty meant was that the Hondas were fast and the Harleys faster.

But there was still some concern. The advisory committee recommended open intakes for the two-valve engines, 36 mm carbs for the four-valvers. But in the official bulletin, the AMA said both engines would be required to use the restrictive tubes for 1988, while the two-valvers would be allowed to pare down to 300 lb. and the four-valvers to 320, both with fuel tanks dismounted.

The AMA introduced a 600 cc single championship, and said that for the coming year, experts would be required to use 750 cc twins in the miles and half-miles, 600 cc singles in TT and short track. Minimum weight for the 600s was 230 lb., which explains why they'd taken over TT.

One in-house high point of the year had to be Bill Werner's fiftieth national win. The statisticians calculated that riders using engines Werner built had racked up a few more than that, but Werner said if he hadn't built and prepared the entire machine, it didn't count.

He explained his working method with his rider: "I don't like being told what to do. I like being given problems, and coming up with solutions."

Werner said Gary Scott always wanted things done his way, which was an irritant, while Springsteen had such natural talent that he didn't care how the bike was prepared, which in time made Springer "his own worst enemy." Parker, said Werner, was the best balance, a rider who knew how to give input and how to take advice.

Werner has never been full of himself. When asked about his philosophy, Werner quoted former champion Dick Mann:

"Circle track racing is so easy, it's hard.

"What you're doing is very easy. You're just turning left two times.

"To do that significantly better than someone else, is very hard."

And he bristled at the notion that the rules had given Harley some sort of edge.

"We were competitive last year. If we didn't have restrictors, we'd still be competitive."

In sum, Harley-Davidson was back in the racing business while Honda, having achieved what they set out to achieve, was essentially out. There had been an escalation, which left the two factories at the top. The restrictors and costs had widened the gap, just as the critics had feared, while at the same time the machines were markedly improved.

It was time for a new chapter.

Chapter 8

Return of the Native, 1988–90

When Cycle Week 1988 unfolded at Daytona Beach, it would have taken a certified weatherman to know which way the wind was blowing. Included in the fine print were entries in the Pro Twins race for Jay Springsteen, Gene Church and Chris Carr.

This was first, a return in force to road racing, even if the entries weren't in the premier class. It was also a variation on the regular factory team, a variation made more normal as the week wore on.

The star of the return was Springsteen and his amazing machine. It came from the fertile minds of Mert Lawwill and Doug Garoutte, a designer and fabricator and the skilled hands that form many of Lawwill's creations.

The Doug Garoutte and Lawwill road racer left no new idea untested. Begin at the front, with the upside-down fork sliders reversed so the axle trails rather than leads. Check the damper for the front brake, with linkage to resist compres-sion on braking. The oil tank is semi-wet sump, with the storage tank below the crankcases, to keep the weight low and free the space usually taken behind the engine. Mert Lawwill

Radical frame moves the swing-arm pivot to within a few inches of the countershaft sprocket, reducing the effect engine torque has on rear suspension. Gearshift is remote, and is done with hydraulics. Note the master cylinder above the rearset footpeg, the slave cylinder above the shortened shift lever. The engine was a normal Lawwill-built XR-750 stroked to 1000 cc. By team accounts it overpowered the chassis. Mert Lawwill

The key was the frame, which was sort of a variation on the tubes from the dirt-track frame and the spars from Rob North's road-race-style experiment. The frame's central tubes formed a backbone, from which the engine was suspended so the engine itself was part of the frame. Rear suspension was mono-shock and the forks were upside-down Simons but with the legs reversed so the axle trailed and was closer to the steering head's axis. The fuel tank conformed to the odd shape of the backbone, the oil tank went below the engine and around all this went the good old bodywork from the good old XRTT.

Church and Carr had the product of Eric Buell, a racer and former Harley-Davidson engineer who'd branched out to produce Buells, the Harley-powered sports bikes, except that they had been highly prepared and fitted with full-race XR-1000 engines, same as used in the Garoutte-Lawwill machine.

Things looked good in practice, for instance Springer was clocked at 165 mph, but the engine cracked its cases. Church fell and cracked his collarbone so Parker subbed but retired the Buell when the rear shock absorber broke. Carr's bike was so far off the pace he didn't start the actual race.

Not a good time for anybody. Later the builders opined that the preparation wasn't good, while the team said the specials had been built too lightly from the beginning, and everybody involved now finds it hard to remember. Or they'd prefer to forget the whole thing.

They got back on the usual track(s). The 1988 factory team was Springsteen and Parker, plus Carr. He was the new kid for the second year, the difference being that in 1987 he and Lawwill hadn't agreed on preparation or strategy. So, for 1988 Lawwill went completely outside, with riders Ricky Graham and Steve Morehead, and Carr came completely inside, to be tuned by Ken Tolbert, a sharp young wizard who was also that rarity, a skilled mechanic who'd also ridden well enough to earn his expert license.

Why the Daytona venture became clear a few weeks later, with the announcement that Harley-Davidson engineers were designing a new racing engine. It would be a V-twin, of course, with an initial displacement of 1000 cc, putting it at the top of the class. The new engine would have many valves per cylinder, twin overhead cams, fuel injection, engine management like the GP bikes and would be water cooled. The press release predicted 130 bhp and said the complete machine had a target weight of 320 lb. The press was shown a computer-generated sketch of the engine and was told the plan was to debut the racer "during the 1989 season."

Right. At this writing in early 1991, the new engine is still on the drawing board. Just like Grandmother said, everything takes longer than you think.

1988: Climbing the Ladder

The second part of the plan, ruling on the dirt tracks, was something else. Harley luck, you could say, had put together Werner, whose scruffy brown notebook held the wisdom of fifteen years at the national level, and Parker, the scrappy kid whose bubbly humor concealed a good mind and a will to win. Parker had been helped along the way. Through loyalty he'd listened to those who knew less than they thought. But now he was teamed with a peer . . . and both knew it.

The official season began in San Francisco, at the Cow Palace, with a short-track-and-TT doubleheader, just like Houston used to have. Bubba Shobert won both.

Daytona we've already talked about. The real season opened at Sacramento. Shobert won but there was a difference in that this time, the Honda snuck into the Harley's draft and Shobert edged Parker by less than 2 ft., with Carr tucked in behind.

Top qualifier was Bryan Villella, 1987's Rookie of the Year, on a private XR. In the hunt was Jay Springsteen, who'd become sort of a team graduate, with factory help but mostly sponsored by Bartel's, a thriving Harley dealership south of Los Angeles. And, in a sense summing up the season, both of Lawwill's XRs were fast but didn't last.

Springer was top qualifier at the Ascot half-mile, won by Carr, who used a low line to nip Parker and his high line. Shobert was third, in a race sadly remembered for the death of former Harley team racer Ted Boody.

Morehead won the San Jose mile for Lawwill, trailed by Shobert and Parker. Shobert had top time and it was the first XR win there in five years, so the makes were in balance.

Shobert won the Springfield mile, with Parker second and Rod Farris, on a private Honda, third. Louisville, always Harley Heaven, went to Morehead, Carr and Springsteen. Morehead was riding an XR prepared by Hank Scott and set up as a twingle. Postrace, Graham said Louisville went to Big Orange rather than Big Red because "the XR's power curve is a little more mellow than the Honda's."

Shobert was plainer spoken: "It's pretty clear the Honda doesn't work here."

Reviewing the miles and half-miles, the winners were Morehead, Parker, Morehead, Carr, Carr, Shobert, Carr and Parker. The last was the Indy mile. The second mile of the weekend was rained out and the calculators showed that Shobert couldn't be beaten for the Camel Pro title, the combined dirt and pavement points, which handed him $100,000. Carr, whose XR broke a crankpin in the race, was unbeat-

Frame tubes wrapped around the top half of the engine and the engine bolted to the tubes with brackets from the cylinder heads. The structure formed the classic straight shot from steering head to swing-arm pivot, which in this case was far forward of the usual location. Brake linkage at lower right looks to have been made from parts of a steering damper. Also in classic style, the builders believe the team didn't prepare the machine right. The team says the thing was underbuilt from the beginning. Interesting experiment, though. Mert Lawwill

Bill Werner, left, and Al Stangler, pose for a semi-formal portrait early in 1988. The shot is formal in the sense that the guys are primed for the occasion, semi-formal because this is another day, another race. Parker's XR has a Knight frame with oil carried in the backbone, the latest in flat-slide Mikuni carbs, dual ignition and a superb example of machine work in the plate that covers the countershaft sprocket and carries the arm for the clutch linkage. But the seat is the old 1970 style and that's as cluttered a gearcase cover as we've seen. Bert Shepard

Chris Carr, a tough kid from central California, became the team's back-up star, challenger to Parker the way Parker had been the junior rider for Springsteen. Harley-Davidson

able in the new 600 cc championship, while the dirt series, known as the Grand National, was still up for grabs.

Parker walked away with Springfield, trailed by Dan Ingram, a former Harley rider who'd borrowed Shobert's own Honda. Just behind Ingram, no kidding, was his sponsor. It was an easy win for Parker, leading Werner to quip that "personally, I prefer a runaway win. It's less taxing mentally."

And team manager Bob Conway revealed that there would be an improved XR-750 engine within a year or two.

The Syracuse mile was a problem. Ingram won on Shobert's RS. Second was Morehead, but on his own, 1979 built XR because he and Lawwill had parted company. Parker's engine blew up, which was rare. And Shobert was first across the line but was

disqualified when a post-race check showed the Honda to be 1.5 lb. less than the required 320.

This can be debated. And it was, for instance Shobert's rear tire was worn to the cords. And while the tank had to come off for the check, Shobert argued that the lines and petcocks, mere ounces but vital here, should have been included.

The suspension was appealed. Meanwhile, at rained-out Hagerstown the tech inspectors weighed Parker's XR: 305.5 lb. At Ascot they tried the scales again, for 306 lb. Bill Werner allowed for tire tread and small parts.

Parker won the Ascot half-mile, with Graham second on Rob Muzzy's Honda, rather than Lawwill's Harley. The points race seemed settled, assuming Shobert lost his appeal of the suspension. Parker, who'd been fourth in 1984, third in 1985 and second

The 1988 season compressed, with Parker (11) leading Steve Morehead (42) on Lawwill's XR, and Carr (20) on the factory bike. Obscured in the middle of the pack are guys like Dan Ingram and Ricky Graham, as the private Hondas are equaled by the private Harleys. Bert Shepard

Did you know that the ancient Greek playwrights were using the fickle finger as a stage gesture 2,000 years ago? True, and between friends, as shown by Parker and Springsteen, it still delivers the message. Bert Shepard

By this stage the XR was evolving slowly. Carr's mount has a Knight frame that's carefully wrapped around the engine; compare the front downtubes and the mounting plates with earlier examples, for instance. The engine also looks slightly lower in front, to keep the weight down. Bert Shepard

in 1986 and 1987, allowed himself to say, "I've been climbing the ladder a long time."

It must have been invigorating at the top. At the last race, back in Sacramento, Parker was fast qualifier, won the fastest heat and won the national with four seconds in hand. It was, as *Cycle News* said, "The stellar performance of his career."

Shobert lost the appeal and both sides agreed that it was better for Parker to win on the track. Further, the maker's series ended with 324 points for Harley-Davidson, 267 for Honda and 16 for Wood-Rotax.

If it was any consolation, the Honda team beat the Harley team in their annual softball game.

1989: Alone at Last

History does repeat itself. Remember Roberts and Yamaha? Late in 1988 Gary Mathers, manager of the ever-smaller Honda racing effort, confirmed a rumor:

"We're spending our budget in Europe with Bubba. . . . Bubba's not interested in doing only dirt tracks, and neither are we."

Several weeks later Shobert was interviewed by *Cycle News*. American Honda had found Shobert a ride in the world championship series, road racing 500 cc two-strokes. He'd run his own Camel Pro team, he'd won the combined titles and the road-race series here. He'd hoped to win Grand National, but he hadn't been able to do it.

Some of the problems were technical. Team Honda had pared the RS750 to 300 lb. fighting weight. Then the AMA imposed the 320 lb. rule on four-valve engines. And then "we hung some weight on it. . . . On the half-miles I never could get it to work the way it had."

Worse, or so it sounds from outside, they didn't do their homework. "I think a lot of it was the

Tammy Kirk, right, was the first woman to earn an expert license in professional dirt track and thus was a symbol whether she wanted that, or not. She qualified for several nationals but never won one, and she was popular with fans and the other racers. But her (and her sponsor/father's) refusal to allow their engine to be inspected cost Kirk her license and caused her to retire under a cloud. Cycle World

Earning the number-one plate showed that Parker had matured into a controlled and thoughtful racer while not losing his willingness to back the bike into a turn in a cloud of dust. Bert Shepard

weights. . . . We never did test with the weights in different places.'' (As we'll see, the details Shobert didn't bother with are the very details that make the difference between first and fourteenth.)

Shobert wasn't happy with the AMA's system of rules, nor with how the races were promoted. He explained Honda's loss of interest as a marketing choice: ''They believe the people who go to the Grands Prix are more sophisticated, and they're the ones who are buying new bikes.''

The first part may of course be true. The second, plainly put, wasn't so. In 1989 *nobody* was buying new bikes.

But anyway, Shobert got a production GP bike and a sponsor. He had the talent and the drive. Tragically, at the 1989 USGP at Laguna Seca, Australian racer Kevin McGee was doing post-race burnouts for the crowd and Shobert, who was on the cool-off lap

and was cruising to the pits with Eddie Lawson, crashed into McGee. Shobert was terribly injured and although he's recovered his mental powers and routine physical skills, his racing career is almost surely over. To their credit, Honda has been fully supportive of the man who did so much for them.

In keeping with motorcycle-racing tradition, Shobert is good friends with Parker and gives all due credit to his rival and the rival factory. Plus, he said in 1989, ''Parker was definitely the hungriest guy out there.''

Perhaps saddest of all, leave out the rules and the money and the career moves, and, as Shobert said, ''There's nothing better than riding those mile bikes.''

Which is just what Scott Parker set out to prove for 1989.

He had help from his friends. The Harley team consisted of Parker, Carr, Springsteen and Kevin Ath-

To see this action is to know that Camel Pro Grand National racing is the best there is. Ronnie Jones (16 Honda) has the inside here, with Carr (20) in the middle and Graham (3 Honda) just behind him. Then Terry Poovey (18 Honda) and (guessing from the leathers) Kevin Atherton on the outside. The experts trust each other and have no qualms about running this tight at 80 mph. Bert Shepard

Kevin Atherton joined the Harley team as the apprentice, the new kid who'd be brought along to replace one of the older members when that rider stepped down or aside, as Jay Springsteen did. The kid's good, witness this feet-up slide with front wheel on the groove and the back in the marbles and digging for traction. Bert Shepard

erton. Except that Parker was the only rider with full-time in-house help all year; Carr, Springsteen and Atherton had outside suppliers like engine builders Steve Storz and Mike Mockabee, and supplied their own helpers. Al Stangler prepped Springer's bikes and Atherton's dad went to the races and so forth.

Reigning champ Parker had the full turnkey operation, with Werner as his full-time tuner and on the factory payroll. Another unique factor had to be that the Harley-Davidson workers' union was a partial sponsor and the guys in the racing shop were union members. Werner, a staunch unionist, enjoyed knowing "we're the only union member crew in the business."

Getting down to business, Werner and the crew had been busy. An outside tuner had come up with some useful improvements to the intake and exhaust ports of the XR heads. The changes had required some radical work, to the extent that the ports broke through walls and passages and had to be extensively reworked. Didn't matter, though, because the changes, with cams and exhaust to match, delivered several more horses. The Honda guys weren't working as hard, witness Shobert's failure to tune his chassis, so the engines were close to parity.

The Harley guys would never make a mistake like Shobert's. Lawwill said with no details that he'd made major improvements in the chassis, mostly a matter of locating the engine where the weight would work for the handling.

And by another happy chance, RJR had redone the Camel marketing plan. There was a new series, for motocross, and the road-racing program was dropped in favor of a combined Camel Pro Grand National championship, backed by Camel Challenges, five-lap sprints for $10,000 and for which, as one racer said, "You have to leave your brain in the tool box."

For 1989 the Grand National Camel Pro schedule was trimmed to seventeen events. Only one was a short track, only one was a TT. The rest were miles, nine, and half-miles, six. It was a schedule made for 750 cc twins.

The season began at Daytona, with a short track in the new stadium. Steve Aseltine on a Wood-Rotax won by 2 ft. gained on the last lap, from Carr. Parker didn't get close.

That was the last time that happened. The defending champ won the Sacramento mile by eight seconds, with Carr second and Terry Poovey on a Honda third. One contender was Steve Morehead, the former Lawwill rider who showed up on a different Honda. Ex-Honda team tuner Skip Eaken had made a new frame, with two shocks rather than the single, at Morehead's request. He asked for it, Morehead said, "because it sets and fits me like a Harley." Flattery comes in odd forms.

Doug Chandler won the Ascot half-mile, after Parker led and his gearbox broke. He took the San Jose mile by two seconds, followed by Chandler and Carr.

Morehead's gambit paid off at Louisville, famous as a Harley track, with Parker second and Carr third.

You can see the pattern. In July the Harley team was granted approval by the AMA for new head castings, ones that took advantage of the new ports and because the material was in different places, didn't need to be patched and filled. They needed new intake manifolds and exhaust pipes because the locations and angles and shapes were different. The new heads weren't, as tuner Ed Adkins said, "a bolt-on job." But they worked.

Pause now for two sad stories.

The first came at the second Springfield mile, the final appearance in Camel Pro of Tammy Kirk. She was the only woman expert, a Georgia farm girl whose dad was her tuner and main sponsor. Kirk wasn't the fastest rider out there but she had spunk and grit; everybody's tomboy sister.

At Springfield she was third in her heat, which qualified her for the national. But one of the guys who finished behind her filed a protest against the engine. There had been rumors but until now, none of the men had felt strongly enough to protest a mere girl.

The Kirks refused to submit their engine for inspection, saying that they were outraged at the accusation and would never race motorcycles again. Because every entrant agrees in writing to allow inspection when a protest is filed, Tammy Kirk's license was revoked.

Now then. Everybody has a right to get angry and have hurt feelings. But other racers, when protested, have proved their innocence by submitting to the rules. That would have been more convincing. Guilty or innocent, Tammy Kirk was a benefit to the sport and it's sad to have her story end on such a note.

The second sad story involves the legend, Springer.

At the end of the 1988 season, Springsteen said the next year would be his last on the factory team.

This was a tough one. He was in 1988 what he'd been since 1976, the star, the incomparable. As Werner said, his illness was "Nature's way of giving the other guys a chance."

But this was a delicate matter. The team is supposed to win races. Jay had been champion three times, then he got sick and was second and third, then disappeared from the top ten. He had bursts of brilliance, as in winning the 1985 Syracuse mile. There were those at the factory who figured loyalty had gone far enough, and Springer's backing had become subtly reduced in the recent past.

In 1989, he was backed by Bartel's. He acquired a new manager, who in turn found a sports doctor with some ideas and different medication, and Springsteen got better. He closed in on Parker, running in front and looking strong.

At Syracuse, he was the best man there and was leading until rain stopped the race. Because not enough laps had been run for an official finish, the race was declared invalid. The AMA wanted to do right, so the prize money was paid and Jay got the winner's share.

He said he'd give back the money in trade for the win, but of course that couldn't be done. Later in this chapter, there will be some ramifications.

Meanwhile, it was a waltz. There were seventeen nationals on the schedule. Syracuse was scratched. Of the sixteen, Parker won ten—yes, ten, a new record. He won all nine of the official miles that season. The only guy even close was Carr, with two wins and a bunch of finishes right behind Parker. Dan Ingram, riding Hondas for Shobert, was more than 100 points out, 136 for the year against 266 for Parker. Harley-Davidson won fourteen races, Honda won two and it's not worth bothering to say who won the manufacturer's contest.

This isn't to say there wasn't good racing. There were close finishes and close passes and narrow escapes, as always. But the best combinations were on factory Harleys, then the better Hondas, then the average Harleys.

Why? To a degree because the XR engine was being improved and had reached near parity with the Honda, and to another degree, because the Harley tuners had more money and knowledge than their rivals. As proof of that, note that for 1990 the AMA decided to require all the 750s, no matter how many valves or cams, to weigh 315 lb. at the finish of the race. Oh, and they all had to keep the restrictors, just in case.

1990: New Engine, Old Tradition

At the conclusion of the 1989 season, Team Harley-Davidson had a party. Everybody was there, plus wives and kids. Conway took the occasion to unveil the new XR-750, actually more a revision than a new engine.

He also said that the Really New Racing Engine was now a 60 deg. V-twin, four valves per, double overhead cams, water cooling, electronic fuel injection, five speeds forward. It was supposed to debut at Daytona in 1991, or so they hoped in late 1989.

The party was also the occasion of Springer's departure from the team, with some hedges.

Jay was given a 1990 engine, to be prepared by the factory's Brent Thompson, who'd done so well for Randy Goss. Jay's tuning and preparation and expenses would be handled by the Bartel's team, with factory help, help that came as a surprise.

This is political. None of the people who cast votes want to talk about which way they voted, nor how the other chaps acted. But as nearly as can be inferred, Springsteen made the first move. He realized his illness was hurting the team, and that the pressure of not living up to expectations was hurting him.

There were those at The Motor Company who would have kept Springer for as long as he'd stay. And there were those who were pleased, if not loudly, that they could replace the old star with a new star. So they accepted Springsteen's resignation.

Then, and this will come as no surprise to students of psychology, with the pressure off, darned if Springer didn't get better! No doubt the medicine and

The Downside, at the Peoria TT, 1990. The tumbling figures on the left are Will Davis and Kevin Atherton. Still in the air are Atherton's machine on the right, Davis' in the center. The collision put Atherton out of action for most of the rest of the 1990 season. Cycle

the doctor were beneficial, but even so, not having to live up to other people's expectations had to help.

Next came a groundswell, first from fans and dealers who simply didn't like the notion that Springsteen's talent and loyalty were being rewarded with the equivalent of a gold watch and a handshake. Then it turned out that maybe he could come back and wouldn't the factory look silly if Springer did what Gary Scott almost did.

Jay Springsteen took it very well. He's a fair and honest man. He seemed—not that he'd say so to a reporter—to accept both those who wanted him on the shelf and those who came to his defense. And deep down, racing is the only thing Springer really wants to do, or knows how to do.

If anybody was unhappy, it would have been Debby Springsteen. She loves her husband and knows the toll taken by the mysterious illness. In the midst of the party, with everybody else saying whoopee, she could only mutter, "Ten wasted years." She has their daughter to care for and yes, she'd like to have her husband at home during those twenty-five or thirty weekends a year. Against that, she wants her husband to do what he wants to do and she's proud of what he's done.

It was awkward, but it came right on the day as the Australians put it. The 1990 season lined up with Parker, Carr and Atherton plus Springsteen, with equal weights and an improved engine.

One can argue some of the justice of this. The 1990 rules required that all the expert 750s retained the restrictors installed back when Honda was making all those moves. As noted, it may be that the restrictors were a handicap because they hurt most the tuners who aren't able to work around them. And the weight rules, 315 lb. at the finish of the race, tank in

Early in the 1990 season Chris Carr led Parker on points, just as he does here on the track. It was a friendly rivalry for the most part but even so, Parker was taken aback when reporters asked how it felt to be the Old Guard. Bert Shepard

place, allowed the teams with money for improvements, or the skill as in Werner, Tolbert, Stangler, Lawwill and others, to trim excess and add strength.

The good part was that it didn't seem to hurt the racing. The 1990 schedule followed the newer format, with seventeen events on the "AMA Grand National Championship/Camel Pro Series." The series was tailored for either the big twins or the fans, with only one short track, one TT, five half-miles and ten miles.

The short track came first, at Daytona Beach's stadium, done in large measure so the dirt racers could have some excuse to take part in Cycle Week. True to form the race went to a privateer, Dan Ingram, on a Honda. Carr was second, Springsteen fourth, Parker fifth and Atherton twelfth, all aboard Rotax-Harleys. The *big* Daytona race was of course for Superbikes, which have their own series and have nothing to do with dirt or with Harleys, sorry to say.

The real season, the spring Sacramento mile, got back on form with a twist: Carr, Parker and Ingram on a Honda, and Springer on form again. At Ascot's demanding half-mile it was Steve Morehead on Lawwill's XR, then Parker, Carr, Hondaman Ronnie Jones and Springsteen.

Back on the mile at San Jose, Parker began a new winning streak, or so he hoped, by motoring away on the fifth lap and pulling into a five second lead. Carr was second, Jones third and Springsteen fifth, keeping the pattern that was to continue all year. There was some surprise at Springfield, with Honda's Terry Poovey on the pole and Dave Durelle on the fastest Harley in time trials. Hondas won three of the four heats, but at the national's finish it was Parker, Carr and Morehead on the box, Jones, Poovey and Ingram fourth, fifth and sixth.

At Louisville, Harley Heaven as always, Carr took the win and the points lead from Parker, who was second in both despite winning the Camel Challenge. Jones, who'd begun to joke about winning the Honda Race, was third.

Albuquerque was bittersweet at best. Carr won the mile after a restart required because former national champion Steve Eklund crashed and was critically hurt. (Eklund was still comatose early in 1991.) The track was rough enough to get Parker, who was rider representative with the AMA, to ask if the others were willing to race. They were and they did, but it was a bad day.

Not only that, problems with the semi-new XR engine came to light for the first time.

Harley's Capital Drive plant, where the racing engines are machined, did four of the five fixtures wrong and the new cases were machined out of tolerance, which put the main bearings out of alignment, which made the connecting rods walk about and shut off oil flow and tighten up. Conway emphasizes that none of the engines actually blew up, but they did fail and the customers were leery to the point many ran their older engines.

Except that some didn't have any older engines and because the new production run was on the way in 1989, the racing department let stocks run out.

Which led Will Davis to claim Parker's engine. True, he said, $17,500 is a lot to pay, "But I can win $20,000 in one day with it."

And so he could, except that as a disgruntled Werner was quick to point out, nobody has ever won a national with an engine claimed from the factory team. It didn't stop the claims, though.

Parker got back into form at Lima, where the half-mile track was severely rained on, then groomed into the widest possible groove, go-where-you-please traction. It suited Parker's cushion background perfectly. He and Carr fought for first, while the third and fourth battle was between Morehead and Atherton. Morehead took it, a useful score because he'd broken the partnership with Lawwill and was running his 1979 XR, *Ol' Paint,* on his own dime. For Atherton it was the best he'd done that year and he edged Springsteen, who in turn was happy because the bike's cracked frame had been repaired in the nick of time and the weld held.

DuQuoin was odd. The Midwest tour is always subject to Midwest summertime, which means rain. Two laps after the start of the main, the skies opened up and because there was no hope of running that night and no open dates on the schedule, prize money was paid on the basis of how the national would have started, with Carr on the pole, then Atherton and Jones. Parker was fifth, because he'd been second to Carr in their heat. Worse than the rain was that Springsteen scratched, a victim once again of the mysterious stomach illness.

Hagerstown had been rained out and rescheduled, in time for Morehead to put *Ol' Paint* into first on the banked and narrow track, after winning the Camel Challenge and collecting the $20,000 Will Davis spoke of. Parker and Carr were second and third, Jones still won the Honda race, with fourth.

Peoria was *the* TT and of course it was won by Carr, who was also on his way to win the national 600 cc championship for the third straight time. He rode his 600 there, and took the national and the Camel Challenge; Parker and Jones were second and third in the former, third and second in the latter. Including heats, Carr had won fifteen races in a row at the Peoria TT track, including eight of the past eleven nationals. All one could do was echo Parker: "He just goes so damned fast."

More to the point, Parker said he'd give away the TT if he could have the miles. Carr's win put him seventeen points ahead of Parker.

Sure enough, up came Indianapolis and Parker won, edging Carr by less than a wheel's length. Back in the pits, Ingram had signed on to replace Morehead on Lawwill's team and Skip Eaken, an ex-Honda team tuner, replaced Ingram with two-time national champ Ricky Graham—except that Graham was barely located in time because he'd gone to visit his former tuner Ken Tolbert, who of course now was working for Harley-Davidson. One big happy family, is what Camel Pro is.

And, back at Peoria the team had cross-claimed each other's engines, to use the rule that says you can only be claimed every forty-five days. At Indy, privateer Randy Texter claimed Springer's XR and then gave it back, putting Springsteen safe by the forty-five-day rule.

Why still claim? First, because the factory had to make new fixtures and have another run by the foundry, then machine the new cases. They couldn't do it in time; in fact, the cases were put into stock October 5, and the last race of 1990 was run October 6. The team obviously had a supply of cases that could be reworked, adapted and used in-house while not being good enough to sell, so the team had engines and the outsiders thought they were better than the old stuff.

The only factor that kept this from seeming foolish was that this is how these guys earn their livelihoods and the last thing Harley needed was to have customers going away angry, or getting even.

Did the new engines make that much difference? George Roeder, a top tuner, had one of the new engines but didn't trust it on the track. His son didn't do well all year. Mike Hale came out of Texas with his dad and a new engine that worked, and was Rookie of the Year for 1990. You can't prove anything by anecdote, but Conway says the new engine runs better longer and so it seems from the stands.

Meanwhile, with new engines and Bill Werner, Parker won Springfield and the Challenge, while Carr was black-flagged for an oil leak. Parker got the points lead, Jones got second which he said was better than third, except that Springer got third and the fans went wild.

Parker made it four straight at San Jose, but not by plan. There was a first-lap crash that put Parker's bike nearly into orbit and threw Graham off hard enough to break his arm. Just about every tuner in the pits jumped in to help replace the broken parts on Parker's XR: exhaust pipes, bars, the rear wheel and one rear shock. Werner told Parker not to look down or think about things like frames. When time ran short the other riders, no matter which brand, found things to pull out of line to inspect so the clock stopped. Parker made it to the line, worked his way through the pack and won, closely pursued by some racers who'd rather lose on the track than win by default. Look for *that* in other forms of professional racing!

Time for the hand-held calculators. There were two races left on the schedule, Ascot and the second Sacramento. Parker was in the points lead with Carr close behind and everybody else hopeless. Ronnie Jones had been on the box nearly every race, missed two of the thirteen. Any other year he'd be champ. In 1990, he won the Honda Trophy. But it could still go to Carr if Parker fell off, and Parker could lock it up at Ascot if Carr did poorly.

Ascot in turn was officially hosting the track's final motorcycle race. From the battered stands you could look over the battered walls and see gleaming office buildings in the near distance. Ascot, once a swamp and then a cemetery for discarded school buses, a rock's throw from the clashing together of three major highways, was prime real estate thanks to Los Angeles and its growth. To anybody with sensitivity, the closing of the track is a loss, that is, how many glass palaces do we need? Ever see people swapping shirts with "Executive Park" lettered on the back? A shame.

The last race was just as controversial. A clean start and look! It's Ronnie Jones in the lead and Carr is leading Parker. Not exactly a fully turned table, but close. During the Camel Challenge, won by Morehead with Parker second, Carr ran a low and tight line, not his usual style. Then, during the junior races, he walked out between Turns Three and Four. He'd seen something, or he and Tolbert had some ideas. They made some changes, without letting on just what, and while the changes didn't keep Carr up with Jones, they did keep him ahead of Parker.

Until Parker, who is nothing if not determined and just as crafty as he is determined, had his eyes open and worked out what Carr was doing and gained back a yard here, two yards there until he pulled even on the front straight, dove inside at Turn One . . . and out came the red flag. Will Davis had gone down coming out of Turn Four, hard enough and in a spot dangerous enough to cause the race to be stopped. With one or two, depending on how you score it, laps left in the national.

Davis' tank had slopped gas on the track. That was set afire and allowed to burn off while the AMA crew made a decision: the race would be official at nineteen laps, Jones the winner, and because the race finish was decided on the last full lap, Carr was second and Parker third.

The crowd booed, but went home. (There were some in the stands who wondered if the whole thing had been done so the fans, never known for decorum, would riot and wreck the stands, saving the owners the cost of demolition. But of course that was just a joke, eh?)

More important, Parker was in the points lead by eleven, rather than by the seventeen he'd have had if he'd been second and Carr third. And that matters, as witness the seasons of Springsteen versus Eklund and Graham versus Goss, where one more or less place would have swapped the title.

It didn't come down to that.

It came down to Sacramento where nobody, not the riders nor the tuners nor the scorers nor the fans, gave one fig about the title.

What they cared about was the race.

It began normally, Parker and Carr and Jones in the front row, then the guys like Springsteen and Ingram and Morehead. They'd had all season to work out what worked and they knew what combinations to choose when the track was slick and the wind blowing. But first, the track was so slick in Turn Two that Springsteen reported having trouble. If *you* have trouble there, the AMA guys said, we'd better check. And they did, to the extent they dug up the corner, removed the goo and packed it back down.

During practice and qualifying and even the heats, Al Stangler and Kevin Atherton had been deep in thought and deep in, well, call it deep yogurt. They had two XRs, new engines and Knight frames, one tuned to steer quickly and the other to steer slower. Atherton tried both, and neither would keep up with the others. So they did their best.

It worked. The Group of Three, Parker, Carr and Jones, became a Gang of Four, with Atherton hanging on and edging ahead as the leaders drafted and calculated and experimented. Stangler had come up with a combination that worked and Atherton, who'd missed much of the season because he crashed at Peoria, had the confidence to use the bike and run with the big guys.

Now. There'd been some talk about how Carr would win the race because Parker had only to keep Carr in sight to win the title. Nor would Parker mind being the fifth man to win the title three times.

But Parker races to win races. Yeah, he said later, he'd kind of figured to sit back in the front and watch how things went and take no chances and keep Chris in sight. But then Atherton came up to the lead pack and that was fun, good for the kid but then it didn't seem as if anybody had any kind of edge so Parker gassed it and got enough lead so the others couldn't stuff a wheel on him. Before anybody remembered to breathe, Carr made that desperate move but instead of getting the wheel inside it slid him to the outside. When the checkered flag waved it was Parker, Atherton, Jones and Carr and we all let out our first breath in fifteen minutes. Then we headed for the party.

What Next?

The action-packed close of the XR-750's twenty-first season perhaps masked some problems with dirt track.

When we began this history the AMA's national championship was *the* championship, the only big league and the test of the best and a format unique in the world.

Now the former European series is truly a world championship and we have a round in the United States. There's motocross and stadiumcross and Superbikes on pavement. The more titles there are, the less each one means. Back on the Camel Pro trail, if you have the skill and machine to win on the half-mile and mile tracks, you can be national champion. Not to take anything away from the guys who do it, it's just that it's neither as wide nor as high as it was.

By one of those odd twists life delivers every so often, the previous decade in world motorcycle racing has been the American Era, with Roberts, Spencer, Lawson and Rainey, dirt-track grads to a man, showing the rest of the world how it's done.

Back home, back at the Harley-Davidson team end-of-the-1990-season party, there was normal news and new news.

The normal part was that Conway expects the team and the operation to carry on as they have during the previous three years, with Parker and Werner, Carr and Tolbert, and Atherton and Stangler as the full team partners. Bartel's will back Springer, and there will be enough engine cases and parts for everybody.

Conway added that there are several more improvements to do to the XR-750 engine, still in the form we see here and now.

This is because of the new news.

Mark Tuttle, head of engineering for Harley-Davidson and the man in charge overall because the racing department is a subdivision of the engineering department, said in reply to a direct question, no, don't count on the Really New Racing Engine taking its bow at Daytona in 1991. That project is still being worked on but it's clear that the new engine will not, repeat not, be used on the dirt. Rather, H-D has plans to begin a road-racing program, which will be separate from the dirt-racing program, and that's all they'll say about that.

Before taking a deep look at what it all means, we need to do more research into how it's done.

Part III Tuning

Chapter 9

Race Preparation

Emboldened by victories on the track, empowered by success in the marketplace, in 1989 Harley-Davidson's managers authorized Bob Conway and crew to boldly go where no dirt trackers had gone before: they commissioned Rob North, builder and designer of world-class road-racing frames, to do a cutting-edge frame for the XR-750.

The result was a beautiful piece of work, fully equal to frames seen in Grand Prix circles. The frame was laid out along what's known as twin-spar principles, sort of a horseshoe pattern with the closed end holding the steering head and the two spars extending down and around the engine to the rear mount and swing-arm pivot. There were extensions for the front mount and for the seat and fender. The engine itself was a partial stiffener. The swing arm was beefy and braced and carried one shock and spring, on the left.

The North frame had one purpose: it was stiff, in torsion and extension and compression. As stiff as it could be, to the extent that the bare frame weighed 8 lb. more than the double-cradle Knight frame used by the team.

Bill Werner took the North frame and fitted it with a good XR-750 engine and with forks, brake, tanks, seat, controls, wheels and tires. Werner installed the usual carbs and pipes and added ballast to the conventional machines so the team milers and the North version weighed the same and were as alike, frames excepted, as they could possibly be.

The team took the twin-spar bike and their team bikes to a track and ran tests: same power and gearing and tires and settings.

(The tests of the North frame needed baselines, so all the team guys rode all the team bikes, under the clocks. When Carr, Parker and Springsteen rode their own machines, Springsteen and Parker were equally best. But when Springsteen and Parker swapped, Springer was the fastest.)

To compress weeks of work, the conventional XRs were faster than the radical one.

No one knows exactly why. The Harley team experience parallels that of the Honda Grand Prix team, where a full monocoque frame was tried and abandoned for a tube frame because the monocoque turned slower times with the same engine and so forth. But the motorcycle results go against those from racing cars, where the stiffer the frame in torsion, the better the car works. And, in more recent times, twin-spar frames have become the thing to use in road racing.

Mert Lawwill bounces the front of his XR-750, one ear cocked to check if the fluids are gurgling just right and to catch any clunks that would indicate trouble.

Rob North's road-race-style frame for the dirt XR-750 bracketed the engine with two huge spars from steering head to swing-arm pivot. Bill Werner

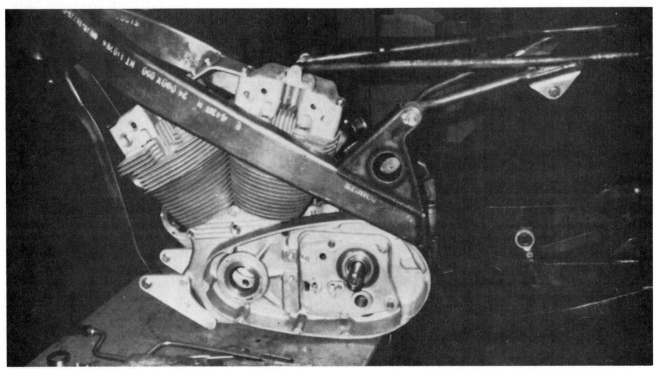

The engine hung from between the spars, with smaller tubes carrying the front mounts and with a subframe for seat, exhaust system and so forth. Bill Werner

The conventional explanation is that this subtle ability to flex in torsion gives what riders call feel, some sense of what the bike is doing overall, while having only the suspension and tires flex takes away feel.

One exception here is Mert Lawwill, who has scant use for conventional thinking on any subject. He says it's more likely that the car people and recently the road-racing people have the sort of control and instrumentation for suspension tuning and behavior to let them track what works and what doesn't. The inflexible frame lets really good suspension work, Lawwill says, while the flexible frame masks the deficiencies of dirt-track suspension.

That's probably the best guess. Meanwhile, the experiment with the North frame is presented as sort of an analogy into the technical care and shaping of the modern XR-750.

Evolution and Experiment

As of 1991, the winning XR-750 begins with more than twenty years of evolution and experiment. Knight and Lawwill and C&J, who are the major suppliers of frames even though demand has slacked to a trickle, all use 4130 chromoly steel tubing. (C&J's Jeff Cole says another reason he leaves in some flex

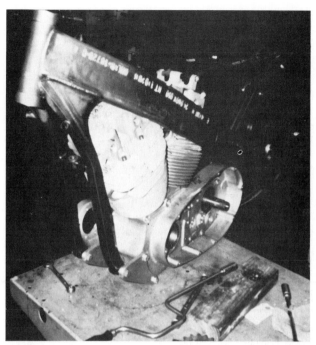

North's frame was compact and extremely strong in compression and twist, the forces most likely to upset handling. Or so it was thought. Bill Werner

The rear suspension was one shock and spring, on the left side of the braced swing arm and feeding a casting mounted solidly against the frame's main tube. The tests, backed up by similar work by other companies, indicated that the off-set suspension worked just like the symmetrical systems did. As a guess, one day soon somebody will make a frame like this work. Bill Werner

is that 4130 will harden and break if it isn't allowed to move about some under torsion.)

The steering head and rear mount/swing-arm pivot will be fabricated, the old castings having been outmoded years ago. Beginning wheelbase will be 55 in. or so, with provision for adding or subtracting an inch or two in either direction. It's worth noting here that the tuners don't talk about this in terms of inches. Rather, they measure in adding or subtracting a link or two of chain.

Now comes the really important part, the locations of the components.

There are guidelines. If you keep the engine low, the center of gravity will be low and the bike will turn easily. If the engine is high, you'll get better weight transfer onto the drive wheel. Plus—this is from Ron Wood—because the wheels and sprockets and flywheels are all forms of gyroscope, the bike will work better if all the gyroscopes are aligned, with front and rear axles, the engine's pinion shafts and the output sprocket all at the same static height. At the same time, the lower the engine the less ground and cornering clearance. And we haven't even begun to think about front and rear weight distribution, the methods used to ensure that under full power the front wheel is just skimming the ground and the rear wheel has all the bike's weight, for better traction.

Obviously, there are lots of theories and practices here.

As one example, in 1990 veteran privateer Scott Pearson had two XRs, a 1980 Lawwill frame and a 1990 Knight version. The Knight had a higher steering head and ride height and the engine was tilted, with the flywheels higher than the output sprocket and the sprocket level with the swing-arm pivot. Pearson runs a longer swing arm than he expected because the 1990 engine has more power and you have to move the engine ahead of the driving wheel to keep the front wheel on the ground.

Back to history and a survey of how different XRs can be. This is Scott Pearson's old-style Lawwill frame, the short chassis with kinked backbone. The engine has an after-market gearcase cover with ignition driven off the former tach gears and minus the housing for the former magneto mount.

C&J's Jeff Cole agrees only in part. His 1990 frame also carries the engine higher and further forward, for the same reasons Pearson expressed. But Cole goes against Pearson and Wood and always has his output sprocket 3/16 in. higher than the swing-arm pivot. Cole says that if you begin with the sprocket and pivot level, as the bike lunges forward and lurches back and hits bumps and so on, the pivots will rise and fall and you get a dead spot: the suspension is one arc, rear axle on pivot, and the drivetrain is another arc, rear axle on sprocket. Cole says that as these arcs cross, the forces change and take away some predictability as to just how much power you can put down.

Cole cheerfully says that while he prefers the raised pivot, Dave Aldana used to win with a dropped swing arm, which also eliminates the dead spot but reverses the effect of the drive chain pulling the rear axle against the pivot. Further, there was a device on

the market not long ago to take the effect of the chain out of the equation, but Werner opined that the best tuners make use of what looks like a handicap and set the suspension to take advantage of it.

The surprise here must be that there isn't a lot of clear difference among the various makers. They all say that it doesn't matter if you use one shock or two, or if you have the single shock in the center or the side.

Next, there is an optimum torsional stiffness, which the builders arrive at with practice.

The XR frame is the result of evolution. Wood and Lawwill and Cole and Knight have all changed the various measurements and locations to fit traction and power and rider preference. Lawwill's early frames for the alloy engine had arched backbones to clear a high engine. It was light and short. Kidd won the title riding it, so the frame had to be a good one.

At top left center of this C&J monoshock frame you can see the reservoir for nitrogen. Barely visible below that is the spring, and behind that is the bracing and mount for the spring to the swing arm. C&J took careful advantage of motocross development and technique when they did this design.

Another C&J, this one owned by Canadian expert Jon Cornwell, from the left side. The center-mount spring/shock lets the exhaust tuck closer to the bike, away from the rider's leg. The primary cover is cast alloy, from tuner Carl Patrick.

Except that other riders didn't feel comfortable and they didn't buy it, so Lawwill's 1990 customer frame is what people expect.

Lawwill adds that the tracks now use more chemicals and have less traction. ("Slime" is the word he uses, instead of dirt.) The engines have more power and there's less grip with the same basic tire, so the bikes are higher and longer and the secrets have changed. He says that the winners he built for Carr and Morehead won because he made a change, moved something less than an inch. It wouldn't have worked five years earlier, Mert grins, and he won't say just what he moved.

And then one remembers that Morehead won in 1990 on his own, riding his ten-year-old frame.

Final point in this vein is that once we get beyond the broad framework (chuckle) we get to the important parts, where the pieces are placed, and we get to the factors about which no two builders agree.

Genius is in the details, somebody once wrote.

So is the winning combination.

The 1990 Engine

This is a typical Harley-Davidson story in that it begins with hope and logic, turns into a semi-tragic

The same cover, in a conventional but nickel-plated frame. The frame carries the oil in its top tubes so the battery is tucked beneath the seat, out of harm's way. The exhaust pipes are stainless steel, which is expensive but durable, and the machined mount for the footpeg is a work of art. Careful scrutiny reveals heads closer to the cases than usual, indicating a short-rod engine.

mess and arrives—or so it looks from here—at a happy conclusion.

When Honda's version of the XR-750 proved to be better than Harley's, the men at The Motor Company knew it, and knew they had to do something. At the same time, there was evidence that road racing was becoming more popular and dirt track less, no matter how we or they felt about it.

So for the long run, management instructed the engineering department to draw up a totally new V-twin racing engine—which has been on the drawing board since. It *probably* will have a vee wider than 45 deg. and will have at least four valves per cylinder and displace 1000 cc with a chance for larger or smaller and perhaps even dirt-track exposure. But the project has been delayed several times and that's all I know as of early 1991.

What did happen was that Conway and Pieter Zylstra were given permission to improve the XR-750 engine.

Officially, it's the *new* engine. Conway says it's called that because the AMA requires all Class C engines to come from stock, certified and recognized castings. The 1990 XR engine used new castings for the cases and heads, thus it's new. The 1990 version was shown to the public at the close of the 1989 season, and was certified as production by the AMA on February 9, 1990.

This is also a Harley-Davidson sort of story in that the 1990 XR is modified to improve the good parts and correct the flaws of the earlier versions, and because much of the gain comes from outside.

The improvement involves the cylinder heads. An outside builder named Ken Augustine did some semi-radical reworking of the ports in his XR heads.

Modern ignition has been grafted onto an old gearcase cover and the mount for tach drive or magneto has been adapted to carry a scavenge pump for the oil system. The sprocket cover has been cut down from the street-bike K version dating back to 1952.

Mert Lawwill prepared this XR for Chris Carr when Carr was a semi-team rider. Those are the Simons upside-down motocross-style forks, and the current Lawwill frame, with oil in the backbone—the filler cap is at the front of the gas tank—and with the frame tubes curled close to the engine.

and got extra power without revving the engine beyond its limits. He submitted the changes to the racing department. The work was checked on the track and in the lab and found to perform as promised. Augustine was rewarded and he in turn gave permission for the team engines to use the changes.

In as few words as possible, the secret of the new ports' success is how they shape and accelerate the columns of air as the mixtures go around the valve guides and seats. The oval port subtly becomes a D on its side, the D being the floor and the place where velocity reaches optimum.

One of racing's technical appeals is that such outside work and thinking and development, works. Shapes and sizes and flows of air relate to cams and timing and compression and ignition and so forth, and even though all that basic work was done for countless hours back in 1970, there's still more being learned in 1990. (The same applies in car racing and in two-strokes, by the way.)

The team had another couple of useful horsepower, which along with the restrictors and the weight handicaps put the Harleys equal to the Hondas.

But there were problems. First, the reshaping of the ports did awful damage to the original head castings. The maximum reworking was interfered with by the headbolts and the size of the head itself. Adding material and moving the other components did violence to the idea of just what a stock casting was (refer back to the later iron heads of 1971), and Harley-Davidson didn't need to be found in violation. Thus, new castings for the heads. And because the bolts would be relocated, the cases had to be changed as well.

With that came some other corrections. Conway knew there were some places he'd like to fix. Zylstra, who'd been in on the original design and the developments since, was even more interested.

A 1985–1988 XR engine producing 90+ bhp is approaching the status of a hand grenade. The lower

Details of the Lawwill-Carr XR include Mert's own gearcase cover and distributor. Plus, the forward portion of the cover and cases has been trimmed off. Because Lawwill thought the crankcase air needed a place to go when compressed, he's installed a compression chamber, bolted to the front of the cover and extending left in front of the cylinder. The sprocket cover that also carries the clutch-activating arm and worm gear has been replaced with a casting that brings the clutch table in from the top.

end, the main bearings, rod bearings and so forth are good for three- or four-mile races before the engine has to be completely overhauled, at a cost of several thousand dollars and within a time frame that means you'd better own more than one engine. Add more power, the 3 bhp from the D-shaped ports for example, and the stress goes up and lifespan goes down.

Zylstra revised the inserts that are pressed into the case halves and carry the main bearings, the Superblend doublewides used since 1975.

Then came the rod bearings. The then-current engines had trouble with flex. The flywheels are pressed onto the crankpin. The distance from the mainshafts to the pin offers leverage and the forces at 9000 rpm have been known to flex the pin and wheels and walk the latter off the former. Some of the problem had been reduced by the development by West Coast wizard Steve Storz of an unbreakable—well, mostly—crankpin. The factory began using the vendor who produced the pin, to Storz' annoyance, but that's another story. More to our point, the team's designers came up with a larger, stronger crankpin.

Tex Peel, hard at work on the rear brake. Peel does things differently: to the right of the rear tire is first, a catch tank for the oil breather and second, the oil tank, shaped sort of like a canteen and with the rear number plate for the outer side.

Lawwill's 1990 XR for Steve Morehead, early in the season. Mert's holding the fuel tank up, so you can see the evolution of the frame backbone and oil tank.

The connecting rods remained the same because Conway found a German company that would supply smaller and stronger rollers and cages for the rod bearings, which are a weak link with a fore-and-aft V-twin.

As explained by science, the larger rollers spin with more velocity at their circumferences and when they reach a critical speed, they can't spin fast enough and they skid, with resulting loss of the oil film that separates the metal parts, which means friction and failure. Smaller rollers have less velocity at the same revs and live longer.

The new heads have dual ignition, a spark plug on each side. And they have what amounts to an ignition for each set of plugs.

The current system is a development of Werner's replacement for the magneto and for the first electronic systems. It's an evolved form of the Spanish Moto-Plat, with drive from the front of the gearcase and with a unit on each end of the driven shaft. There's a set of windings to provide current for the coils that mount beneath the fuel tank, and there are

triggers for setting off the sparks. Each system is single fire, by the way. The trigger housings are slotted so timing can be varied and there's an inspection plug and a mark on each flywheel so timing can be checked and set for each cylinder. There hasn't been a failure for six seasons now, and the system is sold by the racing department to anybody whose dealer will order one.

Removing all other accessories from the gearcase allowed a new, smaller cover, machined from magnesium. Because there's no need for magneto, distributor or scavenge pump drive, the third cam wheel has the same-size outboard shaft as the other three.

Then comes minor improvements. The primary drive consists of the engine sprocket, the three-row chain and the clutch sprocket. The clutch assembly rides on a bearing that slides over a sleeve that's part of the cover holding the gearbox in place. The primary chain's center is slightly outboard of the bearing carrying the clutch assembly, which means a trace of misalignment. The new engine has a revised clutch sprocket-basket and a longer needle bearing, so the

Rows of 1989–1990 XR-750 engines, racked up and ready for delivery, at the racing shop early in 1990. In contrast to the days of selling assembled sets of parts, the department hired outside people and did a full run of completed and tested engines, for selected teams and for private customers. It was a lot of work, and money, and it's a shame that a flaw in the machining process meant that all the engines shown here had to be recalled. Harley-Davidson

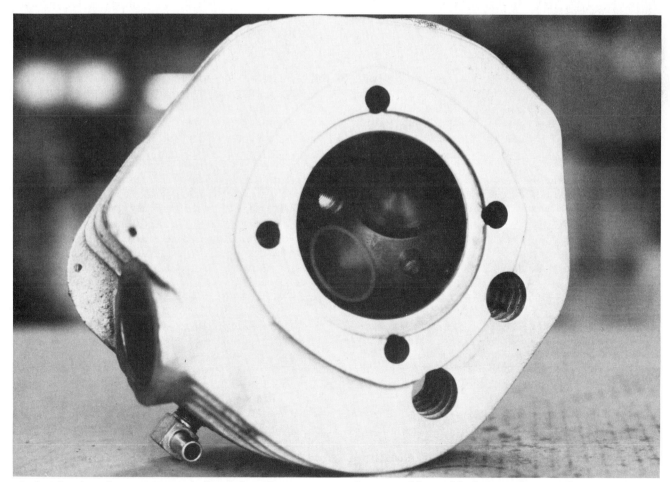

The head-to-barrel connection is a dry seal, with a recess machined into the head and a lip on the cylinder's iron liner. Darkly visible here is the semi-hemi combustion chamber and the two spark plug holes. Steve Storz

New on the left, old on the right. The revised cylinder head is easily identified by the larger flange and the oval intake port. The port changes shape inside and becomes a "D," as the floor is flat just before the port reaches the valve guide.
Steve Storz

pull is straight. (Some tuners trim off the outer third of the primary chain, moving the center of pressure to the center. This saves weight and reduces friction, not by a lot, at a cost of replacing the chain more often.)

The oil system is less worry and less complicated than it was at first. The two-stage oil pump is now driven at half speed, like the road engine and against the quarter-speed gearing used for the KR and earlier XRs: slowing the pump was supposed to reduce cavitation, where the gears spin so fast they don't pick up oil.

The timed breather is now used only for air control, with oil flow regulated by the pumps, drains and scrapers. The new factory engine is tighter, with less room for air expansion when the pistons compress the air in the cases, but Werner says careful routing of oil and use of the breather makes this no problem. Some builders use expansion chambers, tiny boom boxes you could say, at the front of the gearcase, because they believe the squashed air needs a place to go. Each makes a good argument, neither can prove their way is better.

The actual oil pump is a work of art, perfectly machined. The older pumps worked on a ratio of 2:1, meaning twice as much oil could be removed from the engine as was delivered. The new pump's ratio is 4:1, done by making the scavenge gears four times as tall as the delivery gears. Still, the pump can't remove four times as much oil as it delivers; the ratio is there to be sure *all* the oil is pulled from the cases.

The clutch has dry plates, fiber and steel, as used on the KR of 1952. It's still there because it still works, although the springs and pressure plate are stiffer than they were. The only plans for change are a new

material for the fiber plates, which used to contain asbestos.

The new heads and ports naturally required new cams, as in timing and lift. The set carries part number 99442–89RA in case you find some heads at a swap meet.

Attentive readers will recall the problems with the rocker arms and the fact that because each valve was at a different angle to its cam lobe, the original rocker arms had the wrong angles to have the correct lift and location.

This is still partially true. But the designers have come up with improved machining techniques that allow the one casting to be modified so it has the correct angles for the one and four positions: front cylinder exhaust and rear intake. Rockers for two and three, front intake and rear exhaust, must be cut apart and reworked, not to the same angles of course. There's some intensive labor, but it's still cheaper than having four different rocker arms from the foundry.

Conway is especially proud that he's eliminated a total of seven numbers from the parts book. Further, there are now gaskets for just the clutch hub, primary cover, gearcase and sump. There are O-rings for the pushrods. The case halves, the cylinders, the heads and the rocker boxes hold with just a light dab of sealer, or even dry.

The new engine will fit the standard frames. But the parts won't all interchange, a matter of regret. Many of the parts, as in new heads and barrels on older cases, *can* be done, though. But mostly, you need the cases for the flywheels, the flywheels for the rods, the cams for the heads and so forth, or you need a better machinist than most of us can find.

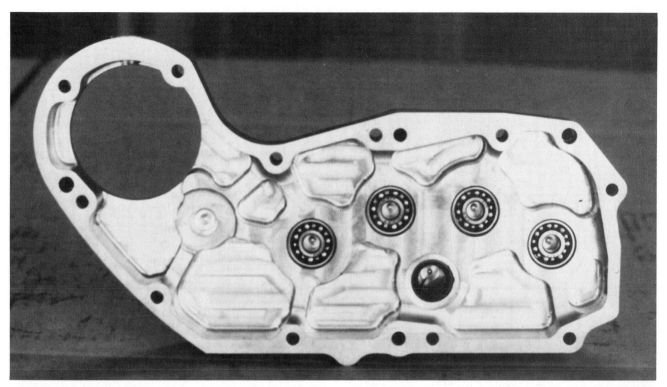

The new gearcase cover, from the inside. Seen here are the four ball bearings that support the outer ends of the cam-shafts, and the intricacy with which the cover fits over the cams and accessory drives. Steve Storz

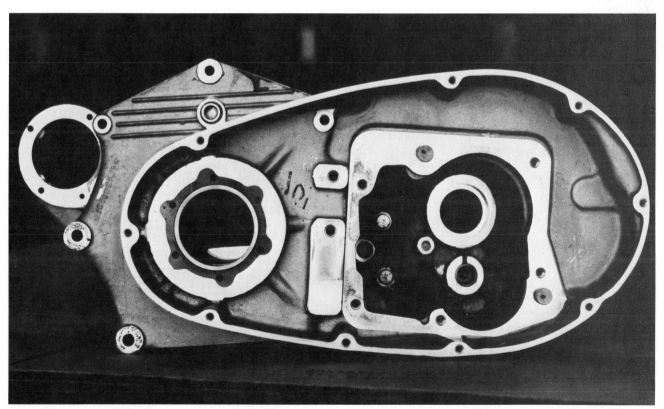

The outer side of the left case half, showing the support and sleeve for the left main bearing and the mounting face for the plate that holds the left side of the gearbox—in Harley parlance, it's the trap door. The shape of the primary housing also dates back to the 1952 K and KR models. Steve Storz

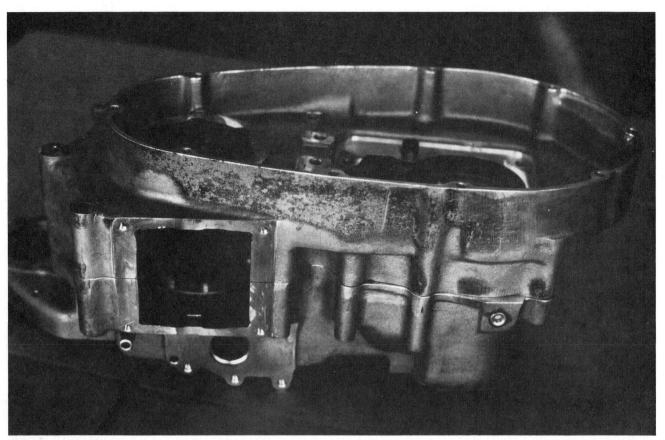

The bottom of the cases has this flat surface and opening, which is where the mini sump goes. The top half of this photo is the left side of the engine, and the mounting flange for the oil pump is below the sump mount. Steve Storz

Historians need to know that although the new engine was certified and went on the market in 1990, the original (a word fraught with portent, as we'll see) cases were stamped in the normal XR way, such as 1C1000J9. That's an old Harley habit, with 1C1 representing a competition engine. R now means the rubberized engine mounts for the big twins. The last two markings are J, the ninth decade and 9, the ninth year of that decade. And before you write, remember that the century's decades begin with the year 1 so the 1910s are the second decade.

Outside Component Suppliers

The new engine was a complicated project. First, the racing department designs and specifies and to some degree stocks parts, but virtually nothing is made in the shop for sale. Instead, there are seventy-plus firms and individuals who supply the team and the parts department: Conway considers Harley-Davidson's Capital Drive plant, which makes some of the parts, a supplier like the others.

Here's how it works. The cases, cylinders and heads are cast by Eck, a foundry with long-standing ties to The Motor Company. The cylinders go to Los Angeles Sleeve for iron liners. The heads get preliminary work in the racing shop, then go to Jerry Branch.

He installs valve seats and guides and the inserts and washers needed to prevent leakage where the ports run squeaky close to the bolts.

Branch does a custom, careful valve job, blends the seats to the ports and installs keepers, valves, springs, collets and shims, then ships the heads back to the team shop for distribution.

The original production run of the new, 1990 engines began with 115 sets of cases. The plans were to build at least twenty-five complete and competitive engines, assembled and tested to make at least 90 bhp. There were twenty-five sets of heads set aside to be sold to tuners who wanted to work their own secrets instead of letting Branch do it. And there were cases stocked by the parts guys, for sale to dealers. Price to dealers is $500 and change, against the $1,000 and change listed in earlier years.

We're setting the stage some here, but the barrels get their liners and are farmed out for final honing and finishing to shops in the Los Angeles area.

This is another special process. It's called Plateau Honing. The liners are honed, cross-hatched in the normal way so there are tiny peaks spiraling around the liners, to be polished and smoothed by the rings during break-in.

Except that for this process the peaks are flat-

154

The cast-alloy cases have a steel insert for the main bearings. This is the inner side of the left case half. There isn't a lot of mating surface, which is why the two halves must be perfectly true. Steve Storz

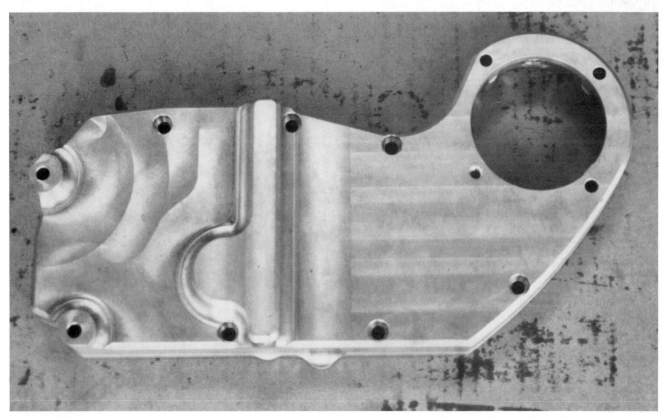

The outer side of the gearcase cover, which is first cast and then machined into this finish. The accessory drive on the top, former home of the tach cable or distributor/magneto, is gone. But the housing that used to take the magneto or the XL generator is still there because that's where the dual ignition mounts. Steve Storz

Remember the mounting flange on the gearcase and engine case? Now work backwards. From the right, there's the shaft that runs across the front of the gearcase, with drive gear and with the ignition windings. Then the twin housings for the triggers, and the outer windings and the covers. There are slots to let each cylinder be perfectly and separately timed. It's been five seasons now since the team had an ignition failure. Steve Storz

For those who put up with the short-lived ball bearings from the old days, this is a miracle. It's the Superblend main bearing, the inner and outer races with barrel-shaped rollers. As you can see, the inner race skews with the outer race fixed so the mainshafts align themselves in the main bearings. Steve Storz

The same connecting rods, which can be used with the new larger crankpin because the roller bearings and cages, in the center, are smaller than the old rollers and cages, on the left. This has a second benefit. The smaller rollers' surfaces are going more slowly at the same crank speed, so they are less likely to skid, that is, stop rolling. Steve Storz

Another major improvement with the 1990 engine is the larger crankpin, left, contrasted here with the old pin. Larger is stronger, meaning less flex and so the flywheels are held in true. As a second note, the designers left out the oil holes at first, as can be seen here. Later troubles persuaded them to return to the old oiling system for the second run of engines. Steve Storz

The gears for the new oil pump. The scavenge set, top, is four times taller than the pressure gears, bottom, so the pump has more capacity for oil retrieval than oil delivery, which is what you need to keep the cases clear of all but an ounce or two of oil. Steve Storz

tened, so there's precisely 0.003 in. between the edges. The flattened peaks allow better oil retention and quicker seating than standard finishing does, or so the department believes.

Lots of care, is what we have here—just as there's one man in the Capital Drive toolroom who makes all the cam lobes. He does them all because he's the best man they've found for the job.

The cases are also finished outside the race shop. This—don't forget this part—is a tricky business. The case halves are difficult to cast. They must hold the cylinders, flywheels and cams and at the same time serve as a stiffener for the cradle and the swing-arm pivot. Each set of cases has to be placed in fixtures for align boring, milling, polishing and so on. When the department decided on new castings, they didn't just have to have molds and boxes, they needed five sets of fixtures to convert rough castings to usable product.

Time for the next odd fact. On the one hand, the racing department has seventy or so suppliers. On the other hand, or side of the counter perhaps, there are only a few hundred customers.

This wasn't intended. When Class C production racing was invented generations ago, the hope was that each dealer would have a team or some guys to be helped and that there would be thousands of racers having fun on Harleys, with parts from the dealer. Then came invasions from both coasts, and the invention of motocross and the use of smaller machines by amateurs. Harley-Davidson racing parts are still sold mostly through dealerships, excepting the team and a handful of privateers who get factory help.

Most obviously, the racing team, department and budget are not what you'd call a profit center.

In the middle, between the suppliers and the budget and design and distribution and the racing fans and Harley fans who are the final target of all this, are those experts and juniors and sportsmen who race Harley-Davidsons. And don't forget, there are outsiders like Lawwill and Storz and Patrick and Neil Keen and Knight with engine and chassis parts. Grand Prix Plastics in California and First Klass Glass in Michigan will meet and beat factory prices for fiberglass seats and tanks.

Add up the buyers. There are a couple hundred experts and juniors with XR-750s or 500-Rs, trailed by a handful of vintage racers—take that either way—with iron XRs, KRs, XRTTs, KRTTs and the like.

Two hundred total? Three hundred? Not even Conway knows for sure.

When I began ordering parts for my iron XR-750 in the early 1980s, I got ticked some days because not everything was in stock right then. Had I known the facts, I would have kept quiet. OK, had I *really* known the facts I wouldn't have begun the project. All I can say, in behalf of all vintage racers and restorers and the man who's rumored to still be racing an iron XR in the expert class in the Midwest, is, thanks.

The timed breather. The XR engine no longer uses the plus and minus changes in air pressure as a means of making oil go in the right place at the right time. But the pressure change that comes from the pistons going up and down in the crowded cases means there's still a reason to let air in and out in sequence. The timer sits in the back of the gearcase, driven off the right-side mainshaft that also drives the cams and ignition. Steve Storz

The aluminum clutch hub. The clutch plates fit inside, the primary chain drives the three rows of teeth on the outside. The new clutch rides on a double row of rollers, moving the support out closer to where the chain pulls it out of line. Steve Storz

Dave Durelle's XR, a good private machine but a bit smudged late in the season. It's got the old-style gearcase cover and ignition, monoshock rear suspension, round-body Mikuni carbs and the lever for the clutch pushrods routes the cable across the back of the engine.

The rest of the clutch, with the cracked fiber and steel plates on the inner hub at right, the pressure plate with springs and mounting bolts at left. A set of four pushrods are moved through the output shaft, right to left, and push the pressure plate away from the driven plates. It's an old system, unique in that the plates run dry, behind a cover in the wet primary housing. It's forty years old and it works just fine, once you learn how to set it up right. Steve Storz

The Bad Part

The 1990 engine was the fourth in the alloy XR series, the third having been done in 1978, 1979 and 1980. There had been a supply of replacement parts since 1980. The records show an average of a dozen or so sets of cases going to private buyers every year. But it's not economic to produce intricate parts in low numbers and because the department began work on the new version in 1988, the supply was allowed to quietly disappear.

The new version was accepted and certified and Conway brought in extra help to assemble and test that first batch for customers. The team tuners, Werner and Tolbert and Stangler, had the new parts as well and did their own engines at the same time.

There were delays and minor mishaps as there must be in such projects, but the team and the racers like Springsteen and Lawwill and the Roeders all had the 1990s installed in time for the beginning of the

1990 dirt-track season.

Bob Conway is quick and careful to point out that none of the 1990 XR engines actually failed, as in ka-pow!

Instead, and reporting well beyond the time of the events, the problem began with the construction of the fixtures in which the new cases were held while being machined. The fixtures weren't quite right. They were supposed to be true to within 0.002 in. and some were more like 0.011 in. out. That doesn't sound like much. It was enough.

More specifically, the left-side case half was bowed when it came out of the jig. Not enough to see, not enough to leak. But when the two halves were bolted together and the faces were flat, the wall of the left half was out of true. The wall holds a steel insert, a permanent fixture, in which fits the main bearing. With the wall out of true the chain of relationships put the insert out, and the bearing and the mainshaft,

159

Secret stuff. This is Parker's miler, with the new engine adapted for Werner's ideas. There's an oil filter at top left of the gearcase, a scavenge pump at middle right and be- *tween them is a sending unit, picking up impulses from the ignition.*

the flywheel and the crankpin. We're speaking here of infinitesimal increments. All the parts whirled freely in test, and the engines happily cranked all the power predicted.

But the fractional misalignment let the rods thrust against one side of the pin, up against the inner face of the flywheel. The oil system routs lubricant into the mainshaft, out the flywheel and into the crankpin, to spray the connecting rod bearings, which, as noted, are high-tech and intricate and fragile. When the bearing cage rubbed against the flywheel face, it shut off lubrication.

The afflicted engines worked just fine, their first race. The second race, they slowed. The third time out they were hopelessly down on power, and it took some time to figure out why and where.

Things could have been worse, in that the engines did work and win races and the guys who could tell early, Lawwill for instance, showed up with 1990 heads on pre 1990 cases.

And there was a cure. Conway found seventy sets of faulty cases. He arranged to have the fixtures made true and then had another production run at the foundry and recast the cases. As a failsafe and perhaps a fix that should have been applied when the engine was built, there are now thrust washers, a special mix of leaded phosphorus-bronze, riding on the crankpin between the bearing cage and the flywheel faces. The washers have flats so when they touch, as they will do with a floating connecting rod of this type, they will burnish on the flat while maintaining clearance for oil flow.

Conway says at least three private 1990 engines have done at least eight national races on the same lower ends. Werner and Tolbert in 1990 went six nationals between lower-end rebuilds. In the old days, three meets was the maximum. An XR rebuild easily gets into four figures' worth of time and parts. The list price for a new XR-750 engine—see your dealer for delivery dates—is $5,995 in 1991 dollars. If normal markup for the department was included the engine would sell for $8,000 or so, and if the old ways were followed you'd have to go through it part by part before it ran in anger. Ron Wood can talk for an hour on what you had to do to the original XRs.

It's worth remarking here that by the end of the 1990 season, the XR's twentieth anniversary if you count the iron version, there was more refinement than experimentation in evidence.

There was a time when guys like Tex Peel built short-rod engines or when Werner slipped twingles into the line-up or Lawwill gained a horsepower lead with a new set of cams.

But it hasn't happened much since 1985 or 1986. Lawwill says he can beat or at least meet the new heads with his version of the old ones. Brent Thompson says his semi-outside engines for Springsteen may not have quite the peak power Tolbert and Werner provide for Carr and Parker, but a check of the qualifying times for the last few years shows more parity than any huge advantage to the factory.

By now there are no flaws in the basic XR-750 engine. There are limits and compromises, as in how fast you can spin the pressed-together flywheels and crankpin, and how much air you can jam through those two valves and their archaic combustion chamber. But the engine by this time is all of a piece.

What next? Conway says there will be more changes and improvements but he won't say in what direction the design will go. Lawwill has designed four-valve heads to fit right on, a kit if you will, but at this writing the chaps in charge don't want to know, even though the rules would probably allow the change with no penalty.

Wheels and Tires

One of the factors the rules people have tried to remove from the Class C equation has always been tires and wheels.

They had good reasons. The tire companies have tried to make commercial use of racing success, which isn't wrong but in other venues it has caused some favored few to have better tires than their rivals can get. That hurts racing in the long run, so the AMA's rules have always required the tires to be certified and available to all, even if the tires are legal only for competition. More to the point, there have been limits on the tread design, mostly meaning no knobbies.

In consequence, there have been tires from Goodyear, Carlisle, Pirelli, Dunlop and peers, as noted in the race results. There are soft, medium and hard compounds. The first move for all racers is to fit the brand and compound that experience has shown works in the day's track conditions. Pirelli's classic MT-53 front tire may keep the front wheel biting at Ascot, for instance, while only the medium-firm Goodyear will work at Louisville and a soft compound is needed at Hamburg, even though all three are half-miles and the latter two are limestone base.

Impulses are sent to this recorder, in a zippered pouch inboard of the rear number plate. Werner knows how fast the engine can rev and thus can be closer to perfect on the gearing. While we're here, that's a rear tire with the inner knobs cut, the outer knobs plain.

Wheels hardly matter at all. They are all 19 in. diameter, an orphan size by 1990, and the Camel Pro crowd uses laced-up wire-spoke wheels almost exclusively.

The design dates back to the days of leather helmets and has been outdated in all other forms of racing for twenty-five years. At least. Car racers and motorcycle road racers went to cast wheels of aluminum and then magnesium and later all manner of exotic compounds and ceramics. They did that because they found them lighter and stronger and better.

Not in dirt-track racing. Morris made cast wheels in Camel Pro size in the late 1970s. The teams tried them, liked them, but didn't adopt them.

The Harley teams and a few other outfits still have the cast Morris wheels, in use. They appear reg-

Parker and Werner like a good, wide front tire for the miles. The forks sport plastic covers to keep rocks from dinging and denting the polished surfaces of the stanchion tubes. And the champ's number plate is blue with a yellow number because that's the Camel team color scheme.

ularly, on front or back, but it's almost always because the tuner wants to change the cross section and thus the contact-patch shape, of a given tire. He might have the same two tires, one on a 2.5 in. cast rim, the other on a 3.0 in. spoked rim, so he'll change from cast to spoked. But the wheel won't matter.

As an educated guess, this compares with the frame question: the spoked-wire wheel has some give to it, while the cast wheel is rigid. It may simply be that because suspension and frame are left to follow their own whims to a degree, that the flexible wheel makes up for, or allows, or enhances, the search for optimum flex. Right or not, the tuners who use the cast wheels say they're good to have around but that when they wear out, there's no grounds for alarm; the spoked-wire wheels and limited-width alloy rims do the job. Where science lags, art and magic—make that black magic—move in.

Wheels need only be round and true, the tires are routine, but in the time before the heats or the race itself you'll see tuners, riders and crewmen crouched over the bike, or a mounted tire, wielding electric knives.

They are carving on the tire treads, the blocks and grooves that comprise the tread of a dirt-racing tire.

Just exactly how this is done, in the sense of taking one long knob and cutting a groove or notching the side of a knob so there's a fresher, sharper surface, is easily seen. What no tuner can explain, or has yet explained to me, is how they learn what works, or just how it works, and if they can prove that it does work.

Surely a fresh tire's treads are better formed to make the tire grip the surface, and one can allow in theory that having two small blocks lets them flex and conform to the track's bumps and ripples. But the time spent on tire cutting is always more than the time working on damping or ride height or any of the other countless adjustments one can make.

No matter. Tire cutting and tuning and carving is one of the things a guy does before the race.

Suspension

This sounds wrong, but the key to winning in dirt track isn't the suspension.

OK, suspension itself, as in telescopic front forks and rear swing arm, is required. Suspension is important. But it doesn't seem to be critical.

There have been changes since the first XR. The components, the fork tubes and swing-arm legs, are larger and stronger now and there have been adaptions and adoptions from motocross, as in the single rear shock, the offset front axle and the upside-down forks, with the axle carried by the sliders. The heavier parts, the stanchion tubes, are more firmly fixed in the clamps. Brands have gone from Ceriani and Girling through Red Wing, Marzocchi, Simons and Works Performance, and the suspension units are adjustable, gas-charged and, well, better.

The Camel Pro crowd discovered at about the same time as the European and Japanese road racers

This is a box of eccentric cones and sleeves which Al Stangler, Kevin Atherton's tuner, carries with him so he can adjust rake and trail and offset of forks to steering stem from the pits.

This is Ken Tolbert, tuner for Chris Carr, right, with helper Scott Scherb, changing the trail in Carr's bike by loosening the steering stem, juggling the cones and tightening the stem. Rake changes steering speed; trail changes the self-centering force of the front wheel and feeds the bars. If you move the right amounts, you can vary each independently from the other.

Mert Lawwill uses dual ignition, but in 1990 it was with a pair of the older heads because he says he can get as much power that way. And the two plugs per cylinder are next to each other on the engine's left, as opposed to the factory's dual plugs being, well, opposed.

did, that just as there is an optimum flex to the frame, so is there one major secret to handling, namely that the front axle be inflexibly fixed to the forks. The relationship between the front axle and the steering head is vital. After that, or perhaps it's aft of that, it matters less.

So the Harley team runs Forcelle Italia (née Ceriani) forks, imported from Italy. Several of the better-budgeted teams use the upside-down and offset forks from Simons, and late-model Marzocchis are standard issue for the journeyman XR. All the brands and models are tunable, by changing damping rates, spring rates, even offset between the legs and the steering stem, along with air pressure and oil viscosity.

Even so, as a rule these settings are made before practice and the make and model doesn't appear to be why one guy wins, or has more cornering speed than the other guy.

Or it may be simply that Lawwill is right in reverse, that because the frame flexes, there's not much difference in how the components react.

Still more Lawwill magic. The mini sump has been replaced with a real sump, a larger oil reservoir that collects the oil from the cases and keeps the weight low and in the center, the better for handling.

Still another variation on the oil crisis, with Al Stangler's scavenge pump and the tightest gearcase cover seen to date. Each of the tuners has his own ideas and team policy lets them experiment, provided the experiments get results.

Gearing

Here's a whole menu of secrets. Gearing has been a Harley-Davidson feature since the introduction of the first WR. The parts books have always listed seemingly endless ratios and the racers have used them. This is so even when the XR is raced only in top gear.

Gearing begins with the engine sprocket, for which the factory lists four choices of size: twenty, twenty-five, thirty or thirty-four teeth. Each sprocket is a different diameter and comes with its own length of primary chain.

There's just the one clutch sprocket, with fifty-nine teeth. Then comes the gearbox, which needn't concern us for the current XR but for the record, the first XR came with standard (XR) or close-ratio (J) gearsets or your combination of the three first gears, two second gears and three third gears. Top was direct, of course.

The factory's selection of output sprockets begins with fifteen teeth and goes to twenty-four, while the rear-wheel sprockets are thirty-six through forty-six teeth.

So first, there's a good range of final drive ratios: the racers speak in final numbers, as in a twenty engine sprocket and fifty-nine clutch sprocket are 1.99:1. Then you've got a twenty on the output shaft and a forty-four on the rear wheel; that's 2.2 times 1.99 equals 4.378, call it 4.80:1. The tuner would tell the rider he's pulling a four-eighty (which would be on the high side, by the way).

There's more to it than that. This is another place Lawwill wonders if the public needs to know, but gearing affects, actually multiplies, torque. And in the frame section we discussed what happens to the rear suspension under engine power.

Changing engine-sprocket size changes the power as it goes to the clutch. The power coming out and the relationship of the output sprocket to the rear-wheel sprocket, even if the actual ratios are the same, varies the compression or extension force going to the rear suspension via the chain. Lawwill says it's one of the ways he controls weight transfer and traction, because the gear selection can aid—and one supposes interfere with—how the suspension works.

But that's secondary. Most important here, the current XR-750 engine can be revved safely to 9300 rpm. Races are won on the straights, speed on the straight depends on the acceleration available coming off the turns, and the final-drive gearing is where you get the acceleration and the top speed.

It all varies with conditions. Springfield is the fastest mile track, routinely run at better than 100 mph. The good guys there, Parker and Graham for instance, simply whack the throttle wide open and hang on, for twenty-five miles. Syracuse is narrow and abrasive and Indy has a head wind at night; you can pull a higher top gear at Springfield than at Syracuse or Indy.

Next, gearing for top speed would mean you'd max out at the end of the straight, too late for a good average. If you gear for punch off the turns, you over-rev the engine halfway down the chute. If there's no traction you gear higher, so your power (and tire tread) doesn't dissipate in wheelspin.

What this explains first, is why all those stacks of sprockets in the pits, and second, why changing the gearing is the most popular change made at the track.

Sources of Confusion

As mentioned with frames, the Harley-Davidson racing department no longer stocks or furnishes every part for the XR-750.

This makes economic sense. It also fits the sporting character of The Motor Company because before the factory *doesn't* stock a part, the part is researched to be sure someone outside does stock it.

Even so, there can be confusion. The twenty years of constant upgrading means that not all the flywheels work with all the cases, ditto for camshafts, rockerboxes and so forth.

More so for the motorcycle parts, for instance hubs. The factory wheels were replaced, in usage anyway, by Barnes wheels and later by Kosman wheels. There have been different brands and models of rear brake.

The original alloy XR used the dished sprocket from the iron XR, which got the thing from the old KR.

The dished sprocket went directly on the splined hub. But it was offset and didn't hold up behind the alloy engine's power and was replaced by a carrier that went on the hub and to which the sprocket was bolted.

Then came aftermarket hubs, and choices of axle diameter to go with the different swing arms. What happens now, and I say this because it happened to me, is when the carriers get worn, which they do, you must buy a complete new wheel or get a hub and have it laced to a rim. Order adapters, spacers, carriers, axle, disc and sprocket, then you and your machinist spend some hours measuring and guessing and trimming and such until the new wheel sits where it should and doesn't foul the chain or the brake carrier. At the other end it's possible to buy, sight unseen, a new front wheel only to learn that it's a spool hub, which means there's no way to attach a front brake disc.

What this comes down to is first, the XR-750 has been the same basic machine since the current version was introduced in 1972. Second, if any two XR-750s have been out of the factory for more than one week, they are no longer identical. Third, everything you need is out there, if you take the time and trouble to find it.

Taking It to the Street

About the time I persuaded a publishing company that I should watch races at their expense, it occurred to me that Harley-Davidson was missing a good bet. The XR-750 was the best-looking scooter ever, most of the parts could be easily produced and racing had made the model famous—in short, why not build a street version, sort of the equivalent to Honda's XR and XL dual-sport lines? I asked them.

As usual, Harley-Davidson hadn't missed a bet. They had entertained the same thought and in fact had built prototypes of a street XR-750 and submitted the prototypes to various tests as per government regulation. This was in the late 1970s and the government hadn't yet dared to interfere, but the handwriting was on the wall.

By the time the air-cooled and ball-bearing engine had been tamed enough to pass the noise and emissions tests, there wasn't enough performance left to make the model fit its intended niche.

Or so H-D brass decided. As a sour note here, Yamaha broke sales records with its cruiser 750 cc V-twin, which didn't have any performance at all, relative to sports models anyway. But it looked bitchin' and sold like hot dogs at half time.

But the idea was too good to waste and the street-equipped XR-750 became something of a cult, a privately performed rite of enthusiasm.

There are a couple of ways to do this. The purist way is shown here; buy an XR or a set of the parts, and put them together. Thanks to Harley's use of Sportster components for those early XRs, it's not too tough to install an XL generator and ignition, nor to have the machine work done to install an XL kick-start clutch basket, shaft and lever. Find a place to hang or hide a battery and you're ready for the Department of Motor Vehicles. But that comes later.

The next way is to buy either a rolling XR chassis with TT stuff, that is, brakes and a Sportster engine, and combine them. There are guys who've taken a complete Sportster and got an XR frame and suspension and combined the two.

The third way is to take the Sportster and install XR tank and seat and replica pipes. Easy, but not quite the real thing.

Some of the convertists make it even easier by leaving off the generator and kick start. That is, if you don't mind bump-starts, and you don't really want a practical bike, one you can ride in rain and at night.

The look-alike Sportster is easy. The combination XL-XR is more work. It's more work than you'd think because, just like when you put different wheels or brakes or suspension on your XR, nothing is as simple as it looked. The XR is a finely crafted instrument. Every piece is just where it has to be. Every component does

Looks like the studio shot of the first alloy XR-750, eh? Closer scrutiny reveals a small but legal headlight, Supertrapps with baffles and Grimeca brakes. What you can't see from here is the kick start, battery and license plate. This is a 1980 frame and engine with the earlier fiberglass tank and snap-cover seat, converted for street operation by California tuner Steve

Storz. There are probably several dozen XRs done like this by now but before you begin, know that the job takes, or took this man and the author, who did the same thing to an iron XR, three years from purchase of the parts to riding the beast. Nick Cedar

its job and nothing else, and that makes it difficult to expand or relocate anything. It can be done. It's just that like the rest of life, it takes longer and is more trouble than expected.

The overlooked handicap is state laws. At the federal level, ever since the rules controlling road bikes were introduced, it's been illegal to make road bikes that don't meet the rules. I'm not a lawyer and don't know how nor would I presume to give advice but it does seem, or so I'm told, that a private party can build a motorcycle and register it in his home state if it meets the rules, or can revise an old motorcycle.

There are fifty sets of rules, no two alike, and I've found that exactly what they are and how they work varies with who's across the counter from you and how they feel about "murdercycles."

In my own case I got a 1970 XR-750 engine with a New York bill of sale, a 1972 XR-750 frame with an Illinois bill of sale, and sent the bills of sale to a chap in Alabama, who registered the two as a 1970 Harley-Davidson. He signed it over to me and I took my Alabama title to the California DMV office, got a frame identification plate installed and there I was, on the road at last, with an XR-750 of my own.

The parts? *Cycle News* has an excellent classified section and so does Chicago-based *Old Time Cycles.* Or check the local track if you're lucky enough to have one. The 100 new XR engines has to mean there's 100 used ones on the block, eh?

Reverse the television cliché: Go ahead kids, try this at home.

Chapter 10

How Winning Works

Design engineer Pieter Zylstra has been working on the XR-750 since he did the basic outline for that first iron-barrel XR. His main hobby is vintage racing and his secondary hobby is collecting details about XRs. Some day, he says, he'll have all the data there is.

Perhaps. If so, it will be a huge book full of facts and even then, I suspect, we won't know as much. Make that, we won't be able to *do* as much as some other guys with the same facts.

The closest analogy is what the computer folks call fuzzy logic.

Here's how it works: If a computer is driving north on Interstate 5, it will see a sign that says San Francisco 305, Sacramento 306. The computer uses digital logic, fact plus fact equals fact and thus will enter into memory that San Francisco and Sacramento are one mile apart. Said so on the sign.

Fuzzy logic is what we use when we see the same sign and know that the highway must divide before it gets to either city. We jump sideways to the correct conclusion, add one and one to get D, you could say,

But then—and I swear Werner and Parker didn't pose for this or even know the camera was on them—Camel Pro *racing is a team effort and each partner has to know where they should be going.* Bill Werner

because we already know facts that don't show in what we've just been told.

How does this apply to dirt track?

Begin with all the bikes being alike. The 1991 weight minimum is 315 lb. at the finish of the race. You'll need to use a gallon or so of fuel, at 6 lb. per gallon. So, when the AMA inspectors weigh the bikes before practice, as they did at Sacramento in 1990, the scales read: Parker's number 1, 324 lb.; Carr's number 20, 325.5; Atherton's number 23, 324.5; and Lawwill's 1990 model as prepped for Morehead, 323. The weight rule was the same for all 750s in 1990, so for contrast know that Ricky Graham's number 3, tuned by a former Honda team member, checked in at a porky 340 lb.

As part of the AMA's economy and safety considerations, on occasion all the bikes will have to use the same tire, as in Goodyear D-8s in the rear and D-5s in front at San Jose; D is for dirt, obviously, while the lower the number, the softer the compound. The softest, D-2, is used only on slow tracks for short races.

And of course all the Harleys and Hondas have to use production castings. As of late 1990, the two brands were close in output, with 100 bhp from the best Hondas, while there was more difference, say

better than that from the team Harleys and the tuners from midpack saying their old XRs topped out at 88 bhp.

Then we come to the differences, in two sections.

First, there are some basic distinctions. Parker and Carr have new Knight frames. Atherton has an older Knight frame, with oil in the backbone instead of a tank. His tuner is Al Stangler, who says he's new to the rider and the engine so he wanted to keep one major factor, the frame, as familiar territory from which to learn.

All the Harley team teams, as it were, got new D-port engines. But each is allowed to install his own variations on the basic parts; Werner may run a higher compression ratio while Tolbert has carbs with venturis bored to the max, and so forth. To further complicate things the outsiders have been claiming team engines all year because, they say, the new ones are superior. Lawwill meanwhile has an engine with the new heads on the old cases, and an engine with the old-style heads and cases. He says first, that Augustine did the work on a pair of heads from Lawwill, so he knows the design and let the factory have it and that he did it because he can match the D-port heads with his techniques on the old-style ports. He adds

A good look at Camel Pro action, with Parker just off the groove, Atherton wide and Carr, who was nurtured on the rough and tough ovals of central California, working the cushion. Poovey (Honda) is right behind Atherton, and Dan *Ingram (31) is on Parker's heels. Dave Durelle (58) hopes to get Ingram before Ingram gets Parker. And so it goes, the most fun you can have with your boots on. Bert Shepard*

that his partner, Charley Gardner, tested one of the claimed engines versus a Lawwill engine on the same dyno and yes, they were equal.

Things are getting complicated. Honda rider Terry Poovey says he'll switch back to Harley in part because he can get 100 bhp from his Honda, but it costs $22,000 to build a good RS750 and you can claim a team Harley for $17,500.

We must allow for some political techniques here, I think. But it's most likely true that with the same restrictors in both engines, the best Harleys will edge the best Hondas. The Honda engine breathes better at high rpm. The more revs, the more air needed. Restrictors cut down on airflow, which means that if everything was equal, the restrictors would hurt the Honda more than the Harley. In actual experience, the numbers and the results seem to mean that the guys with limited resources or talent with flow bench and porting tools will get more power from the Honda.

Which gets us, with our frame, suspension, wheels, tires, spare spark plugs, boxes of jets and stacks of sprockets, to the actual race on the given day, with a track that's unique all the time and which will change minute to minute during practice, time trials, heats and the main event.

Right here is where your keen reporter and/or any rocket scientists in the crowd begin to learn a lesson.

Dialing for the Day

The day begins with the track, so on the occasion of the fall race on the San Jose mile, your keen reporter did a series of surveys, planning to detail how the best guys set up for the race.

San Jose follows Springfield, although in 1990 Springfield's late race was rained out. Springfield and San Jose are both natural miles, two semi-circles joined by straights, and they are different from four-cornered DuQuoin. But Springfield and San Jose aren't the same because the former has wide semi-circles and short straights, and San Jose has narrow semi-circles and long straights.

The teams arrived with bikes prepared for the Springfield they didn't run, and I scurried about asking what they'd change for the different track.

There were some constants. All those asked—Werner, Tolbert, Lawwill, Stangler and Morehead—had fitted twenty-five tooth engine sprockets because that's right in the middle so you can easily gear up or down. The AMA had decreed that everybody would use D-8 Goodyears on the rear, D-5s on the front so that was settled. All the tuners said they'd built as strong an engine as they felt would last the day, with the newest cams, compression ratio approximately 12.5:1, the optimum for life and power with the new lower end. All the builders had 38 mm Mikuni carbs; flat slides for the well financed, older round bodies for the rest. Tolbert admitted his were bored out to 41 mm for extra top end and surely he wasn't the only one.

If there was a difference before practice, it was that the top teams had a choice of two good machines. The middle teams had the miler and the spare, usually prepared for the half-mile and in the pits, just in case. And of course the new guys or the part-time pros arrived with *the* bike, the only one they have.

The secrets, make that the avenues, for dialing in the bike on the day are steering and traction.

Morehead spoke for the group when he said at Springfield, "You're in the corners longer." For that track he had the front end kicked out and the rear lowered, so the bike would hold its line in those long turns. For San Jose he pulled the forks back to quicken the steering and raised the back with longer shocks.

Lawwill says the vital element of handling and traction is the transition, from where you pitch the bike into the turn and hang the back out to scrub off speed, through the apex and back on the power. You should be on the edge every inch, he says, and the transition should be as quick and precise as it can be.

He also made the steering-head angle more acute but when Morehead changed clamps, Lawwill lowered the clamps on the stanchion tubes. And he raised the rear with spring preload instead of longer shocks.

In the same vein, all five were geared in the mid-fives, but one man would do it with seventeen-tooth countershaft sprocket and forty-tooth rear. The next man had eighteen and forty-two, so the overall ratio was the same but torque and suspension loading would be different. Lawwill has one tooth lower than the others, but he pointed out that his rider, Dan Ingram, is heavier than Carr or Parker.

They all went out to practice, they all tried a taller gear and a lower gear, they checked carb mixture and ignition timing and tire pressure and swapped for new tires. Near as I could keep track, none of the five made any major changes or discoveries during practice, time trials or heats. All were fairly close, yet no two bikes were alike and each man had his way of arriving at the combination.

Then, the actual race. On the first lap Parker and Graham tried to avoid another rider and hit each other, hard. Graham's arm was broken, Parker's XR flipped through the air and came down in a tangle.

Werner and a swarm of helpers dragged the thing into the pits and fell on it. They changed the bars, one shock, the pipes and a host of small bits and just barely made the start. The last thing Werner told Parker was, don't look down and don't think about things like the frame.

Parker won going away.

The frame was tweaked so badly that with the wheels pointed straight ahead, the rear was 2 in. out of line with the front.

So much for those tiny increments.

I resumed pondering the next race, Ascot. Ronnie Jones had been lagging a few lengths behind Parker and Carr all year. But at Ascot, he had them even though they hadn't done anything wrong and he wasn't sure just what he'd done right.

At Sacramento, just before the main event Stangler was acting like a man with his hands full of flaming swords. What are you doing? I asked. He said he wasn't sure, that they'd tried both machines, the one that steered quick and the one that steered slow and that for reasons he couldn't catch, neither was working, so he was reaching into the sack of tricks and throwing everything he had at the better of the two.

Twenty minutes later Atherton was on the box, second place. It was his best ride of the season and the first time he'd been able to run with the big guys. Stangler had done the right thing, under intense pressure, without being scientifically sure about what he was doing.

We have a conundrum here. I feel safe in using the last three races of the 1990 season as an accurate compression of the history of the XR-750, and perhaps even racing in general.

There are two sides, what Robert Pirsig would call the Classic versus the Romantic.

After her first season, the bewitching creature who goes to the races with me asked, Why don't they put all that data into a computer program?

Which is why the mention of computer or digital logic. True, you can make the list. You can know all the variables, with cause being steering-head angle or wheelbase and effect being how the bike steers into a turn or snaps out of a slide. You could feed into a program tire size and pressure and trail and what a gearing change does to weight transfer and it would surely fill your data bank to the brim.

But then, as we saw earlier, you can have five of the best tuners in the business and they have five different combinations, five sets of weights and measures to come up with what should be the same total —except it's not, not quite. And the guy who seemingly did the best job isn't sure just how he did it.

And after all that, you have the rider who clearly and plainly, in view of thousands of people, simply transcends himself and his limits, who gets more from his machine than the machine has scientifically got.

Let me begin the summation here by saying that this for me is not a complaint. It's a celebration.

In Conclusion

Motorcycle racing is a sport. True, there are financial aspects, so to a degree it's a business, and because when the race is over all the racers are right back where they began, it's also a game.

But the millions of dollars and the risk of injury and death and the intellectual intensity and clarity

San Jose, 1990 and Parker, with his blue-and-yellow plate, has a short lead on Carr, with Ronnie Jones, the best Honda, tucked in tight and looking for his chance. Then comes Poovey on a good Honda, Mike Hale on his XR-mounted way to Rookie of the Year, and Springer, on a private XR with factory help and going for his best season in ten years.

and dedication to what we can unblushingly call an idea, all make racing a sport. Seldom simple, not always pure, but a sport nonetheless.

I don't think anything has done more for the sport than has Harley-Davidson's XR-750.

To claim that any engine or machine is the world's best is to bring the fans to their feet and logic to a dead stop. What about the Yamaha TZ750? The Jawa speedway engine? The Offenhauser at Indy or the Cosworth-Ford in Formula One? Or, look at the Chevy V-8, a winner out of the box in 1955 and the winner all over the world just last Sunday.

All true. But when the XR-750 began, it was up against a formidable set of rivals, which it equaled and defeated and drove out of the park. Since then it's come up with other, and better, competition and it's done the same to them. Just last Sunday a ten-year-old XR beat a better-than-new Honda RS.

The XR-750 is a work of art, an implement of battle and a rolling laboratory, all in one. It's done the best job for the best racers ever.

And if we all hold our collective breath and buy those tickets, we'll have twenty-one more years of the same.

Tracking the Tracks

At first glance, there should be no problem preparing a motorcycle for a dirt track. The 750s now run the miles and the half-miles, on a surface of packed dirt—how tough can it be?

Tougher than you'd think, and arguably tougher than setting up for pavement racing. You have the weather, as in temperature and humidity, the gearing for turns and so forth, with both.

But to say *the* mile or half-mile is misleading. No two dirt tracks are alike.

First, dirt isn't dirt. The Albuquerque track is a horse track, under control of a state fair board that worries lest the annual motorcycle race damage the horse racing season. Calcium is banned, so Albuquerque needs constant grooming. It can have both a high groove and a low groove, and it can go from too wet to too dry almost between heats.

Louisville is limestone and the limestone dust mixes with water into sort of a paste. Springfield, Illinois, has much the same problem, which is bad for traction and vision.

Ascot is raced (make that was; the official final race on the legendary track was run in late 1990) at least three times each week, by motorcycles, sprint cars and jalopy stocks. When the track was built in the late 1950s, the base and surface were comprised of clay from a nearby swamp and dirt excavated to make a lake in the middle of the oval, plus the usual chemicals. Three times weekly, fifty weeks a year, for thirty years the dirt has been pounded by tires and flung against the retaining walls and mixed with oil and rubber and packed back down. There is no dust left. Ascot is paved, ripply, tacky and slick in different places all on the same day and it took years before a visitor, no matter how brave or talented, could beat the locals there.

Nor is that all. Ascot is poorly lit. Coming out of the north turn onto the front straight is like coming out of a tunnel. Ascot is slightly banked. Harrington is steeply banked, to give the sprint cars more speed. But the half-mile horse tracks aren't banked at all, so they need vast differences in gearing and tires and suspension settings.

Next, the AMA has always been vague about measurement. This surely dates back to the days when it was an accomplishment getting permission to race those dreadful motorcycles in decent towns. But those who have paced the tracks say Ascot is a mighty short half-mile, just as the old San Jose short track was a mighty long quarter-mile.

And there's configuration. San Jose is what's called a natural mile, two semi-circles joined by two long straights. Springfield, the fastest dirt track in the country, has wider corners. DuQuoin has four corners and four straights; instead of a U-turn, there's a 90 deg. corner, a short chute and another right angle.

San Jose is clay, baked like a brick except shade trees keep Turns One and Two tackier than Turns Three and Four. There's no dust, and a blue groove helps traction. Syracuse is abrasive and has a skinnier groove.

You'll usually have wind at Indianapolis at night, but not during the day. Hamburg's limestone demands a soft tire for grip, but wears tires quickly so the soft compound might not last the full national.

In short, if there are fifteen or twenty tracks used for a season, there will be fifteen or twenty different surfaces, contours and distances. And did I mention that the fall race at Syracuse usually runs in cooler weather so the track is tackier, faster and safer and needs different specs than used in the spring?

Index

Adamo, James, 111–112
Adkins, Ed, 135
Aermacchi, 20, 28, 37–38, 48, 51, 53, 57, 104
Agajanian, A. J., 69
Agostini, Giacomo, 57
Aksland, Skip, 84, 88
Aldana, Dave, 145
Alexander, Ron, 25, 45, 88, 106

Beauchamp, Rex, 26, 49, 56–58, 60, 63, 65–66, 70, 78
Belland, Jim, 18, 19, 41, 88
Bolger, Joe, 93
Boody, Ted, 79–81, 84–85, 89, 91, 103, 114, 119, 122, 126, 129
BOTT (Battle of the Twins), 111, 113
Branch, Jerry, 88, 124–126, 154
Brelsford, Mark, 20–21, 25–26, 28, 41, 47–49, 51–53, 57–60, 63, 111
Brow, Garth, 84, 87–89
BSA, 12–13, 21–22, 26, 49–50, 57, 79, 83, 88, 97, 102
Buell, Eric, 112, 128
Bultaco, 69

C&J frames, 63, 109, 116, 118, 143, 145
Can-Am, 100, 104, 106, 108, 118
Carr, Chris, 122, 124, 126–133, 135–138, 140–141, 146, 148, 161, 163, 170–172
Carruthers, Kel, 54
Ceriani forks, 11, 15, 18–19, 49, 52, 63, 81, 91, 96, 98, 106
Champion frames, 63, 97
Chandler, Doug, 109, 116, 118–119, 121–122, 124, 126, 135
Chimiel, Paul, 109, 122
Church, Gene, 112–113, 127
Clark, Ken, 102
Class C, 8–9, 84
Cole, Jeff, 143, 145
Continental tires, 123
Conway, Bob, 5, 113, 125, 136, 138–141, 147–148, 150, 152–154, 147, 159–161
Cornwell, Jon, 5, 146
Cosworth pistons, 123, 173

Darr, Larry, 47, 55
Davidson, John, 81, 87

Davidson, Walter, 14
Davis, Will, 136, 138–139
DeMay, Babe, 56, 111
Denzer, Clyde, 53, 119, 122
Ducati, 98, 111
DuHamel, Yvon, 52
Dunlop tires, 161
Durelle, Dave, 138, 158, 170

Eaken, Skip, 135, 138
Eklund, Steve, 80, 83, 85, 87–89, 91–93, 98, 100–101, 106, 108, 138–139
Erson, Sig, 89

Fairbanks-Morse magnetos, 59
Faulk, Walt, 25, 31–32
Fay, Mickey, 91, 99
Filice, Jimmy, 98, 100–103, 108, 110
First Klass, 157
Fisher, Gary, 50
Fontana brakes, 21
Forcelle Italia forks, 164
Formula One engines, 123
Fredericks, Curley, 6
Fulton, Walt, Jr., 13, 21

Gardner, Charley, 171
Girling brakes, 15, 19, 63, 96, 162
Goliath, 20, 47, 49, 53
Goodyear tires, 88
Goss, Randy, 85, 91–94, 98–100, 102–103, 106, 108–111, 114–115, 118–119, 122, 136, 139
Graham, Ricky, 5, 91, 99–101, 104–107, 109–111, 114, 116–117, 119, 121–122, 126, 128, 130, 134, 138–139, 165
Grand Prix Plastics, 91, 97, 125, 157
Greening, Jim, 31–32, 53
Griffiths, Jerry, 119
Griffiths, Lynn, 69
Grimeca brakes, 167

Haaby, Dan, 13
Habermehl, Don, 111
Hale, Mike, 139, 172
Harley Owners Groups, 108, 112

Harley, John, 28
Harley-Davidson, K, 9–10, 16–17, 36, 153
Harley-Davidson, KR, 9–13, 16–22, 24–25, 29, 34, 36, 96–97, 152
Harley-Davidson, KRTT, 10, 13, 15, 18, 24, 157
Harley-Davidson, RR-250, 58, 83
Harley-Davidson, RR-750, 76
Harley-Davidson, W Series, 9, 10
Harley-Davidson, WR, 10, 96
Harley-Davidson, XL, 11, 15–17, 22, 56, 66, 111, 120, 167
Harley-Davidson, XLR, 11, 16–17, 20, 22, 24–25, 38, 47
Harley-Davidson, XR-1000, 111–112, 116, 128
Harley-Davidson, XRTT 1, 41, 44, 48, 55, 60, 62–63, 81, 85, 88
Harley-Davidson, XRTT 2, 97, 111–112, 128
Haute, Terry, 58
Hearndon, Bill, 103
Highboy frames, 19
Hocking, Rick, 98
Honda, 14, 22, 51, 58, 91–93, 95–96, 98–108, 110–111, 114, 116–124, 126, 129–136, 138, 140, 147, 167, 170–172
Honda Trophy, 139

Indian, 7, 8–9, 102
Ingram, Dan, 130–131, 138, 170

Jawa, 173
Jennings, Gordon, 58
Johnson, Junior, 106
Jones, Ronnie, 99, 134, 138–140, 171–172
Jorgensen, Alex, 84, 88–89, 99, 105–106

Kanemoto, Erv, 63
Kathcart, Griff, 8
Kawasaki, 51–53, 58, 63, 98–99, 103–104, 108
Keen, Neil, 157
Keener, Corky, 4–5, 55, 57–58, 60–61, 63, 65–66, 78–79, 83, 87, 89, 92
Kidd, Mike, 47, 58, 78, 80–81, 89, 91–92, 94–95, 99–100, 102–103, 105–106, 114, 116
Kirk, Tammy, 109, 133, 135
Knight frames, 97, 129, 132, 140–141, 143–145, 170
Knight, Terry, 41, 47, 59, 90, 157
Kosman wheels, 166

Lawson, Eddie, 63, 103, 133, 140
Lawwill frames, 143–145
Lawwill, Mert, 5, 10, 12–13, 18–21, 23–26, 28, 30, 41, 47, 50, 52–53, 55, 57–60, 63–64, 66–67, 69, 73, 79–80, 82, 84, 88–89, 90, 92, 96, 98, 100, 102, 106, 118, 122, 124–131, 135, 138, 141, 146, 14, 157, 159, 161, 164–165, 170–171
Lawwill-Carr XR, 149
Leoni, Reno, 111
Lowboy frames, 19, 21, 28
Lucifer's Hammer, 111–113, 116

Maico, 104
Mallory ignition, 75
Mann, Dick, 12, 26, 51, 102, 126
Markel, Bart, 13–14, 20–21, 50, 53, 55, 85
Marzocchi forks, 96, 98, 101, 105, 111, 162, 164
McGee, Kevin, 133

Mikuni carburetors, 69, 89, 111, 129, 158, 171
Mockabee, Mike, 135
Morehead, Steve, 88–89, 93, 100, 109, 128–131, 135, 138–139, 146, 150, 170–171
Moto-Plat, 92
Moto-X Fox shocks, 111
Muzzy Rob, 108, 124, 130

Neilson, Cook, 20, 55
Nichels Engineering, 41
Nix, Fred, 13
Nixon, Gary, 13, 58
North, Rob, 128, 141–142
Norton, 12–13, 18, 22, 57, 66, 83–84, 91, 99, 102

O'Brien, Dick, 5, 11–15, 17, 19, 20–21, 23, 25, 34, 36, 38, 41, 45, 47, 49, 53, 55, 57, 59–60, 62, 67, 79, 82, 88–89, 92–93, 100–101, 108, 111–112
Offenhauser, 17, 21–22, 173
Ohlins shocks, 122

Palmgren, Chuck, 12, 57
Parker, Scott, 5, 92–93, 100, 104–106, 108–109, 111, 117, 119, 121–126, 128–133, 135–141, 160–162
Pasolini, Renzo, 28, 48, 53, 57
Patrick, Carl, 88, 146, 157
Pearson, Scott, 106, 122, 144–145
Peel, Tex, 5, 88, 92, 99–101, 104–106, 114, 119, 123–125, 149
Perkins, Dudley, 14, 18, 41
Petrali, Joe, 7
Pickerell, Ray, 31
Pirelli tires, 118, 122, 161
Pirsig, Robert, 172
Plateau Honing, 154
Poovey, Terry, 5, 92–93, 105–108, 114, 123, 134–135, 138, 170, 172

Rainy, Wayne, 103, 140
Rayborn, Cal, 11–13, 20–24, 26, 28, 31–32, 45, 48–57, 62–63, 88, 111
Reidel, Jerry, 119
Reiman, Roger, 13, 26
Resweber, Carroll, 5, 79, 111
Rice, Jim, 49, 55–57
Roberts, Ken, 47, 50, 55–58, 61, 63, 65–66, 75, 78, 80–83, 89, 98, 100, 102, 104, 120, 122, 140
Rockwood, Roxy, 69
Roeder, George, 139, 159
Romero, Gene, 21, 57–58, 63, 65, 107–108, 114, 116
Rotax, 100, 109, 114, 116, 123, 138
Rotax/Can-Am, 110

S&W shocks, 106
Saarinen, Jarno, 53, 57
Sassaman, Greg, 57, 60, 62–63, 66, 76, 78
Scherb, Scott, 163
Scott, Gary, 47, 51, 57–60, 62–63, 65–67, 71, 73, 77, 80, 82, 84, 89, 91, 118, 126
Scott, Hank, 57–59, 88–89, 94, 99–100, 102, 107–109, 122, 124
Sehl, Dave, 21, 26, 28, 46, 48, 50–51, 53, 56–57, 92–93, 96
Sheene, Barry, 82
Shobert, Bubba, 106, 108–111, 114, 116–119, 122–124, 126, 129–130, 132–133, 135–136

Smart, Paul, 25, 53, 55
Spencer, Freddie, 63, 102–104, 140
Springsteen, Jay, 31, 59–60, 63, 65–66, 69–73, 76–79, 80–85, 87–91, 93, 99–104, 106, 108–110, 122–123, 126–129, 131, 133–135, 137–139, 145
Stangler, Al, 5, 129, 135, 138, 140, 159, 163, 165, 171–172
Storz, Steve, 5, 79, 84, 89, 93, 97, 123, 135, 149, 157, 167
Superblend bearing, 114, 156
Suzuki, 51, 55, 57–58, 76

Texter, Randy, 139
Thompson, Brent, 5
Thompson, Charles, 33, 47
Thuet, Shell, 81
Tilley, Don, 112–113
Tillotson carburetors, 17
Timkin bearings, 19
Tolbert, Ken, 5, 128, 138–140, 159, 161, 163, 170–171
Trackmaster frames, 63
Triumph, 12–13, 21–22, 25, 31, 49, 51, 55, 57–58, 63, 66, 79, 82, 87, 97, 99, 102, 106
Tuttle, Mark, 140

Villella, Bryan, 129
Vista-Sheen, 60, 63, 104

Week, Clyde, 127
Werner, Bill, 5, 23, 30, 59, 63, 77–80, 82–85, 88–89, 91–92, 101, 103–106, 108–109, 119, 121–122, 124, 129–130, 135, 138–141, 145, 150, 152, 158, 161–166, 169–171
Widman, Earl, 41
Winters, Storm, 91
Wise, Steve, 104
Wixom Brothers, 19, 41
Wood, Ron, 84, 92, 99–101, 109–110, 144–145, 161
Wood-Rotax, 123–124, 132, 135
Works Performance, 162

Yamaha, 22, 50, 54–58, 61, 63, 66–67, 69, 75–76, 79–83, 88–89, 92–93, 95–101, 103–104, 106, 108, 122, 167
Youngblood, Ed, 21

Zylstra, Pieter 1, 5, 15, 36, 41, 44, 59, 75–76, 119, 147–149